# From Protest to Politics

# From Protest to Politics

The New Black Voters in American Elections

Enlarged Edition

Katherine Tate

**Russell Sage Foundation** • New York
**Harvard University Press** • Cambridge, Massachusetts,
and London, England
1994

For my parents, brothers, and sisters

First Harvard University Press paperback edition, 1994

*Library of Congress Cataloging-in-Publication Data*

Tate, Katherine.
  From protest to politics : the new Black voters in
American elections / Katherine Tate. — Enl. ed.
    p.  cm.
  Includes bibliographical references (p.     ) and
  index.
  ISBN 0-674-32540-0 (pbk.)
  1. Afro-Americans—Politics and government.
2. Afro-Americans—Suffrage.  3. Presidents—United
States—Election—1984.  4. Presidents—United
States—Election—1988.  5. Presidents–United
States—Election—1992.  6. United States—Politics
and government—1981–1989.  7. United States—
Politics and government—1989–1993.  I. Title.
E185.615.T38   1994
323.1'196073—dc20        94-29711
CIP

# Contents

# Figures and Tables

## Figures

## Tables

# Preface to the Enlarged Edition

*The view is that Blacks have nowhere else to go but Blacks always have somewhere to go: they can go fishing.*

Ed Brown, Director of the Voter Education Project, 1992

Those who had hoped to see greater partisan diversity displayed by Black voters in the 1992 presidential election must surely be disappointed. Blacks who participated in the 1992 election voted overwhelmingly Democratic, as they had in the last seven presidential elections. Blacks cast Democratic ballots despite the fact that the Democratic presidential nominee, Bill Clinton, had done little to earn their votes. As a self-proclaimed "new Democrat," he campaigned against the old-style liberalism of his party, which is a major basis of Black support. Why did Black voters, once again, vote Democratic in 1992, especially after nearly a decade of rising criticism by Jesse Jackson in his 1984 and 1988 presidential campaigns that the party took Black votes for granted? Why, even as voter participation among Blacks in 1992 increased over 1988, did racial differences in voter participation widen, with fewer Blacks than Whites electing to go to the polls? What impact did the substantial increase in Black representation in Congress have on Black politics at the national level? Although I have chosen not to label the "new Black politics" an authentic political movement, the 1992 elections represented the fruition of Blacks' decade-long struggle to increase their influence and independence in national politics. Recent court rulings on minority voting rights, however, have put in jeopardy the gains made by Blacks through the implementation of the 1982-amended Voting Rights Act.

Perhaps the best theoretical framework for describing Black voting behavior in the three presidential elections I analyze in this book can be found in Albert Hirschman's classic book *Exit, Voice, and Loyalty* (1970). To understand the high level of support by Blacks for the Democratic party, one first must recognize their position as a cohesive political minority whose political options are fewer than they would be in a multi-party system. In a two-party system in which Blacks are ideologically to the left of both parties, Blacks would gain little by moving to the right. Other than voting for the more liberal of the two parties, Blacks can only choose to stay home. In the 1984 and 1988 elections, one can see evidence of both the voice and exit strategies. Jackson's presidential bids, in 1984 as well as in 1988, represented Hirschman's strategy of voice; Blacks backed Jackson's impossible bids for the presidency out of mounting frustration with the rightward drift of the Democratic party. If nothing else, Jackson's campaign gave "voice" to the increasing numbers of Black Democrats who felt that the party took their votes for granted. Although Jackson was unable to push the party onto a more liberal course, he powerfully articulated Blacks' collective grievances, mobilized new Black voters, and stimulated Black interest in presidential politics. "Exit" in this context is the option of nonvoting. To remind the party of the power of their voting bloc, many Blacks denied their vote to the party's 1988 nominee, Michael Dukakis. Although Dukakis won nearly 90 percent of the Black vote in the general election, turnout among Blacks fell to a record low, especially among those who had supported Jackson during the presidential primary contest.

The 1992 presidential election could very well have been a repeat of 1988. As Blacks' enthusiasm for Clinton was perceived to be low, their participation could have likewise remained low. Instead, though Blacks' approval ratings of Clinton were no higher than they were for Dukakis, Clinton benefited from a higher Black voter turnout. Black voting behavior in 1992 was a display of loyalty—not voice as in 1984, not exit as in 1988. In the new chapter written for the enlarged edition of this book (Chapter 9), I identify the set of factors that led to the strong showing of Black allegiance to the Democratic party in 1992 and explain why it is likely that over the short run the Democrats will continue to benefit from Black support.

April 1994

# Preface

The new political power that Black voters wield today and the presidential campaigns of the Reverend Jesse L. Jackson have prompted new interest in the Black vote among scholars and political analysts. Studies of Black voting behavior in recent presidential elections, however, have been slow in coming and have remained fairly limited, often not extending beyond group comparisons between Blacks and Whites. In this book, I analyze the voting behavior of Blacks in the 1984 and 1988 presidential elections. The study moves notably beyond already existing work on Black Americans, as it incorporates a framework consistent with the theoretical approach of most studies of the American electorate and yet still integrates unique aspects of the Black experience as they shape and affect Black political behavior.

I will show in this book, as I have argued elsewhere (Tate, 1991), that Black voting behavior is particularly influenced by the political context. Jesse Jackson, the nation's first non-token Black presidential contender, significantly affected voting patterns among Blacks in 1984 and 1988. With no Black presidential contender in 1992, Black political behavior has been quite different. I will also demonstrate that political context encompasses more than the epiphenomena of the 1984 and 1988 elections. Blacks, no longer excluded as members of the American polity, have amassed tremendous political resources and power over the last quarter-century that have enhanced their political status and affected their political interests and behavior. Voting, always believed to be an important tool in the struggle by Blacks for racial equality, has made electoral politics a collective effort toward egalitarianism.

This book avoids fashioning a composite of the Black voter. Such a portrait would be not only premature, based on only two elections, but inappropriate as well, since American voters have generally defied stereotyping. Nevertheless, from this study, several aspects of Black voting behavior stand out. Most notable are both Blacks' strong group-oriented behavior and their liberal policy interests. Black voters have strong partisan loyalties to the Democratic party, but these do not override their attachments to a formidable Black candidate like Jackson. His race, progressive policies, and strong charismatic personality help explain why a majority of Blacks, although loyal Democrats, reported in both the 1984 and 1988 surveys that they would vote for Jackson over the party's nominee if he ran as a political independent.

I also address the question of how minority groups such as Blacks might best use electoral politics as a means of social and economic group advancement. Black voting did not critically affect the outcome of the 1984 and 1988 presidential elections; nor did Blacks receive many tangible benefits through their participation in Jesse Jackson's two presidential campaigns. Since Blacks have only recently emerged as key players in American politics, however, we have still to witness the long-term impact of the new Black voters on American society and politics. This analysis of Black voting behavior in the 1980s thus contributes to a broader understanding of contemporary American politics.

I first became interested in Black politics as a political science major at the University of Chicago, but I was only able to begin real work on this topic while I was a Ph.D. student at the University of Michigan. I owe a lot, in particular, to those who helped me get started in the field of survey research at the Program for Research on Black Americans (PRBA), the Institute for Social Research, University of Michigan, and most especially, Shirley J. Hatchett and James S. Jackson. Several scholars within the field of Black politics have also helped me along the way. Lucius J. Barker, Hanes Walton, Jr., and Linda F. Williams, in particular, contributed to a great many of the ideas contained in this book. They unselfishly shared insights on the subject and freely gave me advice that enhanced the final product. I am happy to count them as friends as well as intellectual mentors.

The Department of Government at Harvard University provided a supportive environment for me while I began work on this book. I would like to thank especially James Alt, Morris Fiorina, Michael Hagen, Martin Kilson, Gary King, Paul Peterson, Doug Price, Theda Skocpol, and Sidney Verba in the Department of Government at Harvard for their critical readings of the book as it progressed. I would also like to thank Robert O. Keohane, chair of the department, and Randall Burkett of the W. E. B. Du Bois Institute at Harvard for their support of my research. I am very much indebted to my former and current graduate student research assistants, Kevin Hula, David Lublin, and Tonya Jenerette, as well as Vivian L. Johnson, who helped prepare the manuscript. I was able to finish this book while on leave at the Survey Research Center at the University of California at Berkeley, and would like to thank especially David Collier and Laura Stoker for their support during that year.

The Russell Sage Foundation gave me critical financial support in the early stages of this project, and I thank the foundation's former vice-president, Peter De Janosi, and its president, Eric Wanner. I also received some funds for this project from the National Science Foundation (RII 8912870). I acknowledge with appreciation the help of my two senior editors, Lisa Nachtigall at the Russell Sage Foundation and Aïda D. Donald of Harvard University Press. In addition, I benefited from the comments of Paul Abramson, Charles V. Hamilton, Jane Mansbridge, Dale Rogers Marshall, and Aldon Morris. Finally, I also benefited from the assistance of Elizabeth Suttell and from editorial work on the text by Mary Ellen Geer at Harvard University Press, and, especially, from the editorial work by Dr. Sheila McAvey at Clark University.

On a more personal level, I need to thank my family and friends. I am fortunate to come from a large and politically opinionated family of two parents, five sisters, including my twin, and three brothers, all of whom have helped to inspire my work. In addition, friends like Karin Clissold, Steven Corliss, Brenda Norris O'Neill, and Deborah Yarsike Ball have given me unwavering support all through and since my years at Michigan. Karin Clissold, in particular, went well beyond the bounds of friendship in helping me complete this (and other) projects. Finally, J. M. Lélias gave me important support throughout this project. Although his contribution to the book, like my family's, is not easily identifiable, it is still there and was essential.

# From Protest to Politics

*It's like the old preacher says: We ain't what we oughta be; we ain't what we're gonna be; but thank God we ain't what we was.*

Andrew Young

# 1

# The New Black Politics

As a direct result of the 1965 Voting Rights Act, a new stage in Black politics has been reached. In the past half-century, Black Americans have moved from the Republican to the Democratic party and from the disfranchised to the enfranchised. Passage of the voting rights legislation in 1965 led to a 21 percent increase in Black voter registration (Thompson, 1982: 10). The largest gains were recorded in the South, where the percentage of Blacks registered to vote rose from less than 31 percent in 1965 to approximately 66 percent by 1984.[1] The number of Black elected officials since 1965 has skyrocketed as well, from an estimated 500 or so in the early 1970s to over 6,800 by 1988 (Joint Center for Political Studies, 1989). In the aggregate, Black political gains symbolize what political analysts have referred to as the shift from protest tactics to electoral politics (Smith, 1981; Rustin, 1965).

Since 1965, Blacks have been able to use their new voting power with mixed success. There have been stunning political victories at the local level. Beginning with the 1967 elections of Carl Stokes in Cleveland and Richard Hatcher in Gary, Indiana, Blacks have gone on to elect their own representatives in nearly every city in the North and South where they constitute a numerical voting majority or near-majority. There are now Black mayors in most major cities across the country, including Atlanta, Los Angeles, New Orleans, Philadelphia, Baltimore, Birmingham, and, most recently, Seattle and New York. Black women have also been recently elected as mayors in Washington, D.C., and Hartford, Connecticut. Furthermore, Black Americans have been elected to office in all congressional districts where Blacks form a voting majority.[2] Most striking have been the political changes that have taken place in the South, once the bastion of White supremacy. In 1965, only 78 Blacks held elected office in the South, whereas by 1986, Black southern legislators constituted 64 percent of the 6,424 Black officeholders in the country (Williams, 1987b: 77–78). As a result of Black voting power in the South, most Democratic congressional and state representatives now have either been replaced by liberals or have become more liberal on civil rights issues over time (Whitby and Gilliam, 1991). Thus, despite the presidential-led opposition to civil rights legislation in the 1980s, most southern Democrats in Congress gave their support to the designation of Martin Luther King's birthday as a national holiday and to the 1981 extension of the 1965 Voting Rights Act.

However, the significance of these elections has been more symbolic than substantive. Although the elections of Blacks have led to increases in the numbers of Blacks holding municipal jobs (Karnig and Welch, 1980; Eisinger, 1982; Browning, Marshall, and Tabb, 1984; Mlandenka, 1989), they have not translated into a significantly better way of life for those Blacks at the bottom of society. Pervasive unemployment, entrenched poverty, sub-inferior schools, and urban decay remain critical problems within the Black community. In addition, as jobs have become more scarce in urban areas since the 1960s, the percentage of poor people has increased, and Blacks represent approximately 60 percent of the poor in central cities (Sandefur, 1988). Black politicians have seemingly been unable to deal with these problems (Reed, 1988; Bush, 1984; Peterson, 1981). At most, the new Black political representation has benefited middle-class Blacks, providing new economic opportunities through government employment and minority contracting in city governments (Jaynes and Williams, 1989: 251). In contrast, in cities like Atlanta, the problems facing the Black urban poor have worsened over time (Orfield and Ashkinaze, 1991).

At the national level, the Black political record is mixed as well. Jesse Jackson's candidacies in 1984 and 1988 were enthusiastically greeted by the majority of Blacks and broke new political ground for Blacks. Nonetheless, his twice-failed attempts at garnering the

Democratic presidential nomination suggest that there are limits to Black political power. Blacks hold fewer than 2 percent of the total number of elected positions in this country, even though Blacks represent 12 percent of the population. Much of the gain in the number of Black representatives was due to a sizable Black electoral base, and already the impressive gains in the number of Black elected officials appear to be leveling off since many Whites remain unwilling to vote for Black candidates. Few Blacks have made it to national or even statewide offices. Of the few that have, many won in highly contested, racially charged elections, with votes split along racial lines. For example, although Douglas Wilder's victory as the nation's first elected Black governor since Reconstruction made history, he won by the slimmest of margins, 7,000 votes out of the 1.7 million cast.

In addition, the election of Ronald Reagan in the 1980s revealed the marginal status of Black voters at the national level. Reagan was elected with an unprecedented crush of support, enjoying some of the highest popularity ratings among White Americans since President Eisenhower. In contrast, fewer than one in every ten Blacks voted for Reagan. Furthermore, throughout Reagan's eight years in office, Blacks' evaluations of him remained uniformly negative. And as Blacks became alienated from the Reagan administration, they also became increasingly frustrated with their level of influence in the Democratic party. Finally, in spite of the steady gains in Black registration and turnout throughout the 1980s, Black voter participation dropped significantly in 1988—from 56 percent in 1984 to 52 percent in 1988. In contrast, in the same period, White voter turnout dropped by only two percentage points.

The shift from protest to politics clearly represents a new epoch in Black politics that warrants further examination. Past research on Black voting behavior largely covers the pre–1965 voting rights South. Although a number of studies now exist that examine the results of Black electoral participation—how the elections of Blacks to office have affected public policy and government expenditures, for example—little attention has been given to the general impact of these new political changes on the Black electorate itself. How have these changes affected the political behavior of Blacks, their policy objectives, and their orientation toward politics? Using data collected during the 1984 and 1988 presidential elections in a survey called the National Black Election Study (NBES), this book offers a new analysis of the Black electorate in the context of the recent developments in Black politics.

## The New Black Voter and Jackson's Presidential Campaigns

A significant development in Black politics has been the emergence of the "new Black voter" (Preston, 1989). Since 1965, differences in Black and White registration and turnout rates have diminished considerably. In 1984, the gap between Black and White voter registration rates was the smallest ever recorded—2.2 percentage points, compared to 9.2 percentage points in 1968 (Williams, 1987b: 103). Once differences in socioeconomic status are taken into account, Black and White turnout rates are roughly equal (Bobo and Gilliam, 1990; Wolfinger and Rosenstone, 1980), and in some instances Black turnout rates have exceeded those of Whites. In eight states in the 1982 congressional elections, Blacks turned out in larger numbers than Whites, while in seven other states, Black and White turnouts were roughly equal (Preston, 1989).

Michael Preston (1989) writes that the new Black voters can be divided into two groups: newly registered Black voters who now see some link between participation and political output and previously registered Black voters who now possess a stronger sense of political efficacy and group consciousness. The group of newly registered Black voters, which includes the young, the poor, women, and the elderly, represents those who in the past were the least likely to register and vote. Not only are these groups more likely to register, in some instances their registration rates are higher than those of their White counterparts. In 1984, for example, poor Blacks and those having only a grade school education were registered at rates higher than their White counterparts. As Table 1.1 shows, in 1984, 66 percent of Blacks with annual family incomes of $5,000 to $9,999 were registered to vote, in comparison to 56 percent of Whites with similar annual incomes.

In her analysis of U.S. Census Bureau data, Linda Williams finds that Black voter registration gains are largely due to increased registration among southern Blacks and Black women. While Black voter

**Table 1.1**  Whites' and Blacks' National Registration Rates by Education and Income in 1984

| | Registration | | Black-White Gap (%) |
|---|---|---|---|
| | White (%) | Black (%) | |
| EDUCATION | | | |
| Elementary | | | |
| 0–4 years | 32.7 | 51.4 | 18.7 |
| 5–7 years | 51.1 | 64.1 | 13.0 |
| 8 years | 61.5 | 64.2 | 2.7 |
| High school | | | |
| 1–3 years | 54.6 | 60.0 | 5.4 |
| 4 years | 68.2 | 65.8 | −2.4 |
| College | | | |
| 1–3 years | 77.3 | 72.5 | −4.8 |
| 4 years | 84.5 | 79.2 | −5.3 |
| 5 or more years | 88.1 | 87.5 | −0.6 |
| FAMILY INCOME | | | |
| Under $5,000 | 47.1 | 58.7 | 11.6 |
| $5,000 to $9,999 | 56.1 | 65.6 | 9.5 |
| $10,000 to $14,999 | 63.6 | 66.4 | 2.8 |
| $15,000 to $19,999 | 66.2 | 66.8 | 0.6 |
| $20,000 to $24,999 | 70.0 | 67.0 | −3.0 |
| $25,000 to $34,999 | 75.2 | 71.7 | −3.5 |
| $35,000 to $49,999 | 80.8 | 78.0 | −2.8 |
| $50,000 and over | 83.3 | 79.4 | −3.9 |

*Source:* Williams (1987a), Table 6.5, and as reported in U.S. Bureau of the Census, Current Population Reports, Series P-20, no. 405, tables 9 and 14.

registration in the United States increased by only one-tenth of a percent between 1968 and 1984, Black registration in the South increased by 5 percent. Similarly, Black women's registration rates improved sharply during this period. Despite being among the poorest groups in the United States and despite the fact that they are often the sole providers for their families, since 1976 Black women have had higher registration rates than Black men. Between 1976 and 1984, registration rates among Black women increased by 9.5 percentage points, while those for Black men increased by 5.8 percentage points (Williams, 1987b: 103). Preston writes that along with the Black middle class, newly registered Blacks now believe that their participation in politics can make a difference and that these new Black voters now represent a permanent core of the electorate who "will probably never return to the quiescent state in which they existed in the past" (1989: 130).

Because cross-time national studies of the Black electorate do not exist, it is difficult to document long-term change. Nonetheless, in his analysis of national opinion data from 1952 to 1980, Paul Abramson reports that Blacks' feelings of political effectiveness had increased substantially between 1956 and 1960, and that group differences between Blacks and Whites had declined since the 1950s, when most southern Blacks were effectively disfranchised (1983: 174–176). Recent surveys support this conclusion. In a 1980 national survey of Black Americans, the majority of respondents felt that the election of Blacks had improved the status of Black Americans. Furthermore, in a 1984 national telephone survey of Black Americans, the majority (70 percent) strongly felt that the Black vote could make a difference in who gets elected at both the local and national levels, including who becomes president. Similarly, the majority (62 percent) disagreed with the statement "People like me don't have any say about what the government does."

The resurgence of Black voters, according to Michael Preston, is due mainly to three factors. First, a number of voter registration drives, particularly targeting Blacks, were conducted between 1980 and 1984. The largest gains in registration occurred among minority groups, with Black registration in 1984 up by 6.3 percentage points over 1980 (Piven and Cloward, 1988: 182). Second, the surge in the number of Black candidacies in the post–civil rights era also contributed to the growth in the number of Black voters. The number of Black elected officials in the country grew at a phenomenal rate, with more than a 234 percent increase in the number of Blacks holding elective offices from 1970 to 1984. Most notable were the elections of Black mayors in large cities. By the mid-1970s, the racial composition of many large cities had changed as a result of Black migration to northern urban areas from the South during the first half of the twentieth century and because of the White flight from the cities to the suburbs that occurred during the 1960s and 1970s. Blacks emerged as a voting majority or near-majority in these large metropolitan centers and suddenly were able to play a much larger role in local politics, electing their own representatives. In Cleveland, for example, Blacks constituted 40 percent of the city's registered voters, and in 1967, with the support of about 20 percent of the White voters, were able to elect their first Black mayor, Carl Stokes. In 1970, Blacks constituted 51 percent of the Atlanta residents. In 1973, they were able to elect Atlanta's first Black mayor, Maynard Jackson. In Chicago, Blacks constituted 40 percent of the city's voting population, and in 1983 they elected their first Black mayor, Harold Washington. In many of these mayoral contests, Black turnout rates exceeded those of Whites by a margin of 10 to 15 percent.

According to Preston, these victories were significant for a number of reasons. First, they instilled a new, more vigorous sense of group political efficacy within the Black community. Having become voting majorities or near-majorities, Blacks felt more confident in their abilities to produce political outcomes in their favor. Second, in the process of producing these victories, the level of Black political organization increased. Many grassroots organizations developed to elect Blacks to office. These organizations not only registered new Black voters but also helped advance Blacks' level of political sophistication. Blacks learned who their allies were during these electoral contests, but they also discovered which groups were the most hostile to Black advancement. In a number of cases, Blacks had to end their long-time alliance with machine organizations in order to elect the city's first Black mayor. Finally, the victories Blacks were able to achieve, especially the highly publicized elections of big-city Black mayors, changed the national climate for Black political mobilization, inspiring more Blacks to register in order to participate in their own communities and in national politics.

Lastly, the Reagan administration also can be credited with the growth and development of the new Black voters. While incomes for Blacks had risen relative to those of Whites during the 1960s and 1970s, this trend was reversed in the 1980s. As a result of the 1982 recession, family incomes in general declined by 5 percent between 1979 and 1984, but Black family incomes fell by 14 percent (Tienda and Sandefur, 1988: 26). Moreover, the Reagan administration's policies did not help Black Americans economically. The Reagan 1982 budget cuts included reductions in a variety of social welfare policies—job training, food stamps, health services, and guaranteed student loan programs. These cutbacks disproportionately affected the Black community, in which over one-third were living below the poverty line. In a 1982 survey, 85 percent of Blacks felt that the Reagan administration had gone too far in scaling back government spending on social welfare programs, in contrast to 37 percent of Whites who felt this way (Lawson, 1991: 221). Reagan's conservative rhetoric further marginalized Blacks and other minority groups living on the fringes of society; Reagan was widely perceived as being anti-Black by Black Americans. This dissatisfaction with Reagan aided the efforts of voter mobilization organizations and indeed led more Blacks to register and vote independent of these organizational efforts than had occurred previously. In 1984, more Blacks turned out to vote in a collective effort to defeat Ronald Reagan.

A second major development in the new Black politics was the presidential bids of the Reverend Jesse L. Jackson. Jackson's profound influence on the character and shape of the new Black politics necessitates some attention to his 1984 and 1988 presidential campaigns.[3] Although Jackson was not the first Black American to run for president, he was able to mobilize a much higher percentage of the Black community in support of his candidacy than had past Black presidential contenders, including New York Congresswoman Shirley Chisholm, who ran in 1972. As a Black American championing minority causes, Jackson was never seen as able to attain the party's nomination, since Black voters represent only a quarter of the Democratic party's base. Yet millions of Blacks still supported both his bids. Jackson was able to generate massive Black support because he offered Black voters something other than the White House, redefining victory for Blacks into other, more achievable objectives which included increasing Black voter registration, inspiring more Blacks to seek elected offices, articulating a progressive agenda, and, ultimately, expanding the political influence and strength of Blacks within the Democratic party. Jackson structured and maintained his campaign as a bid for the presidency. In reality, however, his presidential bid was a bargaining vehicle for Black Democratic voters. His candidacy was an attempt to move Blacks from a passive to a more active role within the Democratic party.

Political scientist Ronald Walters (1988) believes that in spite of Blacks' minority status as voters, Black empowerment today could be effectively pursued through a Black presidential campaign strategy such as Jackson's. Although the Black vote is not usually large enough to play a determinative role in the outcome of presidential races, it can guarantee a Democratic loss if Blacks choose to vote for an independent party or candidate or to abstain and stay home. Furthermore, a successful Black campaign would be able to deny the Black vote to any of the other candidates and thereby pose a threat to the nomination for the front-runner. Walters contends that Black presidential candidacies can also assist in the institutionalization of Black politics, for not only will such a campaign organize the Black vote every four years, but a Black presidential contender can issue policy statements that could become part of the party's policy platform at the quadrennial national conventions.

In his presidential bid, Jackson's leverage was further enhanced by his decision to run within the Democratic party. Historically, Black presidential campaigns were ineffective as bargaining vehicles for Blacks because, as representatives of minor parties, Black candidates did not carry much influence at the national level. As a major party presidential contender, however, Jackson was able to compete in a number of nationally televised debates involving all the Democratic candidates. Jackson's participation in such debates made it possible for him to acquire more media attention for his campaign issues, and enabled him to make direct appeals to the public in competition with the other presidential contenders.

In 1984, Jackson campaigned with a budget approximately one-third of that of other major presidential contenders. Given that news coverage in nominating contests is allocated on the basis of a mix of primary or caucus victories and press expectations and that Jackson won less than 20 percent of the vote in nearly every state, he was not expected to receive much news coverage. However, Jackson received better than average media coverage than did similarly situated contenders in part because of the novelty of his candidacy as a Black American. But since press and public expectations for Jackson were so low, his minor electoral achievements were often inflated into monumental ones by the press and television. Furthermore, Jackson took risks to "make news." For example, in January 1984 he flew to Syria to win the freedom of Robert Goodman, an imprisoned Navy flyer, an act that not only won him national acclaim and an invitation to the White House from President Reagan, but also boosted his standing in the polls in New Hampshire (Walters, 1988: 170).

Ironically, the most damage to Jackson's 1984 campaign came in the form of media coverage. On February 13, the *Washington Post* published a story claiming that Jackson had referred to Jewish Americans as "Hymies" and referred to New York City as "Hymietown." Having apparently used these terms in a private conversation with a Black *Washington Post* reporter, Jackson initially denied having made such statements. The story still made national headlines. Jackson eventually issued an apology at a Jewish synagogue in Manchester, New Hampshire (Barker, 1988: 71). His apology did not end the controversy. The affair activated a rehashing of his 1979 trip to the Middle East and his embrace of PLO leader Yasser Arafat. The media also spotlighted Jackson's friendship with Black Muslim leader Louis Farrakhan. Appearing at a rally a few days prior to Jackson's February 26 apology, Farrakhan had warned Jewish organizations that there would be "retaliation if they harmed Jackson in any way." Jackson had defended Farrakhan's remarks, saying that they "reflected Black anger at the assassination of Black leadership figures" (Barker, 1988: 74). Milton Coleman, the *Washington Post* reporter who broke the Hymie story, was also threatened by Farrakhan, who said, "One day we will punish you with death . . . we're going to make an example of Milton Coleman." Later, Farrakhan would call Hitler "a great man—wickedly great." Farrakhan's remarks had the effect of keeping Jackson on the defensive, forcing Jackson to distance himself from Farrakhan; Jackson ultimately criticized the Muslim leader's statements as "reprehensible and morally indefensible."

Jackson's political victories in 1984 can be divided into the tangible and the symbolic. His tangible achievements were few. Even though Jackson had captured the lion's share of the Black Democratic vote in the primary contest, his leverage strategy failed miserably. He obtained over 3 million votes in the Democratic primary, but entered the convention unable to wrest concessions from the party. All of the minority planks proposed by the Jackson camp were overwhelmingly defeated by the Mondale-Hart forces at the 1984 convention (Barker, 1988: 156).

One of the vital issues that Jackson raised at the 1984 convention which was soundly defeated concerned the Democratic party's delegate selection system. The current system allocated delegates only to those candidates able to achieve a 20 percent threshold of votes in each congressional district. Moreover, one-seventh of the delegates at the 1984 convention were "super delegates"—elected officials and party leaders who were selected by the party and not elected by the rank-and-file membership. Jackson pointed out that the threshold requirement unfairly penalized minority and urban voters, who were more likely to be concentrated in a few congressional districts. Such a scheme, Jackson also charged, distorted the one-person-one-vote principle. The party responded by committing a few of its at-large delegate slots to Jackson, but the delegate allocation procedures and the threshold rule remained in place. Thus, although Jackson won 18.3 percent of the total primary vote in 1984, he ended up with only 10 percent of the convention delegates (Morris and Williams, 1989: 243).

Another equally important issue for the Jackson camp in 1984 was the run-off primary. The run-off primary system, used primarily in some southern states, is perceived as one of the lingering obstacles to increased Black political representation (Parker, 1990). Ending the run-off system was important to Jackson since one of his stated objectives was to increase the numbers of Black elected officials. To win the party's nomination in a run-off primary system, a candidate has to receive 50 percent or more of the vote. Candidates must compete in successive races until one wins the majority of the vote. This system had traditionally worked to the disadvantage of Black candidates, since Whites would combine their votes to defeat a Black candidate who had won with the plurality of the vote in the initial contest. This plank, however, like all the rest of Jackson's planks, was defeated in 1984.

Another Jackson objective, which he did not raise explicitly at the party's national convention in 1984, was to increase Black and minority representation in the campaign organization for the party's nominee. Again, Jackson was not especially successful in this endeavor. He had been unable to achieve a real bargaining relationship with the party's presidential nominee, Walter Mondale, since Mondale wanted to work with Jackson only after he had secured the nomination. Mondale supporters were fearful that open negotiations and concessions to Jackson would lead the party to adopt ultraliberal positions which would then cost the Democrats the election. Publicly pressing Mondale on this matter, Jackson stated shortly after the convention that his "enthusiasm level would be nil if Mondale had not appointed more Blacks and women to the campaign by Labor Day" (Walters, 1988: 177). In August, Mondale hired a Jackson campaign aide, Ernest Green, to work on his presidential campaign. Furthermore, in his first meeting with Jackson on August 28, 1984, Mondale agreed to hire some additional Blacks for his campaign. The division among Black leaders over Jackson's candidacy and their inability to agree on some general strategy during the convention may have contributed to the failure of Jackson's bargaining strategy with the Democratic party in 1984 (Barker, 1988: 180). Black leadership support for Mondale indicated that the Black vote was divided, and that the Black Jackson supporters could be safely and successfully ignored by party leaders.

Jackson did substantially better in his 1988 presidential bid. He more than doubled his primary vote in 1988 from 3.3 to 6.7 million, constituting 29 percent of the total primary vote. He nearly tripled the number of his delegates at the national convention, from 384 in 1984 to 1,122 in 1988. Jackson delegates constituted a force of 27 percent at the 1988 convention. Furthermore, in contrast to 1984, Jackson received the endorsements of many Black elected officials in 1988. While he ran a distant third in 1984, he placed second out of a field of eight in 1988. Having set out to win a larger share of the White vote, Jackson managed to consolidate his support within the Black community in 1988, winning nearly unanimous Black support. While 77 percent of Blacks supported Jackson in the 1984 primary contest, 92 percent supported him in the 1988 primary contest. Differences among Blacks in their support of Jackson at the primaries were not to be found in 1988. Older and less educated Blacks, who were less likely to vote for Jackson in the 1984 primary season, were equally supportive of him in 1988. Jackson was able to win 13 percent of the White Democratic vote in the 1988 primary election as well (Plissner and Mitofsky, 1988).

Jackson did better in 1988 for several reasons. First, once Gary Hart dropped out of the race, after his relationship with model-actress Donna Rice made headlines, Jackson remained the only presidential contender who had also run in 1984. And in contrast to 1984, he was not competing against nationally established Democratic leaders like Walter Mondale. Second, with the exception of Illinois Senator Paul Simon, Jackson was the only Democratic contender who represented and espoused traditional liberal Democratic policies and values, which enabled him to broaden his base of support in 1988 (Abramson, Aldrich, and Rohde, 1990: 34). In 1984, half of the contenders, including the front-runner, Mondale, had been traditional Democrats. In addition, in 1988 Jackson campaigned on a broader set of issues and themes, avoiding the two issues he had identified as priorities in 1984, namely, the primary threshold rule and run-off primaries. A chief problem with his 1984 campaign focus was that it had been narrowly restricted to voting rights, and, according to Lorenzo Morris and Linda Williams, the run-off issue was a "poor choice for mobilizing black voters and a totally irrelevant choice for mobilizing the rest of [his] rainbow" (1989: 243). The run-off primary, after all, is used only in ten southern states. In addition, Jackson was aided by his decision to hire more experienced and politically seasoned campaign managers to run his 1988 campaign. Finally, in 1988 the threshold for winning delegates was reduced from 20 percent to 15 percent. This change may have also helped Jackson win more delegates in 1988.

Partly because of his larger success and partly because he had a stronger campaign organization in place, Jackson's use of his campaign as a bargaining vehicle was somewhat more successful in 1988 than it had been in 1984. In 1988, Jackson and Dukakis forces reached agreement in advance of the convention on several policies contained in the party's platform. They included the party's endorsement for the designation of South Africa as a terrorist state, same-day voter registration, D.C. statehood, and increased set-asides for minority contractors in federal contracts. Two of the three issues that Jackson supporters would later bring to the floor for discussion and amendment to the party platform at the convention—the call for a tax increase for the wealthy and a U.S. pledge against first use of nuclear weapons—were soundly defeated by a 2 to 1 margin.

The third issue, favoring Palestinian self-determination, was never voted on. Finally, although this issue had not formally reappeared in his 1988 campaign, Jackson still had negotiated with the party for a revision of the delegation selection rules for 1992. The threshold rule was lowered from 20 percent to 15 percent, but the number of super delegates was slightly increased for the 1992 national convention (Smith, 1990: 221).

Even though Jackson's 1988 campaign was more successful than his 1984 bid, his candidacies failed to resolve any of the fundamental political dilemmas that Blacks face today. The vote-maximizing potential of a Black presidential strategy that Walters (1988) outlines did not prove to be especially successful in Jackson's campaigns. The record high Black turnout in 1984 did not affect the outcome, nor did Black voting (or the apparent nonvoting by Jackson supporters) make a difference in the 1988 presidential race. Morris and Williams argue that Jackson's candidacy may have actually set off a new disenchantment with electoral politics among Blacks, arguing that "given the lack of black influence on 1984 electoral outcomes and the rightward drift of Democrats as well as Republicans, one message blacks may well have received is that their embrace of mainstream politics got them little or nothing" (1989: 245). Similarly, Jackson's bids may have exacerbated Blacks' political problems, pushing Blacks further into a marginal and politically impotent corner of the party and in national politics in general. Other analysts have argued that Jackson hurt the party's chances of winning the presidential election, pointing out that conservative and moderate White Democrats are unwilling to vote for a party that is seen as a captive of Jackson and Black interests. Such claims may ultimately harm Blacks politically, since they are used to justify the party's abandonment of Blacks in favor of renewing its courtship of moderates and White southerners.

Yet while neither of Jackson's presidential campaigns resulted in tangible bargaining successes for Black Americans, both nevertheless achieved important symbolic victories for Blacks. Many Blacks considered Jackson's bids for the Democratic party's nomination successful. One reason for this perception is that the press did not award much coverage to the debate on platform issues in 1984 or 1988, focusing instead almost exclusively on Jackson's speeches at the conventions. Jackson's oratorical skills had raised the excitement level in the Black community, so much so that the Black voting public generally missed his failed negotiating attempts at the national conventions, witnessing instead only the great success of his speeches at the conventions. It is unlikely that Jackson's 1984 bid caused Blacks to withdraw from politics. Indeed, as I will show later in the book, Jackson can be credited in part for the development of the new Black voter. Jackson's presidential bids mobilized new Black voters and stimulated Black interest in presidential campaigns.

## The Second Stage of the Civil Rights Movement?

In addition to its focus on the new Black voter, this book addresses a larger theoretical issue, namely, the question whether the new Black politics can be considered in some sense a continuation of the Black protest movement, which most analysts claim ended in 1972. In a 1965 article entitled "From Protest to Politics: The Future of the Civil Rights Movement," civil rights activist Bayard Rustin predicted that the civil rights movement would evolve into formal, institutionalized party politics. The strategies and thrust of the movement would change, he argued, but Blacks would still be engaged in a movement radically oriented toward social change.

It is unclear whether the new Black politics can reasonably be labeled the "second stage" of the Black civil rights movement. Blacks' political orientations and interests, as well as their leadership, have changed over the past two decades. Many political observers of that period felt that Black enfranchisement would restore Blacks' faith in American democracy, putting an end to their movement and their growing political radicalism. Many also believed that with their incorporation, Blacks would eventually become no different from other groups of voters, having interests as individuals in a sound economy, safe neighborhoods, good schools, and lower taxes (Dahl, 1961: 32–62). Furthermore, Black leadership would change. In a letter to President Johnson, one White social scientist remarked that through its support of Black voting rights, the White House could establish a "network of black political leaders from every level of government," thus having a "link to the Negro community and [thereby] effectively bypass the Rap Browns and Stokely

Carmichaels and even the Martin Luther Kings (none of whom have been elected to anything)" (quoted in Lawson, 1985: 13).

Passage of the 1965 voting rights bill did in fact substantially change the structure of Black politics, giving Black Americans new access to the dominant forums within institutionalized politics. The higher levels of Black voting that took place after its passage also created a new class of Black elected leadership. Adolph Reed, Jr. (1986) contends that Black officeholders have largely replaced traditional Black protest leaders as spokespersons for the community's interests. Reed views Black elected officials as politically and morally superior to traditional Black protest leaders, since Black representation is guaranteed through electoral mechanisms. Black leaders today must now adequately represent their Black constituents or face the loss of their office. Blacks' new reliance on electoral politics, however, may also have undermined the racial solidarity they displayed during the civil rights movement. Traditionally, it has been argued that electoral politics suppresses group politics (Piven and Cloward, 1988: xii–xvii). The new emphasis on voting could have moved Blacks away from a group to an individual orientation toward politics. Group consciousness can be undermined by the individualistic (that is, one person, one vote) symbolism attached to voting.

In light of these changes, it is possible that Blacks today may be less politically unified than during the civil rights movement, especially given the increased class stratification within the Black community. Since the civil rights movement, a substantial number of Blacks have entered the middle class. From 1960 to 1980, the proportion of Blacks in middle-class occupations and those receiving middle-level incomes increased from 16 to over 30 percent (Landry, 1987). Yet even though the size of the Black middle class has increased, it has been estimated that over one-third of all Black families currently live below the poverty line (Farley and Allen, 1987). In general, Blacks are three times as likely as Whites to be in poverty (Cotton, 1989). The high incidence of poverty within the Black community is further compounded by the high rate of Black unemployment, which has remained in the double digits since the 1970s. Furthermore, if one takes into account the proportion of discouraged Black workers, those no longer actively seeking employment and classified as out of the work force, estimated at 15 to 17 percent in 1984, Black unemployment figures would double (Farley and Allen, 1987: 211–213). In contrast to the number of middle-class Black families enjoying the benefits of two paychecks, the number of poor Black families lacking adequate incomes and on welfare have led some to conclude that there are, in effect, "two Black Americas." This new Black middle class may have different political interests from those of the Black poor.

Not only is deepening class stratification taking place, but civil rights may no longer represent the central concern of Black voters. Charles V. Hamilton (1986) outlines what he terms a shift from the "politics of rights" to the "politics of resources" that has occurred over the last two decades. Black Americans, he writes, have historically supported both civil rights and social welfare policies, but the problems of unemployment, poverty, crime, lack of education, and drugs have become first-order problems, while civil rights has now become the "symbolic agenda" of Blacks. Recent survey data support Hamilton's claim. Blacks today consider unemployment to be a far more important problem facing Black Americans than race discrimination. In a 1984 national telephone survey of Black Americans, 62 percent named unemployment as the most important problem, followed by racial discrimination. And when the respondents were asked which constituted the second most important problem, crime and race discrimination were closely ranked.

Nevertheless, in spite of these changes, signs of protest remain visible even in this new stage of Black politics. Protest activists have not been wholly replaced by elected officials in some sectors within the Black community, and they have remained credible leaders. Black activists like the Reverend Al Sharpton in New York City still manage to attract large followings of Blacks in spite of the alternative leadership that Black elected officials now present. The transition from protest to politics is neither as sharp nor as irrevocable as political analysts have maintained. Although protest politics and social movements have been strictly differentiated from electoral politics in terms of their goals (the former usually being anti-establishment or anti-institutional), tactics (the former being non-conventional, direct-action), and structure (the former are generally disorderly and nonhierarchical), analysts of social movement now recognize the important continuities between protest movements and institutionalized politics (Tarrow, 1987: 3). The relationship between protest and organized politics most likely fits a continuum (Piven and Cloward, 1988; McAdam, 1982: 36), not a discrete series of stages, as it often is depicted. Indeed, the rising Black voter registration rates suggest a continued collective struggle, evident in Jackson's bids for the Democratic presidential nomination. The strong and unified support that Jackson received has been interpreted by some political scientists as suggestive of a grassroots electoral movement by Black Americans, especially since Jackson's campaign at base has been viewed as an attempt to restructure politics and government to bring about the inclusion of the powerless and politically disadvantaged (Foster, 1990; Thompson, 1990). Moreover, the movement label is given to a wide array of new political groups that emerged in the late 1960s and 1970s that formerly might have been called interest groups. These groups, such as the environmentalists, gay rights groups, and anti-nuclear organizations, have blended the direct-action tactics that had been used in the Black civil rights movement with standard political lobbying practices, such as letter-writing and petitioning (see, for example, Useem and Zald, 1987). In addition, feminists have argued that the "women's vote" (a phenomenon that has yet to be as clearly documented as the "Black vote") represents the continuation of the modern-day women's liberation struggle (see, for example, Klein, 1985). Finally, although unemployment, poverty, and crime now dominate the Black political agenda, research reveals that the majority of Black Americans remain dissatisfied with the amount of progress made in race relations since the protest movement (Schuman, Steeh, and Bobo, 1985). Although they are no longer priorities, racial inequality and racial issues have not lost their political currency within the Black community, especially among its leaders (Verba and Orren, 1985).

Ultimately, the answer to this larger question about the nature of the new Black politics rests on answers to the subset of smaller questions raised explicitly in this book, including the following: Are Blacks still race-conscious? Do Blacks have group interests, or have their policy views become more individualistic? What underlies Blacks' support for the Democratic party, and their support of

Jackson for president? Who participates in politics in the Black community today? Finally, are Black political aspirations firmly planted within the Democratic party, or does the idea of Black political independence through the creation of a Black national political party still generate considerable mass support? These and related questions will be explored in the course of this book.

The book is organized in the following manner. Chapter 2 examines recent claims that Blacks have become more politically conservative and that the deepening class divisions within the Black community have led to a conflict in policy objectives between middle-class Blacks and working and poor Blacks. Chapter 3 investigates the factors that account for Blacks' near unanimous support for the Democratic party today, and how Jackson's presidential bids may have undermined that support. Chapters 4 and 5 examine the attitudinal and demographic variables associated with Black electoral participation. Chapter 5 specifically examines the impact of Reagan, Bush, and Jackson on Black rates of participation in the 1984 and 1988 primaries and presidential elections. Chapter 6 explores Blacks' evaluations of the presidential contenders prior to the general election, as well as their voting decisions in the 1984 and 1988 primaries and presidential elections. Chapter 7 assesses Black attitudes toward politics and Black political strategies in general. Finally, Chapter 8 offers an assessment of the book's implications for the future direction and shape of Black politics in the 1990s and beyond.

The conclusions in this book are based on analysis of the 1984–1988 National Black Election Study (NBES). This study is a large national panel survey of Black Americans conducted during the 1984 and 1988 presidential elections. A total of 1,150 voting-age Blacks were interviewed prior to the 1984 national election, and 872 were reinterviewed immediately after the 1984 election. In 1988, 473 of the original 1984 Black respondents were reinterviewed prior to the 1988 national election; 418 were reinterviewed following this election. A more detailed description of the surveys and data set is provided in Appendix A. This panel study now makes it possible for the first time to document change in the Black electorate over a four-year period.

# 2

# Race, Class, and Black Policy Views

Black Americans experienced considerable change in their political attitudes during the 1960s and early 1970s. The civil rights movement had radicalized them. By the mid-1970s, Blacks were more liberal in their policy preferences than a decade earlier (Nie, Verba, and Petrocik, 1979), and a near-majority now identified with the Democratic party. White Americans had become somewhat more progressive in their political attitudes during this period as well (Schuman, Steeh, and Bobo, 1985; Taylor, Sheatsley, and Greeley, 1978), but by the 1980s, the political differences between Blacks and Whites would become most striking. Where Whites saw that substantial progress had been made in the area of race relations, Blacks saw little progress; where the majority of Whites opposed affirmative action and desegregation programs, the majority of Blacks favored them (Sigelman and Welch, 1991; Schuman, Steeh, and Bobo, 1985). The percentage of Whites who felt that substantial progress had been achieved in race relations rose steadily from 39 percent in 1964 to 63 percent in 1976. In contrast, among Blacks, the percentage who claimed that a lot of change had taken place steadily declined from 60 percent in 1964 to 32 percent by 1976 (Kluegel and Smith, 1986: 185–196). Furthermore, most Whites now believe that Blacks are no longer held back because of race, and that Blacks have no one but themselves to blame for their group economic situation. In contrast, most Blacks feel that structural factors work against their collective advancement in society.

It is possible that the conservatism of the 1980s tempered the political liberalism that Blacks developed during the civil rights struggle. William J. Wilson (1981), a Black sociologist, argued that with the passage of civil rights legislation and with the scope of the changes in race relations, the status of Black Americans was constrained less by race than class. Furthermore, he asserted that race-specific programs and policies would not help the situation of poor Blacks, and that Blacks should move away from such programs toward social welfare programs that would generally improve the lot of the poor. Many Black political leaders and intellectuals have strongly contested Wilson's arguments, particularly the arguments they considered implicit in his analysis, namely, that racial discrimination was no longer a problem for middle-class Blacks and that race-specific programs should be abandoned altogether (see Willie, 1979).

Although Wilson did not speculate directly on the relevance of class in Black public opinion, his arguments concerning changes in race relations and the Black class structure helped promote two new claims regarding the nature of Black politics. First, it is asserted that as a result of changed race relations, civil rights and racial equality are no longer political priorities for most Black Americans, even though their leaders have continued to push for such issues. A second claim is that Blacks as a group are no longer politically cohesive, that middle-class Blacks are now more politically conservative than working-class and poor Blacks. The high public visibility accorded to Black conservatives in the Reagan administration fed media speculation on the possibility of an emerging class of Black conservatives. In this chapter I will assess the validity of these claims and will show that although the issue of race has diminished slightly in its political importance relative to social welfare issues, race remains highly significant and salient to the vast majority of Black Americans, and the majority can be considered race-conscious. However, even though Blacks are united politically by race, Blacks are also divided by class.

## Is the Significance of Race Increasing or Declining?

Throughout the 1980s, race-specific programs were increasingly attacked. Critics of these programs asserted not only that such programs had failed to help the most disadvantaged members of the Black community, but also that the political climate had turned against affirmative action and other special race programs, with the majority of White Americans becoming resentful of such programs. Public opinion surveys bear this out, revealing that the majority of White Americans feel that enough attention has been focused on the civil rights of Blacks; indeed, some now claim that Blacks have received too much attention on this matter (Colasanto, 1989). Furthermore, racial stereotypes have not broken down, since Whites' opinions of Blacks are increasingly strongly negative. A survey conducted in 1990 by the National Opinion Research Center at the University of Chicago found that the majority of Whites surveyed said that Blacks are more violent, less intelligent, and lazier than Whites (Duke, 1991). The resentment of Whites toward affirmative action has been successfully exploited in political contests involving Blacks. In the 1990 Senate race in North Carolina, political incumbent Jesse Helms was able to defeat his Black opponent quite handily after airing a television commercial that showed a Black getting a job through affirmative action even though the White applicant was apparently "better qualified" than the Black and "needed the job the most." Also, although President Bush recently signed into law a new civil rights bill, he vetoed an earlier version of it, labeling it a "quota bill." American politics has become more race-charged, in part, as Thomas and Mary Edsall (1991) claim, because of the open and bitter conflict over affirmative action, the Democratic party's image as the party of the urban poor and Blacks, and the Republican party's easy use and manipulation of civil rights and race as campaign issues.

There is some evidence that suggests Blacks themselves have grown less enchanted with a policy agenda focused exclusively on race. In their comprehensive study of Blacks' and Whites' racial attitudes, Schuman, Steeh, and Bobo found that in the last fifteen years, Black support for government intervention in race relations has declined (1985: 145–152). From 1964 to 1978, Blacks have become less inclined to favor federal intervention to integrate schools and less supportive of the principle of federal aid targeted to minority groups. For example, Black support for federal intervention to integrate public schools fell from 90 percent in 1968 to 60 percent in

1978. Similarly, Black support for efforts by the federal government to improve the social and economic position of Blacks declined by 20 percentage points over a ten-year period. Surveys conducted in 1984 also indicate that Blacks today are less concerned with civil rights as a policy matter relative to other issues. In a 1984 Joint Center for Political Studies/Gallup Organization poll, 65 percent of Blacks felt that unemployment was a very important issue in the presidential campaign, while 45 percent identified poverty as an important election issue. Only 38 percent felt that civil rights was an important issue to be addressed in the presidential election (Jaynes and Williams, 1988: 246). Similarly, in the 1984 NBES, when respondents were asked which of the three problems facing Black Americans today—unemployment, discrimination, and crime—they considered most important, the majority (62 percent) named unemployment, while only 21 percent mentioned discrimination. Furthermore, the majority in the NBES survey felt that the focus should not be on racial discrimination. Sixty percent voiced agreement with the statement: "This country would be better off if we worried less about how equal Black people and White people are."

Schuman, Steeh, and Bobo (1985) note that the slippage in support for busing and minority aid may be a response on the part of Blacks to the current conservative political climate. The current context may have forced a rearrangement of the interests and priorities that Blacks advocated during the civil rights movement. Given the degree of White opposition to such programs, and the past and current Republican administrations' unwillingness to back such programs, Blacks may have retreated from positions on certain race-based programs taken during the heyday of the civil rights movement. The problems of poverty, unemployment, and crime have also increased in magnitude and intensity within the inner cities; thus, Blacks may now be more concerned about these issues than with the less tangible problem of racial discrimination that they still face.

Yet, although support among Blacks for race-specific programs has declined, that support remains considerably higher than Whites' support for such programs. Racial discontent also remains high within the Black community. Although the issue of race discrimination may no longer be a political priority among Blacks, most still feel that racial discrimination remains a substantial problem in the

United States. Sigelman and Welch (1991) find that the majority of Blacks claim to have experienced discrimination in education, housing, employment opportunities, and wages. They write that Blacks today "see racial discrimination as an everyday occurrence, not an historical curiosity" (1991: 59). In the 1984 NBES, approximately 85 percent of the respondents disagreed with the statement that "Discrimination against Blacks is no longer a problem in the U.S.," and, of that total, 65 percent *strongly* disagreed. Furthermore, there is evidence that reveals that a large minority of Blacks are dissatisfied with the amount of racial progress attained since the civil rights struggle. In fact, more than one-third of Blacks question whether any racial progress has been achieved at all. Thus, although 52 percent felt that a lot of progress has been made in getting rid of racial discrimination, 45 percent felt that not much real change had occurred. And while 57 percent felt that the civil rights movement had affected them personally, 40 percent felt that they remain unaffected by the struggle. Furthermore, even though 24 percent responded that Blacks today get a "better break" when asked "On the whole, do you think most White people want to see Blacks get a better break, or do they want to keep Blacks down, or don't they care one way or the other?" 37 percent claimed that "Whites want to keep Blacks down." Thirty-one percent felt that "Whites don't care one way or the other." Finally, a solid 36 percent of Blacks believe that Blacks in this country will *never* achieve full equality with Whites. In contrast, 46 percent express the view that racial equality can eventually be achieved.

Moreover, Blacks are keenly aware of the inequalities that persist between Blacks and Whites. A vast majority of Blacks see substantial and sustained inequalities between Blacks and Whites. For example, 61 percent of the Black respondents said that Blacks are worse off than Whites economically. The prevailing belief that American society remains racially divided and unequal helps to create and sustain a strong awareness of race, which, in turn, helps establish a strong racial identity among Black Americans. Blacks' subordinate position in society, in other words, explains why Blacks identify more closely with their race than Whites do (Gurin, 1985). A number of questions in the 1984 NBES survey reveal the degree of racial affinity among Blacks. When asked how close they feel in "ideas and feelings about things to Blacks," the majority (56 percent)

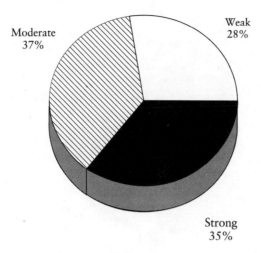

**Figure 2.1**  Strength of Race Identification among Blacks. (*Source:* 1984 NBES.)

responded that they feel very close to Blacks. Thirty-eight percent felt fairly close, with less than 7 percent stating that they were "not too close" or "not close at all" to Blacks. The majority of Blacks believe that what happens to the group affects them personally. Fully 75 percent of Blacks in the survey felt that what happens to Black people will shape their lives. Approximately 30 percent said that what happens to the group affects them "a lot." Blacks apparently also think consciously about race, although for three-fifths of the sample, race was not particularly salient. Sixteen percent reported that they think about race "a lot," and 13 percent think about it "fairly often." In contrast, only 2 Blacks out of the sample of 1,150 voluntarily told interviewers that they never think about their race.

Figure 2.1 displays the distribution of strong, moderate, and weak common-fate identifiers in the 1984 sample. This measure of race identification is closely associated with Blacks' perceptions of group power. Those who feel that Blacks wield less influence and power than Whites in society and politics are more likely to be strong race-identifiers, and vice versa, while those who perceive vast economic differences between Whites and Blacks are also more likely to be strong race-identifiers.[1]

However, even though race identification remains strong, class

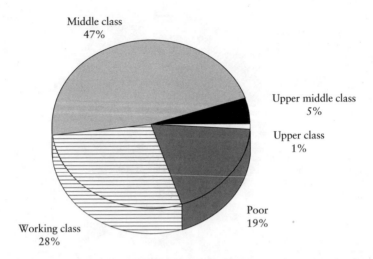

Figure 2.2    Distribution of Subjective Social Classes among Blacks. (*Source:* 1984 NBES.)

stratification has become more pronounced within the Black community. The percentage of Black families living at or below the poverty line has increased, as has the percentage of Black families who can be classified as middle class. While the majority of Blacks today still consider themselves to be neither poor nor middle class but working class, the percentage of Blacks who identify themselves as middle class doubled between 1952 and 1978 (Vanneman and Cannon, 1987: 248). But in the 1984 NBES study, the plurality of the respondents said that they were middle class (46 percent), while only 27 percent were working class and 19 percent poor. The remaining 6 percent of the respondents identified themselves as either upper-middle class or upper class (see Figure 2.2). The higher percentage of self-identified middle-class Blacks in the NBES is no doubt a reflection of the telephone survey design, which tends to produce respondents of higher socioeconomic status than face-to-face survey designs.

Social class identification within the Black community is related to a number of socioeconomic status indicators, including family income and whether the family receives public assistance.[2] Affluent Blacks are more likely to identify with the middle, upper-middle, or upper classes; poor Blacks are more likely to self-identify as poor or working class. Age and gender are also statistically related to Blacks' social class identities. All things being equal, older Blacks are less likely to identify with the higher-status classes than younger Blacks. The Black elderly may be more likely to identify with the poor and working classes, given the employment patterns less than two decades ago that consigned them to the lower rungs of the work force. A greater range of occupations and professions is open to Blacks today, and this may explain why young Blacks are more likely to see themselves as members of higher classes than older Blacks. Farley and Allen note, "A black man who obtains a college diploma is no longer restricted to the public school system, the civil service or the pulpit of a black church" (1987: 278). Black women are also likely to identify with lower-status groupings. This pattern may be a reflection of their subordinate economic status vis-à-vis other gender/racial groups.

Which Blacks are more likely to identify strongly with the race, and how does class identification affect Blacks' racial identities? Bert Landry (1987) maintains that as a result of civil rights legislation in the 1960s, a new Black middle class has emerged, defined as new because its members are increasingly free from the racist social restrictions that the old Black middle class faced. Traditionally, social theorists have maintained that poor Blacks, particularly the urban poor, possess the strongest racial identities within the Black community, given the extent of their racial segregation and impoverished conditions. The one positive effect of their ghettoization has been the freedom to maintain their cultural ties and identities, which Blacks seeking integration must abandon. E. Franklin Frazier, in *Black Bourgeoisie,* harshly characterized middle-class Blacks as lacking in racial consciousness because of their single-minded pursuit of acceptance by White society. In contrast, W. E. B. Du Bois had predicted that college-educated Blacks ("the Talented Tenth") would be the "race men and women" of tomorrow, working toward the liberation of the race.

Of the few empirical studies conducted on this issue, most have found that it is not the poor and working-class Blacks but the higher-status Blacks who possess the stronger racial consciousness and identities (Marx, 1967; Dillingham, 1981; Jackman and Jackman, 1983; Lewis and Schneider, 1983). The Jackmans' study on class

Table 2.1   Determinants of Race Identification (OLS coefficients)

| Independent Variables | B | (SE) |
|---|---|---|
| Region (non-South) | .12 | (.13) |
| Gender (female) | −.59** | (.13) |
| Age | −.001 | (.004) |
| Education | .12** | (.03) |
| Income | .04 | (.02) |
| Urbanicity (low-high) | −.06 | (.05) |
| Social class identification (low-high) | −.30** | (.08) |
| Constant | 5.37** | (.45) |
| Total cases | 713 | |
| $R^2$ | .09 | |

Source: The 1984 National Black Election Study.
*$p < .05$.
**$p < .01$.

awareness and identification in the United States found that race has greater significance among middle-class Blacks than working-class or poor Blacks. More than 60 percent of self-identified middle-class Blacks in their sample stated that they felt closer to their racial group than their class group. In contrast, a mere 5 percent of self-identified poor and working-class Blacks preferred their racial group over their class group.[3]

The determinants of common-fate racial identification are shown in Table 2.1. Social class identification was negatively associated with Blacks' racial identifications. Blacks who identified with the middle, upper-middle, and upper classes were less likely to identify strongly with the race. In contrast, education was positively related to Blacks' racial identities. College-educated Blacks, in particular, possessed the strongest racial common-fate identities. Apparently, upward mobility has a mixed effect on one's racial identity, simultaneously undermining and reinforcing it. Education may make Blacks more aware of the extent of racial inequality in the United States, and, as discussed above, those Blacks more cognizant of racial inequalities are more race-conscious. Income was also positively related to race identification; however, it was not statistically significant. Affluent Blacks may have greater interaction with Whites than poor Blacks, making them more racially aware. But even while the racial experiences of middle-class Blacks help sustain their racial identifications, the act of identifying with higher-status social groups reduces race awareness and group consciousness.

Table 2.1 shows that gender was also related to race identification. Black women have weaker racial identities than Black men. This is somewhat surprising since Black women participated in higher numbers than Black men in the civil rights movement (Giddings, 1984: 284), which suggested that they may possess stronger racial identities than Black men. In addition, surveys from the 1970s demonstrate that Black women are more supportive of the women's movement than White women (Baxter and Lansing, 1983; Fulenwider, 1980). Their higher levels of support for feminist principles might also correspond with stronger racial identities. However, as the Black power movement took off in the urban North, Black identification and consciousness became transformed into an assertion of Black masculinity. Another possibility is that Black women form weaker racial identities than Black men because they are less likely than Black men to see themselves as victims of racial discrimination (Sigelman and Welch, 1991: 71–74).

To summarize, even though a large majority of Blacks continue to express support for race-specific/civil rights programs, longitudinal surveys have revealed that race-specific social programs receive less support in the Black community today than they did two decades ago. Moreover, those Blacks who identify with the middle, upper-middle, and upper classes have weaker racial identities than those who identify with the poor and working classes. At the same time, the majority of Blacks remain race-identified, and within the Black community, college-educated Black males appear to be the most racially identified. Thus, although the issue of race has become less significant as public policy, it has not diminished in its subjective importance among Black Americans.

## Black Political Liberalism and Conservatism

Paradoxically, while Black policy positions became more liberal during the 1960s and 1970s, Blacks' political orientations became more conservative. The number of those identifying themselves as conservative more than doubled, from 12 percent in 1974 to 30 percent in 1980. As shown in Figure 2.3, nearly a third of Blacks

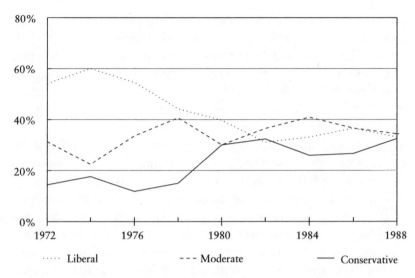

**Figure 2.3**  Ideological Self-Identification among Blacks, 1972–1988.
(*Source:* National Election Studies.)

now identify themselves as political conservatives. At the same time, the percentage of self-identified conservatives in the White community has remained fairly constant, at about 39 percent in 1972 as opposed to 44 percent in 1986. The percentage of White liberals was 23 percent in 1972 and 22 percent in 1986.

In the 1984 NBES, fully 32 percent of the respondents said that they were conservative, while half identified themselves as liberals. Approximately 14 percent were self-identified as strong conservatives, 12 percent moderate conservatives, 18 percent weak conservatives, 16 percent weak liberals, 14 percent moderate liberals, and 20 percent strong liberals. Eight percent were political moderates.[4] The real meaning behind these ideological badges is not clear. Public opinion research has demonstrated that in general Americans do not use ideological terminology in everyday conversations about politics, and most Americans have been characterized as nonideological (Converse, 1964; Kinder, 1983; Smith, 1989). Nonetheless, empirical studies have found that self-identified liberals tend to favor welfare policies and social change, while self-identified conservatives subscribe to free-market economics and are generally opposed to government efforts toward racial integration (Conover and Feldman, 1981). Furthermore, ideological self-identifications are related to voting behavior (Levitin and Miller, 1979). Self-identified liberals tend to favor Democratic candidates, in contrast to self-identified conservatives, who, on the whole, support Republican candidates.

In order to establish the real meaning of these labels for Blacks, in the 1984 NBES those who identified themselves as liberal or conservative (moderates were excluded) were asked a follow-up question: "What sorts of things do you have in mind when you say that someone's views are liberal [or conservative]?" Roughly 30 percent of the respondents failed to define these concepts, even though they had already identified themselves as liberal or conservative. Self-identified conservatives were somewhat more likely to respond "don't know" to this question than self-identified liberals. Furthermore, a large share of the "don't know's" came from the less-educated respondents in the sample. Only 65 percent of all self-identified ideologues having a high school education or less attempted to define either liberalism or conservatism. In contrast, of those Blacks with a college background, approximately 80 percent offered a definition. A variety of factors could explain the failure to answer this question, beyond the fact of ignorance about ideological labels and terminology. In general, poor verbal skills can inhibit responses to open-ended questions. Respondents may also refuse to answer because such a question requires too much effort. However, failure to respond most likely represents unfamiliarity with the terms "liberal" and "conservative" that were used in the question (Schuman and Presser, 1981). Thus, liberalism and conservatism, as concepts, possibly mean very little to the Blacks who failed to define these terms.[5]

The meaningful responses to this question can be placed into three broad categories. These categories correspond with how the respondents have defined conservatism or liberalism, that is, by reference to philosophical principles commonly associated with liberalism or conservatism, in relation to the spendthrift or frugal spending habits of the government, or according to specific social programs and foreign policies. The majority of both liberals and conservatives defined liberalism or conservatism in terms of broad philosophical principles. Self-identified Black liberals tended to define liberals as in favor of "equality," "social reform," or as

Table 2.2  Determinants of Ideological Self-Identification (OLS coefficients)

| Independent Variables | B | (SE) |
|---|---|---|
| Region (non-South) | .05 | (.18) |
| Gender (female) | .28 | (.18) |
| Age | .011* | (.006) |
| Education | .05 | (.04) |
| Income | .05 | (.03) |
| Urbanicity (low-high) | .18** | (.07) |
| Race identification (low-high) | .17** | (.05) |
| Social class identification (low-high) | −.03 | (.11) |
| Church attendance | −.12 | (.07) |
| Constant | 1.52* | (.68) |
| Total cases | 608 | |
| $R^2$ | .07 | |

Source: The 1984 National Black Election Study.
*$p < .05$.
**$p < .01$.

those "who tackle problems quickly." Self-identified conservatives generally said that conservatives were "old-fashioned," "avoided risk," and were "patriotic." Liberals more than conservatives mentioned specific social programs that liberals usually support. In contrast, self-identified conservatives tended to define conservatives as "cautious spenders."

Who within the Black community are self-named liberals, and who are the self-conscious conservatives? Table 2.2 contains the results of the regression of Blacks' ideological self-identifications based on class identification and race identification as well as on a number of demographic variables, including church attendance. The political ideology measure is scaled from strong conservative to strong liberal. While higher-status Blacks were no more likely to identify themselves as conservative than lower-status Blacks, strong race identifiers were more likely than weak race identifiers to consider themselves liberal. Age and geographic location (urbanicity) were also significantly associated with Blacks' ideological identifications. While it is often assumed that people become more politically conservative as they age, there is actually very little empirical support for this assertation. In this case, younger Blacks were far more likely than older Blacks to identify themselves as conservative. This reverse relationship between age and political conservatism within the Black community might help explain the surge in the number of self-identified political conservatives. Over time, older Black Americans who consider themselves liberals are being replaced by a younger generation of Blacks who think of themselves as conservative. Blacks living in rural areas as opposed to urban centers were also more likely to adopt conservative identities. Finally, there was a modest, although not statistically significant, relationship between church attendance and political ideology. Religious Blacks, specifically those who attend church on a weekly basis, were somewhat more likely to consider themselves conservative than those who attend church less often or not at all. In sum, Black conservatives are less race-conscious, younger, tend to live in rural areas or small towns, and are regular churchgoers.

Is the conservative trend in Blacks' ideological self-placement also reflected in their policy views? Blacks, as noted previously, became more liberal during the 1960s and 1970s. Have they moved to the political right in the 1980s?

Group comparisons are difficult to make over time because the numbers of Blacks in a given survey are generally small, and Black opinions are more likely to fluctuate as a result of error. Having noted this, if one compares Black and White opinions on two issues that traditionally divide liberals and conservatives—a federally guaranteed job program and federal aid to minority groups—the percentage of Blacks who express conservative viewpoints still remains considerably smaller than the percentage of Whites with conservative views (see Table 2.3). Whereas nearly half of Whites polled expressed conservative viewpoints on these two issues from 1970 to 1988, roughly a quarter of Blacks expressed conservative viewpoints. Nonetheless, the percentage of Blacks who oppose the idea of a federally guaranteed job program has more than tripled from 7 percent in 1972 to 28 percent in 1988. Black opposition to federal assistance for minorities and Blacks has increased during this period as well, from 6 percent in 1970 to 26 percent in 1988.

Measures of Blacks' and Whites' attitudes toward government spending programs were available only for the 1980s, but relative to Whites a small minority of Blacks felt that spending on social programs should be reduced in the 1980s. The percentages of Blacks

**Table 2.3** Percentages of Blacks and Whites Who Express Conservative Policy Views, 1970–1988

| Policy Statement | | 1970 | 1972 | 1974 | 1976 | 1978 | 1980 | 1982 | 1984 | 1986 | 1988 |
|---|---|---|---|---|---|---|---|---|---|---|---|
| Oppose a Guaranteed Jobs Program | % Whites | * | 49 | 50 | 53 | 58 | 52 | 52 | 48 | 56 | 55 |
| | % Blacks | * | 7 | 10 | 16 | 27 | 21 | 16 | 16 | 24 | 28 |
| | Difference | * | 42 | 40 | 37 | 31 | 31 | 36 | 32 | 32 | 27 |
| Oppose Federal Aid to Minorities | % Whites | 49 | 46 | 49 | 48 | 51 | 52 | 49 | 40 | 48 | 54 |
| | % Blacks | 6 | 9 | 8 | 13 | 19 | 24 | 18 | 17 | 29 | 26 |
| | Difference | 43 | 37 | 41 | 35 | 32 | 28 | 31 | 23 | 19 | 28 |
| Defense Spending Should be Increased | % Whites | * | * | * | * | * | 72 | 34 | 36 | 33 | 33 |
| | % Blacks | * | * | * | * | * | 59 | 24 | 33 | 30 | 32 |
| | Difference | * | * | * | * | * | 13 | 10 | 3 | 3 | 1 |
| Social Services Spending Should be Cut | % Whites | * | * | * | * | * | * | 43 | 36 | 29 | 34 |
| | % Blacks | * | * | * | * | * | * | 20 | 13 | 12 | 15 |
| | Difference | * | * | * | * | * | * | 23 | 23 | 17 | 19 |

*Source:* The American National Election Studies, 1952–1988 Cumulative Data File.
*Data not available.

and Whites who believe defense spending should be increased are equal, while the proportion of Whites who feel that social services should be cut is twice that of Blacks.

When a fuller range of Blacks' policy attitudes are compared to Whites' policy positions in 1984 only, Blacks appear distinctly liberal. Table 2.4 displays Blacks' policy positions in the 1984 National Black Election Study and Whites' policy positions taken from a comparable study conducted in 1984, the National Election Study. Because the policy items were asked in several formats, all of the items were rescaled to range from zero to one, where zero constitutes the most conservative position and one represents the most liberal position.

As revealed in the table, Blacks' policy preferences were fairly liberal across the range of policies available in the data set. All of the mean scores are well above the midpoint of 0.5. Even in the area of foreign affairs, where less is known about race differences, the majority of Blacks expressed liberal opinions. When asked if the United States should become more or less involved in the internal affairs of Central American governments, the majority of Blacks said that the U.S. should be less involved. On the issue of guaranteed jobs and a decent standard of living, along with defense spending, however, Black Americans adopted a more centrist position.

If one compares NBES respondents with White respondents in the National Election Study, Blacks and Whites expressed the least disagreement on federal spending on crime, defense, and U.S. involvement in Central America. Blacks and Whites were somewhat more likely to disagree over the size of federal expenditures on Medicare, public schools, and whether or not the government should guarantee a minimum standard of living and jobs for all Americans. Federal assistance for minorities and spending on jobs programs and food stamps were issues where there was the greatest disagreement among Blacks and Whites; the average racial gap on these issues was twenty points or greater. Jobs for the unemployed and food stamps are closely identified with Black Americans. Since the early 1970s, the Black unemployment rate has remained twice that of Whites, even in periods of high employment. Furthermore, over one-third of Black families live below the poverty line and are more likely to receive welfare assistance. Black male joblessness, some

**Table 2.4** Policy Attitudes of Blacks and Whites in 1984

| Question Wording | Blacks | | | Whites | | |
|---|---|---|---|---|---|---|
| | N | Mean | (S.D.) | N | Mean | (S.D.) |
| Guaranteed Jobs: "Where would you place yourself on this scale where 1 = government should see to it that every person has a job and a good standard of living and 7 = government should let each person get ahead on his own?" | 580 | .56 | (.33) | 1,667 | .45 | (.29) |
| Jobs for the Unemployed: "Federal spending on government jobs for the unemployed should be increased, decreased, or kept about the same?" | 839 | .87 | (.27) | 1,598 | .67 | (.37) |
| Food Stamps: "Federal spending on food stamps should be increased, decreased, or kept about the same?" | 837 | .70 | (.34) | 1,564 | .41 | (.35) |
| Medicare: "Federal spending on Medicare should be increased, decreased, or kept about the same?" | 847 | .88 | (.24) | 1,620 | .70 | (.29) |
| Crime: "Federal spending on dealing with crime should be increased, decreased, or kept about the same?" | 838 | .74 | (.33) | 1,627 | .75 | (.29) |
| Schools: "Federal spending on public schools should be increased, decreased, or kept about the same?" | 847 | .89 | (.23) | 1,629 | .73 | (.30) |
| Government Aid to Blacks and Minorities Scale: "Where would you place the government in Washington's efforts to improve the social and economic position of Blacks and other minority groups on a scale from 1 to 7 where 1 = government should not make any special effort and 7 = government should make every possible effort?" | 915 | .67 | (.34) | 1,681 | .46 | (.26) |
| Government Aid to Blacks and Minorities: "The government in Washington should make every possible effort to improve the socioeconomic position of Blacks and minority groups—do you strongly agree, somewhat agree, somewhat disagree, or strongly disagree?" | 690 | .74 | (.22) | * | * | * |

| | N | Mean | (SD) | N | Mean | (SD) |
|---|---|---|---|---|---|---|
| Affirmative Action: "Because of past discrimination, minorities should be given special consideration when decisions are made about hiring applicants for jobs—do you strongly agree, somewhat agree, somewhat disagree, or strongly disagree?" | 831 | .58 | (.36) | * | * | * |
| Black Self-Help: "The government should not make any special effort to help Blacks and other minorities because they should help themselves—do you strongly agree, somewhat agree, somewhat disagree, or strongly disagree?" | 840 | .71 | (.34) | * | * | * |
| Defense Scale: "Where would you place defense spending on a scale from 1 to 7 where 1 = spending should be greatly increased, and 7 = spending should be greatly decreased?" | 785 | .57 | (.33) | 1,715 | .49 | (.27) |
| Defense Spending: "Federal spending on military and defense should be increased, decreased, or kept about the same?" | 825 | .56 | (.39) | 1,623 | .49 | (.36) |
| U.S. Role in Central America Scale: "Where would you place yourself on a scale from 1 to 7 where 1 = United States should become much more involved in the internal affairs of Central American countries and 7 = United States should become much less involved in this area?" | 605 | .68 | (.32) | 1,508 | .60 | (.29) |
| Importance of South Africa: "How important is it for Black people to bring pressure on Congress to change U.S. policies toward South Africa? Very important, somewhat important, or not too important?" | 843 | .51 | (.45) | * | * | * |

*Source:* The 1984 National Black Election Study (Black sample, weighted means) and the 1984 American National Election Study (Whites only).

*Note:* All items were rescaled to range from 0 (conservative) to 1 (liberal) for comparability. Weighted means were used for Blacks.
*Comparison data not available.

policy analysts have noted, has been redefined as a problem outside the realm of economics and transformed into a welfare problem (Weir, Orloff, and Skocpol, 1988: 425). Even though American welfare programs are not race-specific, welfare has become, in the minds of many Americans, the "special interest" of Blacks.

A different story emerges when the attitudes of Blacks and Whites on social issues are compared, as shown in Table 2.5. Here, the racial gap is not as large. Indeed, on certain issues, such as homosexuality and gender equality, Blacks are somewhat more conservative than Whites. Blacks and Whites respond similarly on the issues of the legalization of marijuana and premarital sex. A higher percentage of Blacks, however, view sexual relations between two adults of the same gender as always wrong. On only one social issue, capital punishment, do Blacks and Whites display significant differences in opinion. Whites, by a margin of 30 percent, are more likely to favor capital punishment. Law and order issues have traditionally divided Blacks and Whites. Although Blacks are more likely than Whites to be victims of crime, the majority of Blacks remain opposed to capital punishment. No doubt their opposition is based on the fact that a disproportionate number of Blacks receive death sentences. Politicians who campaign on the issue of law and order have traditionally been political conservatives, and Blacks have generally not supported such politicians.

To summarize, a comparison of Black and White policy preferences in 1984 supports the general view that Black Americans are extremely liberal, and that on issues that involve race, Blacks and Whites are still widely divided. However, a higher percentage of Blacks today express a politically conservative viewpoint than a decade ago. Moreover, nearly a third of Blacks identify themselves as conservative. If one excludes the issue of capital punishment, Blacks today are no more or no less liberal than Whites on most social issues.

## United by Race or Divided by Class?

The liberal public policy profile of Blacks relative to Whites can be explained by a number of factors. Given the strong identification of Blacks as a race, undoubtedly race and race identification figure

Table 2.5  Percentages of Blacks and Whites Who Hold Conservative Social Policy Views, 1972–1988

| Policy Statement | | 1972 | 1973 | 1974 | 1975 | 1976 | 1977 | 1978 | 1980 | 1982 | 1983 | 1984 | 1985 | 1986 | 1987 | 1988 |
|---|---|---|---|---|---|---|---|---|---|---|---|---|---|---|---|---|
| Premarital Sex Is "Always Wrong" | % White | 39 | * | 34 | 32 | * | 32 | 30 | * | 29 | 28 | * | 29 | 28 | * | 27 |
| | % Black | 23 | * | 30 | 22 | * | 28 | 22 | * | 29 | 23 | * | 20 | 28 | * | 24 |
| | Difference | 16 | * | 4 | 10 | * | 4 | 8 | * | 0 | 5 | * | 9 | 0 | * | 3 |
| Homosexuality Is "Always Wrong" | % White | * | 71 | 70 | * | 70 | 71 | * | 73 | 72 | * | 71 | 74 | * | 75 | 75 |
| | % Black | * | 83 | 75 | * | 75 | 77 | * | 79 | 82 | * | 88 | 84 | * | 85 | 90 |
| | Difference | * | -12 | -5 | * | -5 | -6 | * | -6 | -10 | * | -17 | -10 | * | -10 | -15 |
| Favor Capital Punishment "for Murder" | % White | * | * | 70 | 68 | 71 | 75 | 73 | 75 | 81 | 80 | 79 | 82 | 79 | 78 | 81 |
| | % Black | * | * | 40 | 36 | 43 | 46 | 46 | 43 | 49 | 50 | 47 | 57 | 48 | 48 | 48 |
| | Difference | * | * | 30 | 32 | 28 | 29 | 27 | 32 | 32 | 30 | 32 | 25 | 31 | 30 | 33 |
| Oppose Legalization of Marijuana | % White | * | 81 | * | 79 | 72 | * | 71 | 75 | * | 80 | 76 | * | 82 | 83 | 82 |
| | % Black | * | 81 | * | 77 | 64 | * | 61 | 71 | * | 72 | 77 | * | 78 | 83 | 79 |
| | Difference | * | 0 | * | 2 | 8 | * | 10 | 4 | * | 12 | -1 | * | 4 | 0 | 3 |
| Women Should "Take Care of Home, Not Country" | % White | * | * | 34 | 35 | * | 37 | 31 | * | 26 | 23 | * | 25 | 23 | * | 20 |
| | % Black | * | * | 44 | 41 | * | 45 | 38 | * | 34 | 30 | * | 38 | 31 | * | 25 |
| | Difference | * | * | -10 | -6 | * | -8 | -7 | * | -8 | -7 | * | -13 | -8 | * | -5 |
| Oppose Abortion for "Any Reason" | % White | * | * | * | * | * | 62 | 67 | 58 | 58 | 65 | 60 | 63 | * | 58 | 63 |
| | % Black | * | * | * | * | * | 69 | 66 | 66 | 71 | 68 | 73 | 66 | * | 65 | 64 |
| | Difference | * | * | * | * | * | -7 | 1 | -8 | -13 | -3 | -13 | -3 | * | -7 | -1 |

Source: General Social Surveys, 1972–1988.
*Data not available.

prominently in their policy outlooks. Strong race-identifiers should be more likely to adopt liberal views not only on race-specific programs such as affirmative action but on social welfare programs as well. In addition, the ideological orientations of Blacks might greatly shape their policy attitudes. Self-identified Black liberals may be more liberal on a variety of public policy issues than self-identified Black conservatives. Given that the near-majority of Blacks are Democrats, party membership might explain their liberal policy attitudes, since Democrats tend to be more liberal than Republicans on a wide variety of public issues. Finally, given the growth in the number of middle-class Blacks and the more conservative political environment of the 1980s, some have speculated that middle-class Blacks have become more politically conservative on a number of social policy matters. Social class might also affect Blacks' policy positions. Affluent, self-identified middle-class Blacks might be more conservative than poorer, self-identified working-class and poor Blacks.

Table 2.6 contains the results of an analysis of the independent effects of race, ideological, party, and social class identifications on Black policy positions (see the first section of Appendix B for a full account of the analysis). The contributing effects of certain social variables, including income, education, and region, were also estimated (shown in Table 2.7). Only the policy measures available in the 1984 NBES data set were examined; thus, the effects of race and class on Black attitudes on the social policies reported in Table 2.5 cannot be ascertained.

Of the four identification measures, race identification had the strongest and most consistent effect on Blacks' attitudes toward social services and race-specific programs. Blacks who were strong race-identifiers were more likely to endorse the idea of guaranteed jobs and a minimum standard of living, and to advocate increased federal spending on social welfare programs such as jobs for the unemployed, food stamps, and, to a lesser degree, Medicare. Yet, while strongly race-identified Blacks were more likely than weakly identified Blacks to feel that government spending on programs to combat crime should be increased, they did not show any difference of opinion on government spending for public schools. Race identification had the greatest impact on Blacks' attitudes concerning all

**Table 2.6** The Impact of Social Class, Race, Ideological, and Party Identification on Blacks' Policy Attitudes (maximum likelihood estimates)

| Dependent Variables | Social Class Identification | | | Race Identification | | | Ideological Identification | | Party Identification | | SMC/(N)* |
|---|---|---|---|---|---|---|---|---|---|---|---|
| | B | (SE) | Total Effect | B | (SE) | Total Effect | B | (SE) | B | (SE) | |
| Guaranteed Jobs | -.10 | (.07) | -.15 | .14 | (.05) | .24 | -.14 | (.03) | -.01 | (.05) | .07/(580) |
| Jobs for Unemployed | -.03 | (.04) | -.06 | .10 | (.04) | .14 | -.00 | (.03) | -.10 | (.04) | .04/(839) |
| Food Stamps | .08 | (.06) | .04 | .19 | (.05) | .20 | -.10 | (.03) | -.12 | (.05) | .10/(837) |
| Medicare | .06 | (.04) | .04 | .07 | (.04) | .08 | -.04 | (.02) | -.11 | (.04) | .03/(847) |
| Crime | -.08 | (.06) | -.11 | .10 | (.05) | .15 | -.03 | (.03) | .03 | (.05) | .04/(838) |
| Public Schools | -.08 | (.04) | -.11 | .01 | (.04) | .08 | -.06 | (.02) | -.10 | (.04) | .06/(847) |
| Minority Aid Index | -.04 | (.04) | -.09 | .19 | (.04) | .26 | -.06 | (.02) | -.12 | (.04) | .09/(690) |
| Affirmative Action | .09 | (.06) | .04 | .25 | (.06) | .24 | -.02 | (.04) | -.03 | (.06) | .03/(831) |
| Black Self-Help | -.19 | (.06) | -.25 | .18 | (.06) | .32 | -.06 | (.03) | -.14 | (.06) | .06/(840) |
| Defense Spending Index | -.10 | (.06) | -.13 | .00 | (.05) | .10 | -.10 | (.03) | -.23 | (.05) | .12/(785) |
| U.S. Role in Central America | -.07 | (.06) | -.08 | .05 | (.05) | .02 | -.07 | (.03) | -.11 | (.06) | .03/(605) |
| Importance of South Africa | .03 | (.07) | -.06 | .33 | (.06) | .38 | -.12 | (.04) | -.07 | (.07) | .15/(843) |

*Source:* The 1984 National Black Election Study.

*Note:* The probability value ($p$) is less than or equal to .05 when B/SE $\geq$ 1.96.

*SMC is the squared multiple correlation for each policy variable. N is based on the total number of complete cases in each model.

of the racial policy items. Strongly identified Blacks were more likely to support group entitlement programs. Similarly, while race identification had no effect on Blacks' attitudes toward defense expenditures and U.S. involvement in Central America, it turned out to be an important predictor of Black attitudes on South Africa. Strong race identifiers were more likely to feel that South Africa was an important issue, in comparison with weak race identifiers.

In contrast to race identification, class identification had a weaker effect on Black policy preferences. Self-identified higher-status Blacks were more likely to oppose the concept of guaranteed jobs and a good standard of living for every American. The impact of class identification on attitudes toward federal spending on jobs programs, food stamps, and Medicare, although positive, was negligible and nonsignificant. Yet self-identified lower-status Blacks were slightly more likely to favor increased spending on community issues such as federal aid for crime prevention and public schools. In the area of racial policies, social class identification had a nonsignificant effect. Finally, higher-status Blacks were slightly more likely to desire cuts in government spending on defense than lower-status Blacks. Class identification had no meaningful effect on Blacks' attitudes about Central America or South Africa.

Liberal/conservative self-identifications had a modest effect on almost all of the policy items in the study, with the exception of jobs for the unemployed and affirmative action. Self-identified conservatives and liberals were strongly divided on two social welfare issues, guaranteed jobs and food stamps, as well as defense spending, with conservatives more likely to oppose increased spending on jobs programs and food stamps, but more likely to favor increased spending on defense. Conservatives were also more likely to oppose affirmative action and government aid to Blacks and minorities, and they were in favor of an interventionist policy in Central America and less likely to think that South Africa was an important foreign policy issue.

Like ideological self-identification, party identification had a modest to strong effect on almost all of the policy items as well. It played a particularly strong role in shaping Black policy attitudes on issues where race identification had no effect: defense spending and U.S. involvement in Central America. Strong Republicans were far more likely to desire increased spending on defense and the military while favoring a larger U.S. role in the affairs of Central American governments.

The effects of the social background variables on the policy attitudes are presented in Table 2.7. Family income turned out to be an important determinant of the majority of Blacks' policy preferences. Affluent Blacks were opposed to the principle of a minimum standard of living for every American as well as the expansion of most welfare programs, with the exception of Medicare. This finding stands in contrast to the previous studies that have suggested that Blacks are not divided by class (for example, Gurin, Hatchett, and Jackson, 1989; Welch and Foster, 1987). Although family income had a less consistent effect on Blacks' attitudes on racial programs, affluent Blacks were more likely to oppose government aid to Blacks and other minority groups. Family income had no effect on Blacks' foreign policy attitudes.

Education was a source of both liberal and conservative attitudes among Blacks. College-educated Blacks were more likely to oppose a guaranteed jobs/standard of living program as well as increased spending on food stamps and Medicare. At the same time, they were more likely to support increased spending on public schools. Although no educational differences among Blacks could be found in their support of affirmative action and minority aid, college-educated Blacks were more likely to push for a smaller defense budget.

The remaining demographic variables had little effect on Blacks' policy attitudes. The analysis found no evidence of a generational or gender gap within the Black community on policy matters. Older Blacks were somewhat more likely to oppose minority aid and were more likely to support a larger defense budget. And although Black women have in general greater financial burdens than Black men, they were not more likely to advocate increased spending on welfare programs or racial policies. Black women, however, were somewhat more likely to oppose U.S. intervention in Central America in comparison to Black men. Blacks in the South held somewhat more conservative views on the food stamps program and defense than Blacks in other regions of the country. Rural Blacks were slightly more supportive of increased spending on crime and schools, while

Table 2.7 The Impact of Social Background on Blacks' Policy Attitudes (maximum likelihood estimates)

| Dependent Variables | Income | | Education | | Age | | Gender | | Region | | Urbanicity | |
|---|---|---|---|---|---|---|---|---|---|---|---|---|
| | B | (SE) | B | (SE) | B | (SE) | B | (SE) | B | (SE) | B | (SE) |
| Guaranteed Jobs | -.13 | (.05) | -.10 | (.09) | -.04 | (.07) | .03 | (.03) | -.01 | (.03) | -.03 | (.04) |
| Jobs for Unemployed | -.12 | (.03) | .01 | (.06) | -.01 | (.04) | .01 | (.02) | -.01 | (.02) | .04 | (.03) |
| Food Stamps | -.12 | (.04) | -.30 | (.08) | -.06 | (.06) | .03 | (.03) | .11 | (.03) | -.10 | (.04) |
| Medicare | -.03 | (.03) | -.16 | (.05) | -.06 | (.04) | .00 | (.02) | -.03 | (.02) | .01 | (.03) |
| Crime | .08 | (.04) | -.05 | (.08) | .06 | (.06) | .03 | (.02) | .05 | (.03) | .07 | (.04) |
| Public Schools | .06 | (.03) | .10 | (.05) | .00 | (.04) | .01 | (.02) | .01 | (.02) | .04 | (.02) |
| Minority Aid Index | -.13 | (.03) | .02 | (.06) | -.08 | (.04) | -.03 | (.02) | .01 | (.02) | -.03 | (.03) |
| Affirmative Action | -.07 | (.04) | -.04 | (.08) | .06 | (.06) | -.00 | (.03) | .01 | (.02) | -.08 | (.04) |
| Black Self-Help | .04 | (.04) | .19 | (.08) | -.05 | (.06) | -.00 | (.03) | .01 | (.02) | -.07 | (.04) |
| Defense Spending Index | .03 | (.04) | .24 | (.08) | -.12 | (.06) | .04 | (.03) | .09 | (.03) | .01 | (.04) |
| U.S. in Central America | -.01 | (.05) | -.01 | (.09) | -.01 | (.06) | .06 | (.03) | .04 | (.03) | .01 | (.04) |
| Importance of South Africa | .03 | (.05) | .49 | (.10) | .38 | (.07) | -.10 | (.03) | .03 | (.03) | .07 | (.05) |

Source: The 1984 National Black Election Study.
Note: The probability value ($p$) is less than or equal to .05 when B/SE $\geq$ 1.96.

at the same time they were opposed to more spending on food stamps.

The strong effect of racial identification on Blacks' party and ideological identifications makes its total effect twice as large as its direct effect. In contrast, social class identification had no effect on Blacks' partisan ties and political orientations. Consequently, its total estimated effect on Black policy positions is not much different from its direct effect.

In brief, racial identification had the strongest overall liberalizing effect on Black policy preferences. But its effect was limited mainly to issues that affected the well-being and status of the group, especially racial programs, social welfare policies, and the matter of South Africa. Social class identification had the weakest overall effect on Black political attitudes of the four identification measures, although the general direction of its effect suggests that, on the whole, self-identified higher-status Blacks are more conservative than self-identified lower-status Blacks.

Blacks' ideological and partisan ties, in contrast, had a much wider impact on their policy preferences than race identification. Blacks' party and ideological identifications structured many of their policy attitudes, with ideological identification having a slightly weaker effect than party identification. The partisan and ideological ties of Black Americans, however, are based on their racial identities (see Tables 2.2 and 3.2). In this way, race identification has an indirect role in shaping Black policy preferences on issues that are unrelated to race, like defense spending and U.S. involvement in Central America.

Family income exerted a strong conservative effect on Blacks' policy attitudes. Affluence therefore leads to greater political conservatism among Blacks. Education, in contrast, had a mixed effect on Black public opinion. The total conservative effect of education on Blacks' attitudes toward social welfare programs was undercut by its enhancement effect on Blacks' racial identities and its liberalizing effect on Blacks' ideological identities.

## Summary and Conclusion

Civil rights and race discrimination appear to occupy a less central place on the political agenda of Blacks today than a decade ago.

The diminished salience of race discrimination and civil rights may be a reflection of the new conservative political climate that emerged during the 1970s and 1980s, where civil rights and racial equality are no longer defined as national priorities. Alternatively, Blacks may be less preoccupied with civil rights issues than with the problems of poverty, unemployment, teenage pregnancy, crime, and drug use and addiction, which have increased in magnitude and intensity.

Nevertheless, racial inequality and race discrimination remain central concerns of many Blacks today. A large minority of Blacks continue to feel that not enough progress in the area of race relations has been achieved. Blacks believe that as a group they are economically disadvantaged and wield less influence and power in American politics and society than Whites. A substantial minority, in fact, feel that Blacks may never catch up to Whites. These perceptions of group inequality promote a strong awareness of race and racial identification with the group. The majority of Blacks in 1984 closely identified with their race, and felt that what happened to their racial group would have an impact upon their individual lives, which, in turn, fostered a liberal orientation toward politics. In the 1984 NBES study, racial identification was found to promote a liberal self-identification and was related to a wide variety of Blacks' policy preferences. Race identification rivaled party and ideological identifications as alternative sources of Blacks' policy positions. Strong race identifiers were much more liberal than weak race identifiers, particularly on issues that are closely connected to the welfare of the group, for example, affirmative action and social spending programs. Race identification, however, had no direct effect on Black attitudes on defense and other social spending programs, such as Medicare and aid to public schools. On these issues, party and ideological identifications largely structured the attitudes of Black Americans.

Although social class identification had little to no effect on Black policy preferences, in contrast to previous analyses, socioeconomic status, as measured by family income and education, strongly affected Blacks' policy attitudes. Affluent Blacks tended to be more conservative on policy matters than their poorer brethren. Nevertheless, affluent Black Americans are still very liberal in comparison to their White counterparts (Gilliam and Whitby, 1989; Welch and

Foster, 1987; Gilliam, 1986). Middle- to high-income Blacks were less likely than low-income Blacks to endorse increased federal spending on food stamps, Medicare, public schools, and so on. Finally, even though some political analysts and scholars have suggested that economically advantaged Blacks may be more supportive of affirmative action and federal minority set-aside programs, the analysis found no evidence of this. Indeed, income had no effect on Blacks' attitudes on the issue of affirmative action.

How can these findings be interpreted more broadly? First, the widening economic rift in the Black community appears to have had a mixed effect on Blacks' racial identities. The changing fortunes of Blacks, specifically, the rising numbers of middle-class Blacks, have both weakened and reinforced Blacks' racial consciousness. On the one hand, self-identified middle- and upper-middle class Blacks are less race-oriented than self-identified poor and working-class Blacks. On the other hand, affluent Blacks and those having a college education are more likely to be strong race-identifiers in contrast to low-income and less-educated Blacks. Although much more empirical research is needed in this area, it appears that race identification is based on Blacks' racial experiences. Bert Landry argues that in spite of the changed racial environment for today's Black middle class, middle-class Blacks are still very racially sensitive. He writes, "Like the old black middle class that preceded them, these young members of the new black middle class find all too often that though the racial climate improved, it is still not color blind" (1987: 112). He concludes that the lifestyles of those in the new Black middle class are "somewhat tarnished" by the racism still active in American society. Nevertheless, there appear to be two types of middle-class Blacks: those who remain racially identified and may even misidentify with working-class and poor Blacks, and those who identify with the upper classes and, as a result, are less race-conscious, viewing their lives as fairly independent of the group.

Second, even though civil rights is no longer considered to be a priority issue among most Black Americans, Blacks have become somewhat more conservative in their policy outlook. Not only did the percentage of self-identified Black conservatives grow during the 1970s, but a higher percentage of Blacks today oppose a guaranteed jobs program and federal assistance to minorities than a decade and a half ago. Still, Black conservatives are in the minority. On the basis of the 1984 NBES, only 10 percent of the Black community may be true economic conservatives. Only 10 percent in 1984 desired cuts in the food stamps programs, and fewer than 5 percent advocated a reduction in government spending on Medicare and on jobs training programs. A much larger percentage of Blacks are social conservatives, however. But even on public morality issues where Blacks express more conservative viewpoints, Blacks are no less liberal on public policies concerning AIDS and public day-care facilities for children. Although the 1988 reinterview is not necessarily an actual reflection of Black opinion at this time, 74 percent in that study felt that federal spending on AIDS research should be increased, and 80 percent felt that the government should spend more on children's day-care facilities.

It is possible that in the 1990s conservatism could develop within the Black community, but not on the issues, such as the role of the federal government, that have commonly divided liberals and conservatives. A number of new issues have arisen that have pitted Black communities against liberals and civil libertarians. These new issues range from the constitutionality of locker searches and the presence of metal detectors at public schools, to the eviction of accused drug dealers and their families from public housing, to publicly funded schools for Black boys. The temporary curfews on teenagers imposed by Black mayors of large cities have similarly divided Black communities from their traditional liberal allies. It is possible that while Blacks generally oppose capital punishment, they may come to support capital punishment for drug dealers. Since these issues are considered to be community ones, Black public opinion on these matters at the national level has not been as carefully monitored as it should be.

Finally, the analysis presented here has established that race identification promotes a more liberal political perspective among Black Americans. This liberal agenda, however, should not be confused with support for more radical political programs. For all intents and purposes, strong racial identifiers, a large percentage of whom are college-educated, may be armchair liberals—doing what they can for the race within the confines of the existing political structure.

Even though Black leaders consider themselves to be extremely liberal, Verba and Orren (1985) in their survey of national leadership found that the majority of Black leaders rejected radically redistributionist views—policies and programs aimed at reducing the income gap between the extremely wealthy and the very poor in the United States. Thus, even while the racial identities of Blacks enable them to transcend their middle-class class positions, their political liberalism may extend only as far as addressing the problems of race, not those of class inequalities.

# 3

# Blacks and the Democratic Party

Since 1964, Black Americans have come to represent one of the largest blocs of the Democratic party, approximating one-quarter of the party's membership base. Although discussed widely, the factors that explain Blacks' overwhelming support of the Democratic party have rarely been identified through empirical means. A number of basic questions regarding the nature of Blacks' support for the Democratic party, therefore, have gone unaddressed: Which Blacks are more likely to be Democrats? Since affluent Americans are more likely to affiliate with the Republican party, are high-income Blacks more inclined toward that party? Can Black support for the Democratic party be linked to Blacks' liberal policy preferences, or are the majority of Blacks Democrats simply because they lack a better alternative? As a political minority, Blacks have traditionally found themselves supporting the major party that constituted the "lesser of two evils"; thus, it is possible that Black support for the Democratic party is merely driven by the current nonattractiveness of the Republican party. Finally, it is necessary to consider how Jackson's candidacies have affected Blacks' support for the Democratic party. I. A. Lewis and William Schneider (1983) contend, in their analysis of Black Democrats, that even though Blacks constitute a large percentage of the party's base support, Blacks are nevertheless a "restive element"—that is, in light of their ideological intensity and critical stance toward Democratic leadership, they are quite willing to abandon their party in favor of Jackson or an alternative pro-Black third party candidate. Did Jackson, having capitalized on Blacks' discontent with their status within the party, undermine Black support for the Democratic party, or did his candidacies actually revitalize it?

## A Historical Overview

When Black Republicans began voting Democratic in national elections during the 1930s and 1940s, their alliance with the party was not considered to be a permanent one. Blacks originally voted Democratic during that period out of economic necessity (Weiss, 1983). Few could forget that the Democratic party was largely controlled by the South, which depended on lynching, supremacist violence, and legal devices to disfranchise Blacks. Most Blacks were, in fact, Roosevelt Republicans. Not only did the majority of Blacks not consider themselves to be Democrats, given their small numbers within the party and disfranchisement in the South, but the Democratic party did not consider them to be an important component of the New Deal coalition forged by Roosevelt. Blacks received little in return for their votes. Although widely perceived as the champion of the poor and the downtrodden, Roosevelt had a dismal record on race. During his administration, not one of the more than 150 civil rights bills introduced in Congress passed into legislation. It was only much later, in his third term of office, that Roosevelt issued an executive order making discrimination in government employment illegal and establishing a Committee on Fair Employment Practices to enforce a nondiscrimination policy in defense programs (Carmines and Stimson, 1989: 31). In fact, Roosevelt had acted only in response to Black protest. Earlier, A. Philip Randolph had threatened to organize a mass march on Washington if the government continued to ignore Blacks' demand for new civil rights legislation. Randolph then cancelled plans for this march as a result of the new executive order (Nieman, 1991: 139–140).

Although a new and growing majority of Blacks had voted Democratic during the New Deal era, the Republican party still remained an attractive political alternative for many Blacks. In the 1952, 1956, and 1960 presidential elections, Blacks remained slightly independent of the Democratic party, dividing their votes between the two parties (Walters, 1988: 28). Dwight Eisenhower, for example, received about 40 percent of the Black vote in 1956, while Richard

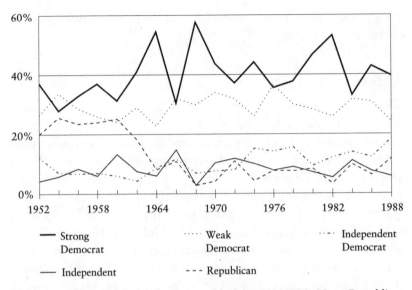

Figure 3.1    Party Identification among Blacks, 1952–1988. *Note:* Republican category includes self-identified weak, strong, and independent Black Republicans. (*Source:* National Election Studies.)

Nixon netted almost one-third in 1960 (Huckfeldt and Kohfeld, 1989: 11). It was not until the 1964 presidential election that the overwhelming majority of Blacks began to identify themselves as Democrats. From 1952 to 1962, somewhere between 56 to 66 percent of Blacks identified themselves as Democrats or political independents leaning toward the Democratic party. The 1964 presidential election was a pivotal election, however. By the time of this election, a full 80 percent of Blacks identified with the Democratic party or as independents favoring the Democratic party (see Figure 3.1).

The surge in Black identification with the Democratic party in the 1964 election was largely the result of the new racial liberalism of the party, and more specifically, the enactment of civil rights legislation during the Kennedy-Johnson administrations. President Kennedy, like Roosevelt before him, had initially chosen the strategy of ignoring the call for civil rights legislation. For example, he refused to endorse a civil rights bill introduced in May 1961 that he himself had asked be drafted (Lawson, 1976: 288). Democratic presidential contenders had learned during the Truman years that they could not afford to respond to Blacks' civil rights demands because it would antagonize their White southern supporters. When, at the end of his first administration, President Truman sent the first civil rights bill since Reconstruction to Congress, southern Democrats walked out of the national convention. Although he was reelected, Truman's action cost him the electoral votes of Alabama, Mississippi, Louisiana, and South Carolina (Carmines and Stimson, 1989: 34–35). Kennedy's own strategy might have worked, but the civil rights movement had emerged, elevating civil rights from a regional interest or the special interest of Blacks to a national issue. In the summer of 1963, in response to widespread racial violence, demonstrations, marches, and boycotts, Kennedy announced on national television his intention to submit sweeping civil rights legislation to Congress. In addition to the voting rights bill enacted in 1965, Kennedy's successor, Lyndon Johnson, would later sign into law a number of civil rights bills, including the 1964 Civil Rights Act, an omnibus bill that included a mandate for implementing school desegregation, and the 1968 Civil Rights Act, which targeted housing discrimination. He would also initiate the War on Poverty, a set of federal programs aimed at creating new social service structures that would greatly benefit poor Blacks.

In their book *Issue Evolution,* Edward Carmines and James Stimson attribute Kennedy's inability to keep race from the political agenda and the transformation of the party from racially conservative to racially liberal to a number of factors. They point out that by World War II, southern Blacks' migration to the North meant that northern Democrats, especially those in large urban centers, had become dependent upon Black votes. Suddenly, "for a Democratic presidential nominee to win Illinois meant, in other words, that he had to win big in Chicago, which meant he had to do very well among black voters in the city" (Carmines and Stimson, 1989: 33). The civil rights movement was another politically destabilizing factor. As the movement pushed forward, Whites' attitudes on race had become more sympathetic toward Blacks' demands for equal rights. Senator Barry Goldwater was also instrumental. Between 1950 and 1960, race had been a nonpartisan issue. Goldwater was one of the six Republican senators who voted against the 1964 Civil Rights Act. With this vote as well as his selection as the Republican party's choice for president in 1964, Goldwater made race into a highly partisan issue, with Democrats now squarely occupying the pro–civil rights side and Republicans in the anti–civil rights camp. The public, who until 1964 had seen no real difference between the parties on racial matters, now recognized the Democratic party as the more racially liberal.

Carmines and Stimson, however, overlook the critical role of Blacks as agents of change *within* the Democratic party. At the center of their thesis is their belief that party elites, generally operating independently of Blacks, managed to transform the Democratic party's position on race and that this, in some sense, was accidental. They note that up until 1958, racially liberal Republicans had always outnumbered racially liberal Democrats. In that year, Senate elections altered the mix of liberal Republicans and liberal Democrats when eleven Republicans were replaced by Democrats, ten of whom were racial liberals. Because race was not yet an election issue in 1958, this replacement, according to Carmines and Stimson, occurred simply because 1958 was a bad year for Republicans in the Senate. The next big wave of liberal Democrats came in the 1968 elections, both in the House and Senate. In these elections, race, which was now a major political issue, did affect the outcome. Yet Blacks themselves had always maintained a role in affecting the transformation of the Democratic party from the conservative to the liberal party on race issues. From the 1920s onward, the political influence of Blacks within the Democratic party grew, and by the mid-1960s, they were able to push the Democratic party toward the left on racial issues.

The watershed year in Black politics is often identified as 1965, when the voting rights bill was enacted. The Voting Rights Act enabled Blacks to move away from direct-action techniques and protest to electoral political activities and involvement in the party. However, Black political power predates the 1965 Voting Rights Act (Walton, 1972b). Black voter power was felt within the Democratic party structure as early as the 1920s. As Carmines and Stimson note, Blacks' migration to the North altered their political status, giving them more influence within the party. However, the Black vote in the North was also highly concentrated. In his work on the development of the civil rights struggle, Doug McAdam notes that between 1910 and 1960, 87 percent of the total number of Black immigrants from the South settled in seven key northern and western industrial states: New York, New Jersey, Pennsylvania, Ohio, California, Illinois, and Michigan (1982: 79). This northern Black political power was not without its consequences. Newspapers of the day attributed to the Black vote both the failure of the Senate to confirm Hoover's Supreme Court nominee, John J. Parker, and the defeat of several senators who had supported Parker (McAdam, 1982: 80). However, the move to the Democratic party was especially critical in the development of Black political power, for as long as the majority of Blacks remained Republicans, they could exert little political leverage in the South (McAdam, 1982: 81).

The three decades preceding the civil rights struggle were marked by a steady accumulation of Black political resources. Not only did many Blacks relocate from the South to the North, enjoying the franchise for the first time as well as freedom from the coercive control of the sharecropping system, but Black organizational strength improved as well. Black college enrollment increased sharply, particularly after 1940, and local NAACP chapters expanded rapidly throughout the 1930s, 1940s, and 1950s (McAdam, 1982). Furthermore, during the civil rights movement, Blacks began to use their newly acquired power to play an even larger role within Democratic party politics at the national level.

The 1964 election solidified Blacks' relationship with the Democratic party, even as it closed off the Republican party as an option for Blacks. The mean affect measure shown over time for Blacks and Whites in Figure 3.2 represents the total number of positive statements made about each party minus the total number of negative statements. Blacks' evaluations of the two parties would differ markedly from Whites' evaluations. Beginning in 1964, Blacks would view the Democratic party far more positively and the Republican party far more negatively than Whites. Whites' attitudes toward the two major parties are fairly neutral. By 1972, however, the huge gulf separating the parties among Blacks had begun to close slightly. Blacks still view the parties in radically unlike terms, but less dramatically so than during the mid-1960s.

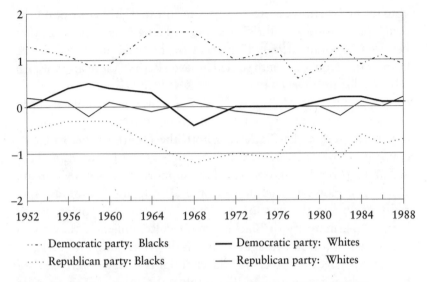

Figure 3.2   Affect toward the Major Parties by Race, 1952–1988. (*Source:* National Election Studies.)

With major differences between the parties on civil rights and racial issues emerging during the civil rights era, Blacks came to view the Democratic party as pro-Black and the Republican party as anti-Black. In the 1984 National Black Election Study, when asked how hard each party works on issues that Black people care about, more than one-fourth of the respondents stated that the Democratic party works very hard, and 45 percent claimed that it works fairly hard. In contrast, only 9 percent said that the Republican party works very hard, and fewer than 15 percent felt that it works fairly hard. In fact, roughly 36 percent of the respondents felt that the Republican party does not work hard at all on Black issues. (See Table 3.1.)

In 1965, the year when voting rights legislation to protect Black voting rights in the South passed Congress, civil rights activist Bayard Rustin, in an article published in *Commentary,* advocated greater Black involvement in Democratic party politics. By the mid-1960s, the prospects for Blacks in electorally based party politics looked extremely promising. Rustin, in particular, felt that the landslide election of President Johnson in 1964 signified the defeat of

Table 3.1   Blacks' Assessments of How Hard the Parties Work on Black
Issues (weighted percentages)

|  | Democratic Party | Republican Party |
|---|---|---|
| "How hard do you think the Democratic/Republican party really works on issues Black people care about?" | | |
| Very hard | 28% | 9% |
| Fairly hard | 45 | 15 |
| Not too hard | 20 | 37 |
| Not hard at all | 6 | 36 |
| Don't know | 2 | 3 |
| Total | 100% | 100% |
| (N) | (863) | (864) |

Source: The 1984 National Black Election Study.

political conservatives, whom he predicted would align themselves
with the Republican party. However, Rustin's hope for a liberal
majority, which would then work exclusively through the Democratic party, never materialized. If Johnson's landslide victory was
the triumph of liberalism over conservatism, it was a very short-
lived one. For a number of reasons, including very low public
approval ratings, President Johnson did not seek reelection, and a
Republican was to be the voting public's choice for president in
1968. Furthermore, by 1968, the escalation of the Vietnam war had
overshadowed the civil rights movement; King had been assassi-
nated, and civil rights groups were unable to act, given deep divisions
over the movement's next steps and objectives. Conservatism had
been rekindled within the American electorate in the aftermath of
the urban riots and as race issues moved from the South to the
North in the form of busing and affirmative action. To remain
competitive in presidential elections, the Democratic party elected
to seek the center ground of politics and not to remain on the left,
as Rustin had predicted. Thus by 1980, instead of belonging to a
liberal-progressive coalition within the Democratic party, as Rustin
had hoped, Blacks found themselves constituting a political minority, isolated and increasingly marginal both within the Democratic
party and in national politics in general.

Political inclusion would dominate the agenda of Black Democrats
from 1964 to 1976. Up until the mid-1960s, Blacks in the South

were effectively locked out of the Democratic party and politics in general. But as the 1964 national elections approached, the Mississippi Freedom Democratic Party (MFDP), an offshoot of the Council of Federated Organizations (COFO), a multi-racial civil rights organization, formed to challenge the all-White primary delegation in Mississippi to the Democratic party's national convention. At the convention, the MFDP was offered two at-large seats and promised future party rules that would prevent the seating of groups that discriminated against minority groups, while the all-White delegation retained their seats as representatives of the state of Mississippi. Most political observers and activists outside the MFDP, including Martin Luther King, welcomed these steps as a fair compromise (Lawson, 1976). But even though the Democratic party later initiated important reforms to increase minority and Black participation at conventions, the perception that Blacks were still locked outside the party lingered. All-White delegations from Mississippi continued to be sent to the Democratic party's national conventions until 1976, even though the party refused to seat these delegations, recognizing instead the alternative, biracial party group from that state that was organized by the NAACP. Finally, in 1976, Governor Cliff Finch of Mississippi persuaded the two groups to merge, ending Black isolation from Democratic party politics in that state (Parker, 1990: 147–151).

In *Black Presidential Politics in America: A Strategic Approach,* Ronald W. Walters describes the efforts of Black activists to achieve greater representation and influence within the Democratic party. Although by 1964 Blacks represented 12 percent of the party's base support, they constituted fewer than 6 percent of the delegates at the 1968 convention. By 1972, the percentage of Black delegates at the national convention had increased to 15 percent, but this figure was still out of line with the 25 percent Black share of the party's voting base. In response to the MFDP challenge and the general pressure applied by Black Democrats, however, the Democratic party committed itself to increasing minority (Black) and female representation at the national conventions. In 1972, the delegate selection rules were revised to include language in support of affirmative action policies to increase minority representation at the national conventions. The rule changes included a statement that "minorities, young people, and women" should be represented in state delegations to the national conventions in "reasonable relationship to their proportion in the state." But even while these changes were approved, a debate developed within the party over the specific wording of the affirmative action mandate and whether or not the party should impose a quota system on the state parties in their selection of national convention delegates. In drafting the new delegate selection guidelines in 1973, new language was inserted that shifted the burden of proving that racial discrimination existed at the state level from the state party to challengers. The draft proposal read, "If a State Party has adopted and implemented an approved Affirmative Action Program, the Party shall not be subject to challenge based solely on delegation composition or primary results" (Walters, 1988: 58).

Black Democrats mobilized during this time in an effort to increase their numbers and influence within the party. A Black caucus had already existed in the Democratic party, but in 1973, a new Black Democratic Caucus (BDC) was formed (Walters, 1988: 60–61). Responding to what the BDC members perceived as a weakening resolve to bring Black representation in line with their proportion in the electorate, the BDC issued a statement in 1974 that read, "If the Party leadership continues to insist on further compromises on Party Affirmative Action provisions, *we have no alternative but to reassess our involvement in and support of the Democratic party*" (emphasis by Walters, 1988: 61).

By the time Jesse Jackson appeared on the national political scene in 1983, substantial integration by Blacks, in fact, had been achieved. Walters reports that Black membership on key standing committees of the party increased on average from 7.7 percent in 1972 to 20 percent in 1984 (1988: 65). Walters contends that the new involvement of Blacks in party affairs, however, had not yielded Blacks the level of influence they sought in presidential nominating politics. He writes: "It is striking that the participation Blacks have won within the institution appears not to have been translated into influence with the presidential nominees and their campaign organizations" (1988: 83). It had been assumed by Black Democrats that political integration into the national Democratic party would automatically yield greater influence in the political decision-making process within the party. Even in 1980, however, bargaining results between Black Democrats and party leaders, according to Walters, were "vague and unsatisfactory" (1988: 84). In particular, Black Democrats were angered by Senator Edward Kennedy's endorsement of Mayor Jane Byrne for reelection and Vice-President Walter Mondale's endorsement of Richard Daley, Jr., in Chicago's mayoral primary election in 1983. The absence of a major party endorsement for Black Congressman Harold Washington, the eventual winner of the Chicago mayoral race, Walters notes, "sent a powerful signal to Blacks" (1988: 161). Thus, although Blacks were generally successful in their efforts to achieve greater representation within the party, many Black party activists felt that their loyalty and numbers had not translated into real influence within the party.

At the grassroots level as well, frustration with the party began to swell during this period. Blacks began to feel that their vote was being taken for granted by the Democratic party. In a 1983 *Los Angeles Times* survey, while 44 percent of the Blacks interviewed felt that "most Democrats are sincerely committed to helping Blacks get ahead," a nearly equal percentage thought that "most Democrats don't really care much about Black people" (Lewis and Schneider, 1985). Still, Black voting for Democratic presidential candidates remained consistently high, and Black identification with the party remained constant at or above 80 percent throughout the 1970s and 1980s. Indeed, in the 1980 presidential election, Ronald Reagan was elected with the lowest percentage of Black votes of any previous Republican presidential candidate (Carmines and Stimson, 1989: 54). Fewer than one out of every ten Blacks had voted for him. The Reagan administration proved to be disastrous to Black economic interests, but the Democratic party failed to serve as an effective counter to the administration during this period.

When Jackson announced his intention to seek the presidency, many saw him as the candidate who would speak to those outside national politics, especially Black Americans (Barker, 1988). Jackson's 1984 candidacy was also viewed by Blacks as a way for them to bargain more effectively with the Democratic party. Jackson sought the party's nomination at exactly the right moment. Since the civil rights struggle of the 1960s, Blacks had become an important and formidable voting bloc. The defection to the Republican party of White southern Protestants, who had originally been the largest and most important constituent group member of the New Deal coalition, sharply increased the party's dependence upon the Black vote. Although Blacks still represented a minority voting power, the Democratic party stood to lose every presidential election if it did not receive the lion's share of the Black vote in each election year. Moreover, just as the Supreme Court decision on *Brown* had encouraged early Black civil rights activists, the successive gains in the number of Black elected officials, and especially the election of Black mayors in cities like Chicago, helped generate widespread feelings of new political optimism among Blacks. Blacks felt more politically effective. In the 1984 NBES, a large majority (72 percent) strongly agreed with the statement: "If enough Blacks vote, they can make a difference in who gets elected President." Fewer than 11 percent disagreed.

In his mobilization of Black voters, Jackson hoped to activate Blacks politically. At the same time, he hoped to establish a different, more reciprocal relationship—"a new covenant, as he put it," states Barker (1988: 183)—between Blacks and the Democratic party. His 1984 efforts in this direction were less than successful. All of Jackson's minority policy planks were defeated by the Mondale forces at the national convention. Furthermore, Walter Mondale refused to meet and negotiate with Jackson until after the convention, and even then, in their mid-August meeting, he only agreed to hire a few of Jackson's campaign workers and to recognize Jackson as the head of the Rainbow Coalition within the Democratic party. In 1984 Jackson's "victories," including his highly celebrated speech at the 1984 national convention, were largely symbolic.

Nonetheless, Jackson received 3.3 million votes in the 1984 nominating contest. Given the high participation rates of Blacks in the Democratic presidential contest, he had successfully mobilized an important unit within the Democratic party whose members would no longer remain passive. Indeed, the new Black voting bloc that emerged by 1984 was an entirely different entity from the one that had helped return FDR to office three additional times, despite the fact that Roosevelt had refused to support any of the 150 civil rights bills sponsored in Congress. First, the Black electorate had clearly matured. Second, Blacks had become an extremely active force within the Democratic party. Indeed, in 1983, it was their new voting clout both within and outside the Democratic party that served as the trump card in Jesse Jackson's hand. The 1984 Jackson candidacy had both initiated and joined a movement on the part of Black Democrats to redefine their relationship with the party.

### Explaining Black Support for the Democratic Party Today

According to the historian Nancy Weiss (1983), Blacks abandoned the Republican party and began voting for the Democratic party for purely economic, not racial, reasons. Nonetheless, Black identification with the Democratic party did not reach its peak until the 1964 presidential election. Civil rights and race issues were undoubtedly critical to Blacks in their identification with the Democratic party. Today, eight out of every ten Blacks are Democrats. In the 1984 NBES survey, 83 percent of the sample identified themselves as Democrats or as independents who favored the Democratic party. By contrast, approximately nine percent of the sample were Republicans, with roughly four percent of these Republicans representing political independents who favored or leaned toward the Republican party. What factors account for Blacks' loyalty to the Democratic party today? Is race still an important component of Black support for the party?

*The American Voter* (1960) by Campbell, Converse, Miller, and Stokes defines partisanship as a psychological attachment to one of the two major parties. Apart from voters' assessments concerning the economy, it may be the most important predictive variable in American politics today, with considerable effect on the political attitudes and behavior of American voters. Of all the partisan social groups in the United States, Black Americans remain the most consistently loyal to their party (Rosenstone, Behr, and Lazarus, 1984: 169–170). Even in an era of weakened political parties, as more Americans split their votes and exhibit new independence from the major parties (Wattenberg, 1984), Black Americans have remained steadfast in their preference for the Democratic party. Furthermore, they have remained loyal Democrats even as a number of traditionally Democratic groups, including southern Protestants, Jewish

Americans, and labor, have increasingly voted Republican (Huckfeldt and Kohfeld, 1989).

Recent empirical studies of Black partisanship have failed to explain why the majority of Blacks are Democrats. Researchers have been unable to find, in fact, any critical differences between Black Democrats and Black Republicans (Cavanagh, 1985; Lewis and Schneider, 1983). Although income divides White Americans along party lines in that working-class and poor Whites are more likely to identify themselves as Democrats, Blacks at all income levels are all equally likely to be Democrats. Similarly, Black men and women are equally likely to identify with the Democratic party. Nor does region appear to make a difference. Blacks residing in the South as well as outside the South are disproportionately Democratic in identification. Furthermore, not much variation is found in the policy attitudes of Black Republicans and Democrats. Black delegates to the Republican and Democratic national conventions in 1980, for example, did not have significantly different policy views (Walters, 1988).

Still, it may be that a mix of racial and ideological concerns, rather than social characteristics, serves as the foundation of Black support for the Democratic party. Lewis and Schneider (1983) argue that the economic concerns of lower-status Blacks drive their support for the Democratic party, while support for the Democratic party among higher-status Blacks stems from their racial liberalism. They contend that race and class "operating at different levels with the Black community" together account for the overwhelming support of the Democratic party within the Black community today.

Table 3.2 presents estimates of the relative impact of class, race, and ideology on Black partisanship. The effects of socioeconomic status (as measured by separate indicators of family income and education), age, gender, region, urbanicity, and union membership are also included. The table contains ordinary least squares (OLS) regression coefficients together with their standard errors (SE). The measure of party identification employed here is standard: respondents were asked which party they belonged to, and then the strength of that affiliation. The range of party identification, therefore, includes strong Democrat, weak Democrat, independent-Democrat, independent, independent-Republican, weak Republican, and strong Republican. The analysis reveals that ideology and class

Table 3.2   Determinants of Blacks' Party Identification

| Independent Variables | B | (SE) |
|---|---|---|
| Social class identification (low-high) | .01 | (.07) |
| Race identification (low-high) | −.08** | (.03) |
| Ideological identification (conservative-liberal) | −.03 | (.03) |
| Income | −.03 | (.02) |
| Education | −.02 | (.02) |
| 18–29 years old | .54** | (.16) |
| 30–54 years old | .22 | (.15) |
| Gender (female) | −.34** | (.11) |
| Urbanicity (low-high) | −.04 | (.04) |
| Union member | .01 | (.03) |
| Region (non-South) | −.06 | (.11) |
| Constant | 3.39** | (.44) |
| Total cases | 581 | |
| $R^2$ | .07 | |

Source: The 1984 National Black Election Study.
Note: The 55 or older category is the excluded dummy variable in this analysis.
*$p < .05$.
**$p < .01$.

identification had no effect on Black party identification (see Table 3.2). Self-identified liberals and self-identified poor and working-class Blacks are no more likely to identify with the Democratic party than self-identified conservatives and middle-class and upper-middle-class Blacks. Of the three identification measures, only race identification had an effect. Strong racial identifiers are more likely to identify strongly with the Democratic party than weak racial identifiers.[1]

Socioeconomic status, approximated by family income and education, had no effect on Black partisan ties whatsoever. But gender and age strongly affected Black partisan support. Black women are more likely to identify strongly with the Democratic party, while Black men are more likely to be weak or independent Democratic supporters, political independents, or Republicans. Surprisingly, young Blacks, those aged 18 to 29, had weaker identifications with the Democratic party, being more likely to identify themselves as weak Democrats or as Republicans, than older Blacks. Those 30 to 54 years of age were no different in party membership and identification than those 55 years of age or older. Even though young voters are not generally noted for their political loyalties, it may be that many young White Americans will eventually affiliate with the Republican party given the strong popularity of Ronald Reagan. Voter surveys conducted during 1984 by the media revealed that the young, traditionally Democratic in preference, split their votes between the parties in the 1984 presidential election. At the same time, given the uniformly unfavorable evaluations Reagan received within the Black community, it is unlikely that younger Blacks might be more inclined toward the Republican party than past generations of Blacks. Young Black voters may be less partisan simply because they lack political experience, and thus may be less likely to identify strongly with parties (Converse, 1976). Eventually, they might align themselves with the Democratic party.

In short, race identification appears to be the major component of Black partisanship today. Middle-class Blacks and working-class and poor Blacks are all equally likely to identify with the Democratic party. However, there appears to be a gender and generational split within the Black community in terms of party preference. Black men and younger Black Americans are less likely to identify with the Democratic party than to be political independents or Republicans.

## Impact of the Reagan Presidency and the Jackson Candidacies

Past characterizations of party identification have implied that party membership is more or less a lifetime commitment, undone or reversed only by rare cataclysmic or catastrophic events like wars or depressions. Morris Fiorina (1981), however, has found that although party preferences are generally stable, the strength of that commitment can vary in response to political events. Weak Republicans, therefore, can become strong Republicans over a short period of time, while weak Democrats can come to view themselves as political independents leaning toward the Democratic party. In spite of their unwavering support for the Democratic party over the past two decades, Black Americans should not be viewed as an exception: their support for the Democratic party may have shifted in response to the political environment and recent events over the past four years, most specifically Jackson's 1984 presidential bid and the Reagan presidency.

Inasmuch as Jackson's 1984 campaign was a political bargaining vehicle for Blacks, it was also aimed at reducing Blacks' dependence on the Democratic party. Dissatisfaction with the party had grown among its Black members because of their belief that the party took their votes for granted. A chief reason given by Jackson for his entrance in the race in 1984 was to help Blacks renegotiate their contract with the party to achieve more favorable terms. Jackson, in fact, made the most of this issue in his early campaign speeches, declaring, "The message to white Democrats is that black voters can no longer be taken for granted because they have 'nowhere else to go.' We had to break the dependency syndrome. We moved from a relationship born of paternalism to one born of power" (quoted in Walters, 1988: 179). Most Black Democrats responded favorably to this message.

Jackson's bid made possible new alternatives to the Democratic party. For example, Hanes Walton, Jr., writes that the Jackson campaign could help Blacks move to "an independent voting position in all elections," or to a third party (1990: 62). A majority of Blacks would have chosen to abandon the party to vote for Jackson. In the 1984 NBES, over half (53 percent) of the respondents claimed that they would vote for Jackson as an independent over Walter Mondale or Ronald Reagan. Furthermore, the percentage of those in the NBES panel study willing to support an independent Jackson bid increased to 65 percent in 1988. Jackson, however, chose neither political independence nor the third party option. He decided against running as a third party candidate in the 1984 and 1988 presidential elections, and pledged to support the Democratic party's presidential nominees in both these elections.

However, even though Jackson ultimately rejected these options, it is possible that his candidacies had a negative impact on Blacks' relationship with the Democratic party. After all, Jackson's candidacy clearly raised Black expectations to a level many felt was not realistic. It was often repeated throughout both his campaigns that Jackson was in no position to win. Black Democrats who supported Jackson may have felt bitter not only about Jackson's loss, but also about the way the party treated him. In fact, the NBES survey shows that some Blacks did feel that Jackson had been mistreated by the party in 1984. Slightly more than one-fifth (21 percent) of the 1984 survey respondents claimed that the Democratic party treated Jackson worse than the other candidates in the race for the party's presidential nomination.

The experiences of Jackson delegates at the 1984 national convention were especially disillusioning. All of Jackson's minority policy planks were soundly defeated. As Black political scientist Lucius Barker, in the published account of his experiences as a Jackson delegate at the 1984 national convention, observed: "Mondale people wanted to show their control of the convention, particularly to show how badly he could beat Jackson . . . Along with many other Jackson delegates, I personally resented deeply this kind of treatment" (1988: 156). Jackson delegates felt that the party's treatment of their candidate at the convention was an indication of the party's attitudes toward Black Democrats in general. As Barker later explained, "As the convention moved toward an end, it became increasingly and painfully clear—at least to me—that, for whatever reason, Mondale and party leaders were not disposed to reach out to Jackson and to blacks generally" (1988: 181). Given their perceptions of how Jackson was received by the Democratic party, those most alienated might be less supportive of the party both in identification and voting behavior. Furthermore, in 1988, Jackson supporters felt even more strongly that Jackson should have been given the opportunity to be the vice-presidential candidate on the party's ticket. That he was not chosen may also be a factor in the decline in party support among the Jackson enthusiasts.

The panel study reveals, however, little movement of Black Democrats toward political independence or the GOP. Over the four-year period, there was, in fact, a slight increase in the percentage of strong Democrats among those reinterviewed in 1988, from 51 percent in 1984 to 55 percent in 1988. As Table 3.3 shows, 81 percent of those who said that they were strong Democrats in 1984 identified themselves as strong Democrats again in 1988. Partisan movement as such suggests that additional numbers of Black political independents and weakly identified Black Democrats in 1984 became stronger Democrats in 1988. The percentage of those re-

**Table 3.3** Cross-Tabulation of Blacks' Partisanship in 1984 by Partisanship in 1988 (weighted percentages)

| 1984 Partisanship | 1988 Partisanship | | | | | | |
| --- | --- | --- | --- | --- | --- | --- | --- |
| | Strong Democrat | Weak Democrat | Independent Democrat | Political Independent | Republican | Total Percentage | N |
| Strong Democrat | 81 | 16 | 3 | 0 | 1 | 100% | 232 |
| Weak Democrat | 36 | 43 | 16 | 1 | 4 | 100% | 94 |
| Independent Democrat | 37 | 19 | 25 | 4 | 15 | 100% | 51 |
| Political Independent | 23 | 12 | 34 | 8 | 22 | 100% | 17 |
| Republican | 0 | 18 | 10 | 16 | 55 | 100% | 24 |

*Source:* The 1984–1988 National Black Election Study.

*Note:* Given their small numbers within the Black community, self-identified strong Republicans, weak Republicans, and independent Republicans were combined to form a single Republican category.

interviewed in 1988 who claimed to be political independents decreased from 5 percent in 1984 to 2 percent in 1988, while the percentage of Republicans remained the same at 8 percent. There is little indication, therefore, that Jackson's 1984 bid had a negative impact on Black support for the Democratic party. Black identification with the Democratic party remained generally stable, with a limited movement, in fact, away from political independence.

Given the stability and modest growth in pro-Democratic identification among Blacks in 1988, it is also quite possible that Jackson actually strengthened Blacks' ties to the Democratic party. Even while Barker, as a 1984 Jackson delegate, wrote of his growing and real resentment against the party because of its treatment of Jackson, he noted his pride in being able to participate in Jackson's campaign. In his reaction to Jackson's convention speech on July 17, 1984, he remarked: "Here was a man who had been beaten by the sheer power of Mondale—and, I thought, Hart—forces but whose support all knew would be needed in November. Jackson's head was not bowed . . . His speech that night was a masterpiece. It will forever give him a medal of honor in my book" (1988: 157).

Most Blacks supporting Jackson did not learn of his defeat at the convention. The press gave this issue little coverage, focusing instead on Jackson's speech and the party's positive reception to it. It was, by all accounts, a celebrated occasion. For many Black Americans, Jackson represented the first Black national political leader since Martin Luther King, and he was considered to be a national and prominent figure within the Democratic party. Thus, the enthusiasm that his 1984 candidacy generated may have had the revitalizing effect on Blacks' Democratic commitment that Roosevelt and Johnson had on past generations of Blacks.

To examine more closely the effect of Jackson's 1984 bid on Black partisanship in 1988, a structural equation model was developed that estimated the impact of Jackson ratings in 1984 on Black party identification in 1988. Further details of this analysis are provided in the second section of Appendix B. Because Blacks' negative assessments of President Reagan might have also critically affected their partisanship, Reagan ratings in 1984 and 1988 were also included in the model. The analysis, as shown in Appendix B, found that Jackson had no independent effect on Black partisanship.[2] In other words, those who rated Jackson most favorably were no more or less likely to move toward or away from the Democratic party in identification. Reagan evaluations in 1984 had, however, a significant effect on Black partisanship in 1988. Blacks most critical of Reagan in 1984 were more likely to be strong Democrats in 1988 than those less critical.

Ronald Walters maintains that the Reagan presidency greatly "devalued" the Republican option for Black Americans, and feels it is unlikely that there will be any appreciable growth in the percentage of Black Republicans "as long as the party's presidential candidates maintain the current profile of policy positions" (1988: 188). The analysis here supports Walters's claims. Rather than benefiting from the tensions Jackson's candidacy had produced between Blacks and the Democratic party, the Reagan presidency helped to strengthen Blacks' loyalty to their party.

## Conclusion: Blacks' Partisan Loyalties in 1992 and Beyond

A review of the history of Blacks' political activity in the twentieth century reveals a marked growth in political power and influence in national politics. Black migration to the North, beginning in the 1920s and continuing unabated up to World War II, as well as the accumulation and concentration of political resources during the civil rights struggle, fundamentally altered Blacks' political status. Blacks no longer played a quiescent role within the Democratic party. As more Blacks became Democrats, their activism also helped to transform the Democratic party from a racially conservative to a racially liberal one. Furthermore, having facilitated the party's transformation, Blacks then became more politically active within the Democratic party, emerging as its progressive wing. Jackson's 1984 candidacy no doubt played a significant part in promoting the growth of Black political activism and the expansion of Blacks' political aspirations. His candidacy alone, however, cannot account for the new power relationship that Blacks have within the Democratic party. Even without Jackson, Black Democrats would probably still have pushed for greater visibility as well as more responsiveness from the party. Furthermore, even without Jackson in the race, Black political aspirations are headed toward a Black presidential candidate, or at least, a candidate who more clearly articulates and supports their interests.

As the primary vehicle in electoral politics, Blacks have become increasingly frustrated with their place in party politics, however. A large part of their frustration is due to the spread of conservatism that occurred over the past two decades and their politically marginal status during the Reagan years. Blacks were effectively locked out of power during the 1980s. Moreover, many Blacks felt that the Democratic party did not help to alleviate their situation either. As Walters notes, "The Democratic party has responded to being out of power for twelve of the past sixteen years by vacillating between the politics and policies of the New Deal and those of the new Republican era" (1988: 189). The abandonment of the civil rights/social welfare agenda created during the Kennedy-Johnson era, in particular, has produced negative feelings on the part of Blacks toward the Democratic party. The selection of Ronald H. Brown, a Black American, as the party's national chairman has been interpreted by some as both a move by the party to appease Black Democrats and a reaffirmation of the party's long-term commitment to Blacks.

Blacks' new influential position within the Democratic party has been a source of concern among Democratic party leaders. The Jackson candidacies, and Blacks' support of his candidacies, have made it more difficult for the Democratic party to manage its unstable coalition of Blacks, White liberals, and southerners. Some have asserted that these difficulties stem from the new and growing dominance of Blacks within the party. One group of political scientists describes the situation quite frankly: "As the Democratic coalition becomes blacker, whites become less willing to participate" (Huckfeldt and Kohfeld, 1988: 184). Apparently, even as early as 1964, an assistant to President Johnson is reported to have said that the 97 percent of Black support that Johnson received was "too much." The political analysts who reported this story liken Blacks in the Democratic party to the New Right of the Republican party and Jesse Jackson to Jesse Helms, noting further that "in politics, as in love, total allegiance can be difficult to handle" (Lewis and Schneider, 1983: 59). Clearly, some put the burden for the party's problems in winning presidential elections directly on Blacks: if only Blacks would participate less or become less visible supporters of the Democratic party, then the party would not lose its White supporters. Since the party depends on Black votes in close races, the real hope, of course, is not that Blacks would participate less but that they would become less visible. But a return to a quiescent state in electoral and party politics for Blacks is highly unlikely. Thus, even though the Democratic party's current racial dilemma appears intractable, successful management of its coalition will not be possible without taking full account of the new political clout that Blacks now wield.

Bipartisanship and even realignment toward the Republican party remain much-discussed options for Black voters. In a thoughtfully provocative essay, however, Dianne Pinderhughes summarily dismisses the possibility of a Black/GOP alliance because Black voters are too liberal; she writes, "A small shift to the right does not necessarily increase [Blacks'] bargaining power because as a group they are too far from the center to affect the overall balance of power" (1986: 86). She contends that the only real alternative to the Democratic party for Blacks is third party formation. Still, immediately following the election of George Bush to the presidency in 1988, the Republican party's national chairman, Lee Atwater, publicly announced that he would like to see the Black support for the Republican party in future presidential elections increase to the double digits. Moreover, the Republican party has aggressively recruited Black candidates, and in 1990 a Black Republican from Connecticut, Gary Franks, was elected to Congress. However, Republican opportunities within the Black community have never appeared bleaker than they are today. Black support for the Republican party reached its lowest levels, just below 10 percent, in the 1964 and 1980 presidential elections. The candidates in these two elections, Barry Goldwater and Ronald Reagan, were widely perceived by Blacks as racial conservatives. Franks is the first Black Republican elected to the House since Oscar DePriest in 1929, but unlike DePriest, he was elected in a congressional district that is only 4 percent Black. Franks is also a self-described "staunch conservative," much like his White predecessor.

As the analysis presented in this chapter revealed, Blacks' racial orientation represents a large component of their partisan identities.

Although Black Republicans tend to be less racially identified than Black Democrats today, no real growth in the percentage of Black Republicans is possible without some modification of the Republican party's conservative stance toward racial policies and civil rights. The Republican party, in other words, must undo the damage to the party done by its racial conservatives and initiate a return, of sorts, to the party of Lincoln. In her discussion of Blacks and the GOP, Pearl Robinson argues that to become an attractive alternative for Blacks once more, the party must "provide options that are congruent with the gains of the civil rights movement," reinforcing Black economic and social mobility through "government-backed antidiscrimination and employment activities" (1982: 218).

Thus far, George Bush has sent a number of conflicting messages to the Black community. As the Republican party's presidential nominee, Bush had forcefully attacked Dukakis for being soft on crime. For Black Americans, the Bush campaign theme of crime closely resembled Nixon's successful law and order campaign in 1968, which some Blacks perceived as anti-Black. During the 1988 campaign, a conservative group, independent of the official Bush campaign organization, had circulated fliers bearing the picture of Willie Horton, a Black Massachusetts resident currently serving time for raping a White woman. The flier claimed, "Dukakis' election would set murderers and rapists free across the country" (Germond and Witcover, 1989). The Bush campaign organization had publicized the Willie Horton case, but had not revealed his race. As a result of this, Bush's political campaign in 1988 was attacked as racist. Donna Brazile, a former campaign aide to Michael Dukakis, had in fact accused the Bush campaign of using "every code word and racial symbol to package their little racist campaign."[3] However, unlike Ronald Reagan, Bush did not campaign as an economic conservative. Indeed, his acceptance speech at the Republican national convention revealed deep differences between the policies and interests he would represent and those that Ronald Reagan had represented. Furthermore, in a speech made to the NAACP in mid-July, before the national convention, Bush said that he would protect the rights of all Americans and that he favored the concept of affirmative action (Germond and Witcover, 1989: 367). Finally, as president, Bush has appointed more Blacks to federal positions than did Reagan. Moreover, Black Bush-appointees, unlike the extreme conservatives whom Reagan had favored, tend to be political moderates, such as Dr. Louis Sullivan as Secretary of Health and Human Services.

Nevertheless, within a few months of holding office, Bush strongly advocated a reduction in the capital gains tax, an act that clearly would work to the benefit of wealthy Americans. Furthermore, although in November 1991 he ultimately signed into law the first piece of civil rights legislation to pass Congress since the heyday of the civil rights era, he had vetoed an earlier version, attacking it as a "quota bill." Finally, the Department of Education under the Bush administration shocked liberals and Blacks with the announcement that it would withdraw federal funds from universities that continued to provide minority students with special scholarships, which the department held were "racially discriminatory." This new policy toward minority scholarships, however, was quickly withdrawn for further study under pressure from the White House. Even though George Bush has softened the Republican party's image on race, using rhetoric highly supportive of civil rights for Blacks, a Republican record in favor of civil rights and race has not (yet) been established. It seems unlikely that rhetoric alone will be enough to lure a substantial minority of Blacks away from the Democratic party. With race and civil rights issues still highly significant within the Black community, it appears for now, at least, that the lion's share of the Black vote will continue to go to the Democratic party.

# 4

# Group Resources and Black Electoral Participation

The overwhelming majority of Black Americans believe in voting as a means to achieve group empowerment. In a 1980 national survey of Black Americans, in response to the question whether Blacks should be active in politics or demonstrate to gain equal rights in this country, 85 percent chose politics over protest. Only 13 percent opted for demonstrations and protest in place of politics.[1] Those able to join in protest politics, like the poor and the young, however, may be less able to participate in traditional politics. Electoral participation, including voting, requires individual resources such as skill, knowledge, and initiative. Socioeconomic status, age, and civic and political orientations have been shown to be the major determinants of political participation (Verba and Nie, 1972; Wolfinger and Rosenstone, 1980). In general, those who are familiar with the political process—usually older, better-educated, and affluent Americans—are more likely to participate in politics. Those with a strong sense of civic duty, those with faith in their individual abilities to influence politics, and those having a general interest in politics are also more likely to participate. These material and psychological resources are related. Higher-status individuals are more likely to feel that they have a stake in politics, are more efficacious, and are more politically aware.

Because of their low socioeconomic status, Black Americans as a group are expected to participate in politics at lower levels than White Americans as a group. Blacks are not only "resource poor" in that many lack the necessary political skills, information base, and levels of education that Whites generally possess, but also, like the poor in general, many Blacks lack the necessary psychological attributes and basic motivation essential for political participation. Given their long history of exclusion from politics, Blacks are often more alienated and less efficacious than Whites. Nevertheless, though Blacks are clearly handicapped by their social status in politics, empirical studies conducted in the late 1960s found Blacks to be more politically active than Whites as a group once the factor of socioeconomic status is taken into account (Verba and Nie, 1972: chap. 10; Shingles, 1981).

Obviously, then, socioeconomic status and civic and political attitudes alone cannot explain the racial differences found in political participation. Social scientists have argued that Blacks are able to participate at such high levels, in spite of their political disadvantages, through the utilization of nontraditional group-based political resources. These resources, which were critical to explaining the emergence of the modern-day civil rights movement (McAdam, 1982), include the development and maintenance of a racial ideology that encourages political action (Verba and Nie, 1972), as well as membership in indigenous community and political organizations, which in turn enables Blacks to participate at greater levels than Whites of comparable social status (Oberschall, 1978).

With the exception of group consciousness, however, group-based political resources have not yet been formally defined, let alone incorporated in empirical investigations of Black electoral behavior. Research in the field of Black voting behavior, in fact, has not moved beyond the identification of structural factors—for example, legal barriers and election laws that limit the participation of Blacks—to specifically individual factors, such as socioeconomic status, which are important to explaining participation in general. In this chapter, using data from the 1984–1988 NBES panel study, I present a model of Black electoral participation that, in addition to the standard predictors of political participation, incorporates the collective resources of Blacks as factors which explain their current rates of participation. These collective resources include: (1) race identification, (2) membership in Black political organizations, (3) church membership, and (4) Black officeseeking.

## Black Collective Resources

In their important book, *Participation in America* (1972), Sidney Verba and Norman H. Nie found that Blacks possessing a strong racial orientation to politics (those who in their study frequently mentioned race in their discussion of political matters) were more politically active than Blacks lacking a racial orientation to politics. They argue that Blacks' self-awareness of their status as a disadvantaged group leads them to be more politically active than other disadvantaged groups, like the poor, who lack a comparable collective identity. In this regard, group consciousness helps to reduce racial disparities found in participation based on status. Other studies have since shown race consciousness to promote Black participation as well (Gurin, Hatchett, and Jackson, 1989; Shingles, 1981; Miller, Gurin, and Malunchuk, 1981).

Black political organizations and institutions, including the Black church, have been identified as crucial to the success of the modern-day Black civil rights movement. While these organizations gave structure to the protest movement, many, operating well before the passage of the 1965 Voting Rights Act, also helped register and mobilize Black voters (McAdam, 1982; Morris, 1984). Although religious groups, such as those affiliated with the Christian Right, have recently become active in national politics, Black churches have traditionally been involved in politics. Contrary to their depiction as separate spheres, Black religious life and political life have historically commingled. It is well known that the Black church served as the "institutional center" of the Black civil rights movement (Morris, 1984: 4). Most recently, Black churches have been active in electoral politics. Jesse Jackson's 1984 bid for the Democratic party's presidential nomination was greatly aided by the Black church. Jackson relied upon a network of Black ministers and churches to raise campaign funds and mobilize Black voters (see Cavanagh and Foster, 1984). Churches have also been instrumental in the recent elections of Black mayors.

In general, organizational membership has been shown to be one of the most powerful predictors of political participation (Verba and Nie, 1972: chap. 11). Members of voluntary associations, both political and social, are more likely to be politically active than nonmembers. Participation is promoted by organizations either through the dissemination of political information, or, as in the case of political organizations, through the involvement of members in activities that are explicitly political. Black organizations, especially, have the potential for offsetting the disadvantages that individual Blacks carry within the political arena. Black organizations can pool scarce resources, such as money and time, educate their members about political matters, and provide additional incentives and motivations for getting involved in politics. Studies of urban politics have demonstrated that Black organizations continue to be politically important. Registration efforts by national organizations throughout the 1980s increased the numbers of Blacks registered to vote (Piven and Cloward, 1988). Local voter registration drives have also been frequently undertaken in order to elect Blacks to office. In his analysis of the 1983 election of Chicago's first Black mayor, Paul Kleppner found that over 200 Black grassroots organizations worked together to register new Black voters (1985: 146). Prior to this critical election, White registration and turnout had always been consistently higher than Black registration and turnout. Largely through the efforts of these organizations, Black participation was 5.8 percentage points higher than White participation in the 1983 mayoral primary (Kleppner, 1985: 148). Yet, as one study implies, voter registration efforts are generally more successful when they take place in localities where community and political infrastructures already exist (Cavanagh, 1987). Thus, organizational membership, in addition to race consciousness (or identification), can serve as an alternative political resource for Blacks.

While there is evidence that suggests that Blacks continue to rely upon group-based political resources in order to boost their participation levels, the nature of the changes that have taken place in Black politics calls into question their continued role in explaining Black rates of participation today. One significant change is the recent finding that Blacks apparently no longer "outparticipate" Whites. In a recently published article, Lawrence Bobo and Frank Gilliam (1990) have found, utilizing data collected in the mid-1980s, that once group differences in socioeconomic status are taken into account, the racial disparity in vote participation disappears (see also Wolfinger and Rosenstone, 1980). Given that the concept of group consciousness as a stimulus of Black participation was developed and tested during the late 1960s and early 1970s, at a time when Blacks were engaged in a large-scale protest movement, the positive effect of race consciousness on Black participation may have been wholly the product of the protest atmosphere of the 1960s. Given the magnitude of Black electoral successes, Bobo and Gilliam suggest that race consciousness may no longer work to mobilize Blacks politically.

In spite of the church's historically documented role in the civil rights struggle as well as its recent activism in the 1984 presidential candidacy of Jesse Jackson, the notion of the Black church as a source of Black political activity has always been questioned by some social analysts. Beginning in the 1930s, a number of sociologists, including E. Franklin Frazier, have argued that the Black church's "pie-in-the-sky," other-worldly orientation and its emotionalism work against the development of a Black political consciousness and "this-world" concern with social change. Most recently, a political scientist, Adolph Reed, Jr. (1986) has asserted that the Black church is at odds with the principles of democracy. He claims that despite the church's involvement in Jackson's presidential bids, church political activism is incompatible with modern, democratic political processes, given that the Black church is intrinsically "nonpolitical," authoritarian, and conservative.

Critics of the Black church base their arguments on the claim that religion is often depoliticizing, that is, "the opiate of the masses." Gary Marx's book, *Protest and Prejudice* (1967), is frequently cited as empirical documentation of the antithetical relationship that exists between religion and politics for Blacks. Marx found that religious Blacks were less likely to be supportive of Black civil rights militancy than nonreligious Blacks. This negative association between religiosity and militancy held even when other factors such as age, region, and social class were taken into account. More surprising than this, however, was his discovery that pro-militant Blacks were more likely to belong to conventional religious denominations, including interracial churches, such as Episcopal, Presbyterian, and Catholic churches. Marx concluded that the nature of religion found in independent Black churches is "an important factor working against the widespread radicalization of [Blacks]" (1967: 105).

In spite of the fact that his study is frequently presented as empirical evidence that the Black church has a strong depoliticizing effect, Marx does not actually examine the effects of religiosity and church membership on Black voting behavior. It has not been established in any published account that religious Blacks are less likely to be active in politics than nonreligious Blacks. In their new book, *The Black Church in the African American Experience,* C. Eric Lincoln and Lawrence H. Mamiya seriously challenge the sociological studies of the Black church that characterize it as a nonpolitical and conservative institution. This view of the Black church, they write, represents "a serious misunderstanding of the relationship between religion and politics and a gross distortion of the political functions which the black churches have performed historically" (1990: 198). Throughout the period of slavery, they argue, many Black clergy were active in the cause of emancipation. Moreover, the church has also served as a training center for Black leaders and has always stressed participation in the political process to its congregants in order to fulfill their duties as "responsible American citizens" (1990: 215).

A further problem with Marx's analysis, highlighted in the Lincoln and Mamiya study but originally identified by Hart and Anne Nelsen (1975), is that it fails to differentiate between the sect-like and the church-like dimensions of religiosity. Sectarianism, or the dimension of religious beliefs that embodies a strong other-worldly orientation, tends to depress civil rights militancy and political activism, while religious beliefs per se are not in conflict with a protest orientation. And currently it seems that Black religious sectarianism is in decline. According to Lincoln and Mamiya, Black Pentecostals, such as the Church of God in Christ, have moved closer to Black mainstream churches in doctrine and teachings. Furthermore, in their 1983 survey of 1,894 Black clergy, Lincoln and Mamiya found an almost absolute majority to be supportive of social change achieved through political action. Nine out of ten clergy whom they interviewed said that they would approve of clergy in their churches taking part in protest marches on civil rights. Furthermore, 92 percent felt that churches should express their views on day-to-day social and political questions. Though a slightly smaller percentage, fully 80 percent of the Church of God in Christ clergy responded positively to these questions as well. Lincoln and Mamiya recognize that the high levels of support for protest in Black churches today could be the legacy of the Black civil rights and Black power movements. They write, "Of course, the passage of time and successes of the civil rights movement may have helped to legitimate a more active role in the secular arena on the part of churches and clergy" (1990: 227).

Other factors, nevertheless, may better account for variations in Black participation today than either socioeconomic status, political dispositions, or group-based political resources. One major difference between the civil rights era and this new electoral period is the absolute numbers of Blacks now seeking office. Black officeseeking, particularly in elections involving Blacks as political newcomers, seems to be associated with astoundingly high Black turnouts. During the late 1960s and 1970s, Blacks registered for the first time in unprecedented numbers. Not only did this encourage Blacks to seek office for the very first time, but the presence of Black candidates further inspired additional numbers of Blacks to register. One can quite easily observe this phenomenon in the past elections of Blacks in mayoral contests. For example, in 1967, when Carl Stokes was elected mayor of Cleveland, roughly 80 percent of Blacks who were eligible to vote did vote (Nelson, 1987). In the 1983 general election of Harold Washington in Chicago, approximately 82 percent of voting-eligible Blacks turned out (Preston, 1987; Kleppner, 1985). Blacks presumably turn out and vote in greater numbers when a Black is running for office because of greater group loyalty, pride, and interest, given the historic nature of the event (the candidate may be the first Black to seek such an office). Black turnout may also be higher in such elections because Black candidates often campaign more intensively and spend greater resources in Black communities precisely to get out the Black vote. Clearly, then, Black officeseeking should be associated with higher rates of participation and campaign activism. It too, then, should be viewed as a collective political resource of Blacks.

## Who within the Black Community Participates?

Empirical investigations of Black voting behavior, as mentioned earlier, have failed to offer models that extend beyond the standard socioeconomic status (SES) model/group consciousness model introduced by Verba and Nie in their book *Participation in America* (1972). The ability of Blacks to mount a large-scale protest movement, however, was clearly aided by the resources they possessed within the community. It seems likely that many of these same resources serve to promote Black electoral participation as well. Before the effects of these group resources (race identification, organizational and church memberships, and Black officeseeking) can be ascertained, it is important first to identify those who participate in politics within the Black community and those who do not. Although participation can involve a number of acts, from contact with a political official to picketing a business to joining a political organization, this chapter focuses on two of the most basic modes of political participation: voting and campaign activism.

*Registration, Voting, and Campaign Activism*
Voting is considered to be the easiest and, therefore, the most popular mode of political participation. In the 1984 NBES survey, 91 percent of the respondents said that they were registered to vote, and approximately 65 percent of the respondents reported voting in the 1984 national election; this figure, however, contrasts with the Census Bureau's Current Population Survey, which estimates that 56 percent of the voting-eligible Black population voted in the 1984 election. The high percentage of NBES respondents who voted may be due to the fact that these are self-reported measures of voter participation. In general, studies have found that self-reported measures of participation overestimate participation levels because roughly 10 to 15 percent of those who report that they voted in a given election did not, in fact, do so (Sigelman, 1982). Obviously, some overreporting of voting is present in the NBES, although the actual extent is unknown.[2] The high proportion of Black voters may also be a reflection of the survey's design. The NBES surveys were conducted by telephone, and, in general, telephone surveys obtain respondents with a higher than average socioeconomic status profile, as well as respondents who, because of their backgrounds, are more likely to vote. It is assumed that the unknown ratio of Black "nonvoting voters" and "voters" in the 1984–1988 NBES panel study, however, is not a problem in the analysis of the voting data. Sigelman (1982) found that the use of self-reported measures of participation,

as opposed to validated voter behavior measures, did not lead to different or biased results.

To better identify those within the Black community who are more likely to vote in and across all types of elections, respondents were assigned to one of three mutually exclusive categories: core voters, peripheral voters, or nonvoters. Core voters are those who vote regularly in all types of elections. Specifically, core voters were defined as those who said that they voted in the 1980 presidential election and the 1984 presidential, Senate, House, and local elections. Slightly over half (52 percent) of the Blacks interviewed in 1984 were core voters. Peripheral voters were those who said that they did not vote in 1980 but voted in all of the 1984 elections *or* those who voted in the 1980 and 1984 presidential elections but did not vote in the 1984 Senate, House, or local elections. Approximately 39 percent of Blacks in the sample were peripheral voters. Nonvoters are those who did not vote in either the 1980 or the 1984 presidential elections. Nine percent of the sample were classified as nonvoters.

Presumably, core voters will be better educated, older, and more affluent than nonvoters. Peripheral voters, although not necessarily better educated than core voters, will be decidedly less partisan than core voters. Peripheral voters are more likely to vote in response to national election forces, while core voters, having committed to a single party, are more likely to be loyal voters who consistently turn out to vote for their party's candidates (Campbell, 1960). In light of the degree of Blacks' loyalty to the Democratic party, it is not surprising that the ratio of core voters to peripheral voters is higher.

Voting, of course, is not the only mode of political participation. Citizens interested in affecting the outcome of an election beyond voting can work for their party's candidate, influence others in how they should vote, donate money to a campaign, and so on. Campaign acts are closely associated with the act of voting, since both take place during an election period (Verba and Nie, 1972). While the majority of Blacks in the 1984 sample were registered to vote and did vote, considerably fewer were campaign activists. As shown in Table 4.1, only 22 percent attended political meetings or rallies in support of a candidate, and fewer than one in every five helped with voter registration (19 percent) or donated money to a campaign (19

Table 4.1    Measures of Campaign Activism (weighted percentages)

| Question Wording | Yes (%) | (N) |
|---|---|---|
| "Did you talk to any people and try to show them why they should vote for or against one of the parties or candidates?" | 40 | (866) |
| "Did you go to any political meetings, rallies, speeches, dinners, or things like that in support of a particular candidate?" | 22 | (866) |
| "Did you help with a voter registration drive or help get people to the polls on election day?" | 18 | (865) |
| "Did you give any money to or help raise money for any of the candidates?" | 19 | (865) |

Source: The 1984 National Black Election Study.

percent). Close to 40 percent, however, tried to influence others with respect to their vote.

*Factors Affecting Political Participation*

To determine which Blacks are more likely to be registered, to vote, and to participate directly in political campaigns in 1984, multivariate analysis was performed on a set of participation measures utilizing a number of demographic variables known to be associated with voting as predictors—such factors as gender, age, and educational level—as well as a number of attitudinal variables such as partisanship, political interest, and trust in government. A campaign activism scale consisting of the four items as displayed in Table 4.1 was constructed.[3] This scale reflects the total number of campaign acts a respondent engaged in during the election year, and ranges from zero (no acts) to four (engaged in all four acts). The mean number of acts a respondent engaged in was less than one. Table 4.2 contains the estimated effects of the predictor variables and their standard errors. The determinants of "registered to vote" and "voted for president" were calculated using logit analysis, while the determinants of the voter type and campaign activism scales are ordinary least squares (OLS) regression coefficients and standard errors.

**Table 4.2** Demographic and Attitudinal Determinants of Black Electoral Participation

| | Logit Coefficients | | | | OLS Coefficients | | | |
| | Registered to Vote | | Voted for President | | Voter Type Scale | | Campaign Activism | |
| Independent Variables | B | (SE) | B | (SE) | B | (SE) | B | (SE) |
|---|---|---|---|---|---|---|---|---|
| Constant | -.14 | (1.65) | -1.60 | (1.30) | -2.32** | (.21) | -.39** | (.39) |
| Gender (female) | .95* | (.36) | .28 | (.24) | .05 | (.05) | -.10 | (.09) |
| Age | .031* | (.015) | .02* | (.01) | .005* | (.002) | .003 | (.003) |
| Education | .03 | (.09) | .02 | (.05) | .01 | (.01) | -.03 | (.02) |
| Family income | .06 | (.06) | .02 | (.04) | .02* | (.01) | .02 | (.02) |
| Region (non-South) | .77* | (.35) | .07 | (.24) | .11* | (.05) | .18* | (.09) |
| Homeowner (yes) | .07 | (.39) | .15 | (.26) | .09 | (.05) | .16 | (.10) |
| Urbanicity (low-high) | -.29* | (.14) | -.04 | (.09) | .00 | (.02) | .01 | (.03) |
| System responsiveness (low-high) | .31* | (.15) | .01 | (.10) | .02 | (.02) | .09* | (.04) |
| Political trust (low-high) | .06 | (.17) | -.10 | (.11) | .01 | (.02) | -.07 | (.04) |
| Political interest | .49** | (.13) | .35** | (.08) | .10** | (.02) | .10** | (.03) |
| Partisanship | .78** | (.21) | .60** | (.14) | .13** | (.03) | .13* | (.05) |

*Source:* The 1984 National Black Election Study.

*Note:* Included as independent variables in the four models but not shown are the group-based determinants shown in Table 4.3.

*p < .05.

**p < .01.

Since the enfranchisement of women, women's rates of participation have traditionally been lower than men's. Past research has documented the existence of a gender gap in participation within the Black community as well. However, this gender gap in Black participation has been something of an anomaly since it was found that Black women typically participate at higher levels than Black men (Baxter and Lansing, 1983; Shingles, 1981; Cavanagh, 1985; Verba and Nie, 1972). Many of these researchers argue that Black women's high rates of participation are largely the expressed outcome of their "dual oppression" as Blacks and as women. If race identification promotes Black political participation in general, then a gender consciousness combined with a race consciousness works to the extra advantage of Black women in participation.

More Black women were likely to be registered to vote in 1984 than Black men, but gender was not related to actual voter participation in 1984. Once other factors such as income, home ownership, and political interest were taken into account, Black women did not "outparticipate" Black men. However, Black women tend to be more politically engaged than Black men, not only having higher rates of voter registration, but generally being more interested in political campaigns and more partisan than Black men (see the final section of Appendix B).

Of the various indicators of socioeconomic status, education is viewed as the one most powerfully related to political participation. Education is positively related to participation, Ray Wolfinger and Steven Rosenstone claim, because "schooling increases one's capacity for understanding and working with complex, abstract, and intangible subjects, that is, subjects like politics" (1980: 18). Income, by comparison, usually has a much smaller, although still significant, effect on voter turnout. One of the reasons that Wolfinger and Rosenstone offer to explain why personal finances are tied to participation is the fact that poor people probably have less time and energy for the "nonessentials" in life, including politics and voting.

Among Blacks, however, education was not directly associated with electoral participation, although it was indirectly related to voter participation through its effect on Blacks' political orientations, as shown in the last section of Appendix B. Black electoral participation was strongly related to political interest, partisanship, and to a lesser extent, Black attitudes toward the general responsiveness of government. College-educated Blacks, in particular, were more likely to be interested in political campaigns and to feel that they have voice and representation in government. For example, 57 percent of Black college graduates reported being "very much interested" in the 1984 political campaigns in comparison to 34 percent of Black high school graduates. Similarly, only 21 percent of respondents having college degrees agreed with the statement that "people like me don't have any say about what the government does," in contrast to 37 percent of high school graduates. Through its effect on such attitudes that strongly affect Blacks' rates of participation, then, education is an important determinant of Black political participation. When these attitudinal measures are not present in the analysis, education has a strong and statistically significant effect on all four forms of Black political participation assessed here. (See the last section of Appendix B for further analysis and discussion of education's effect on Black participation.)

Income was related to the frequency of Black voter participation, while home ownership was related to campaign activism. Thus, poor Blacks were less likely than affluent Blacks to participate in all types of elections, while homeowners were more likely to be campaign activists than were renters. Participation in all elections and direct involvement in political campaigns are, no doubt, more difficult to manage for the Black poor. In some sense, they clearly represent the "nonessentials" of politics and are regarded as different from voting in a single election, even though such acts maximize the individual's influence in politics.

Age, region, and urbanicity are other factors shown to be related to participation. Research indicates that participation in electoral politics increases with age, although it may drop off slightly among the elderly. Age was strongly related to Black political participation, except for campaign activism. In general, older Black Americans were more likely to be registered and to vote in 1984 than younger Black Americans, but no more likely to participate in political campaigns. Past research has also found that southern Blacks and those living in less populated areas of the country are less likely to vote than Blacks living outside of the South and those residing in urban areas. In the 1984 NBES, Blacks residing in the South and those living in rural and less populated areas were less likely to be registered to vote than those outside of the South and living in urban areas. Still, once registered, southern and rural Blacks were no less likely to be active participants than non-southern and urban Blacks. Geographic differences in voter participation rates, frequency, and type failed to emerge among Blacks in the 1984 presidential election.

Four standard attitudinal predictors were also included in the analysis: partisanship, political interest, political trust, and system responsiveness. The partisanship measure has three levels: (1) strong partisan of either major party; (2) weak partisan of either major party; (3) no party affiliation (independent) or other party affiliation. The measure of political interest is a standard one. Blacks were asked, "Would you say that you have been very much interested, somewhat interested, or not much interested in the political campaigns so far this year?" The overwhelming majority (82 percent) of Blacks were very much or somewhat interested in the 1984 political campaigns, with 18 percent expressing "not much" interest. Political trust is a mean sum index of responses for two questions: (1) "How much of the time do you think you can trust government to do the right thing?" and (2) "Would you say the government is pretty much run by a few big interests . . . or is it run for the benefit of all the people?" This indicator is scaled from low trust to high trust. Presumably, Blacks who feel that the political system is not responsive or who are less trusting of government and government officials are less likely to participate than those who feel that the system is responsive and who are trusting of government. Finally, Blacks were asked how strongly they agreed or disagreed with the following three items: (1) "People like me have no say in government"; (2) "Public officials don't care"; and (3) "White officials always get their way." System responsiveness, therefore, is the mean sum index of these three items. It is expected that Blacks who feel that the political system is closed to them are less likely to make an effort to participate in politics than those who feel that the political system is open.

Of all the attitudinal variables, the two most strongly and consistently related to Black participation were also the most explicitly political measures: political interest and partisanship. Those who expressed a strong interest in politics were more likely to be registered, participants in the 1984 presidential election, regular voters, and campaign activists than those expressing weak or no interest in politics. Similarly, strong partisans tended to be more politically active than nonpartisans. The majority (62 percent) of strong partisans, for example, were core voters, while only 3 percent were found to be nonvoters. Among the nonpartisans, those having no attachment to the major parties, 43 percent were core voters while 17 percent were nonvoters. System responsiveness was also related to Black electoral participation and campaign activism. Those who felt that they had a voice in politics and that the government was responsive to Blacks and their interests were more likely to be registered voters and campaign activists than those who felt that they had no say in government and that government was unresponsive to Blacks. The other social-psychological variable, trust in government, was completely unrelated to Black election participation. Political trust (or distrust) may no longer be a relevant factor in explaining Blacks' rates of political participation.

To summarize, political interest and partisanship strongly predict who participates in electoral politics and who does not in the Black community today. As shown by the 1984 NBES, Blacks lacking a strong major party affiliation and those uninterested in politics were more likely to be politically inactive than party members and those absorbed by politics. Young Blacks were less likely to vote than older Blacks. Income also affected Black participation; affluent Blacks were more likely to participate across all types of elections than poor Blacks. Homeowners were more likely to be campaign activists than renters. Still, a critical determinant of Black participation is one that did not directly affect Black participation in 1984: education. As shown in Appendix B and other sections of this book, college-educated Blacks are more likely to express strong interest in politics and believe in the effectiveness of their participation than less-educated Blacks. Thus, Black participation is strongly conditioned by individual differences among Blacks, including social class.

## The Impact of Group-Based Political Resources on Black Participation

Verba and Nie were primarily interested in how race consciousness as a participatory mechanism works to reduce the racial disparities found in voting and other forms of political participation. It is also of interest to investigate whether these participatory mechanisms or collective resources help in any way to mitigate the differences in Black participation based on social class.

To estimate the effects of the group-based political resources presented earlier (race identification, Black organizational membership, and church membership), these factors were included in the logit and regression models developed and presented in the previous section. Their coefficients and standard errors are shown in Table 4.3. Given the inadequacy of its current measurement, Black office-seeking as a group resource could not be included in the model, and thus its unique contribution to Black participation was not estimated. Nevertheless, a discussion and preliminary analysis of the potential of Black officeseeking to boost Black participation are presented in the next section.

Of the three group-based political resources, only membership in a politically active church most consistently promoted Black participation. The other two, race identification and Black organizational membership, were slightly less effective resources in the political mobilization of Blacks.

### Race Identification

The group identification measure in this analysis, one used throughout this book, is an additive index of two questions which separately measure the degree to which respondents felt that what happens to Blacks in this country affects their lives and the degree to which respondents thought consciously about being Black. The estimated effect of group identification on Black political participation was mixed. Strongly race-conscious Blacks were no more likely to be registered voters or to be regular participants across different types of elections than less race-conscious Blacks. However, strongly race-conscious Blacks were more likely to vote in the 1984 presidential election and to be campaign activists than more weakly race-conscious Blacks. Race identification, therefore, should be counted as an alternative political resource for Blacks that continues to raise their participation rate in politics.

Nevertheless, the importance of group consciousness in Black politics can be exaggerated. As a number of social movement theorists have maintained, Blacks' collective grievances over their sec-

**Table 4.3** Group-Based Determinants of Black Electoral Participation

| | Logit Coefficients | | | | OLS Coefficients | | | |
| | Registered to Vote | | Voted for President | | Voter Type Scale | | Campaign Activism | |
| Independent Variables | B | (SE) | B | (SE) | B | (SE) | B | (SE) |
|---|---|---|---|---|---|---|---|---|
| Race identification (low-high) | .06 | (.10) | .15* | (.07) | .02 | (.01) | .07** | (.03) |
| Black organization (member) | 2.00 | (1.06) | .35 | (.36) | .09 | (.06) | .50** | (.11) |
| Political church (member) | .53 | (.34) | .51* | (.24) | .14** | (.06) | .49** | (.10) |
| Log likelihood | −125.08 | | −296.64 | | — | | — | |
| Predicted correctly | 92% | | 82% | | — | | — | |
| Total cases | 610 | | 610 | | 595 | | 605 | |
| $R^2$ | — | | — | | .25 | | .25 | |

Source: The 1984 National Black Election Study.

Note: Included as independent variables in the four models but not shown are the demographic and attitudinal determinants shown in Table 4.2.

*$p < .05$.
**$p < .01$.

ond-class citizenship in the United States have been fairly constant over time. Since Blacks have always demonstrated a great deal of group identification, its role in accounting for increases in Black participation should be minimal (Walton, 1985: 75). Doug McAdam (1982) argues that Black discontent was equally insignificant in the emergence of the Black protest movement. For McAdam, the significant attitudinal transformation that took place within the Black community prior to the civil rights movement was expressed in their collective assessments of the political opportunities for social change. As other social movement analysts—notably Frances Fox Piven and Richard Cloward (1977)—have argued, political insurgents must be convinced that action taken as a group will have an impact before they will act.

Race identification probably led to higher levels of Black political activism in the late 1960s, as past studies have shown, given the political context of that time. Political context may hold the key to explaining when and how race identification may stimulate Black activism. Race identification may play a more prominent role in local elections where race is a politically salient issue, as in the case of the 1983 Chicago election of Harold Washington (see Preston, 1987).

In this new formulation, race identification might be considered a "soft" political resource compared to other Black collective resources such as Black organizational and church memberships. Its power resides in an ideology that encourages the participation of minority groups. As an ideology, however, it is less reliable than the two other "hard" resources of Blacks (organizational membership and church-based political activism) that appear to help Blacks overcome the structural and individual barriers to participation.

### Organizational Membership
In the 1984 NBES, organizational involvement was not measured as extensively as in the seminal Verba and Nie study. Blacks were not asked if they belonged to political or other designated organizations. Instead, they were asked if they belonged to an organization "working to improve the status of Black Americans." Nearly a quarter of the sample said they belonged to such an organization. When asked to identify this organization, many named national civil rights orga-

nizations such as the NAACP and the Urban League, but a few respondents mentioned social organizations such as Black fraternities and sororities, Jack & Jill, and the Black Elks. Of the quarter of the sample who were members of a Black organization, approximately 38 percent reported being active members, while 33 percent said they were fairly active; 24 percent were not very active, and 4 percent were not very active at all.

As an alternative mobilizing mechanism within the Black community, Black organizations can have a quite limited political impact. First, a racial disparity exists in organizational participation. Once socioeconomic status is taken into account, Blacks are not more likely to be members of organizations than Whites. Furthermore, among those who belong to organizations, Whites are more likely to be active members and to have multiple memberships than Blacks (Verba and Nie, 1972: 206–207). Second, the mobilizing potential of Black organizational membership is not fully realized because the types of Black organizations operating today are not likely to be at the grassroots level; it appears that they recruit and involve solely the members of the Black middle class.

One must consider which Blacks are likely to be members of Black political organizations. As Table 4.4 reveals, poor and less-educated Blacks are not to be found in their membership ranks. Fewer than 10 percent of those who did not complete high school were affiliated with a Black organization. Similarly, fewer than 12 percent of those earning $10,000 a year annually and fewer than 14 percent of those earning between $10,000 and $20,000 a year were members. Those who do not own homes and are on welfare assistance were far less likely to join Black political organizations. Nor were young people likely to be members. All of these are groups that tend not to be politically active. The existing Black political organizations, therefore, currently enhance, rather than diminish, the political participation gap within the Black community based on social class.

Organizational membership had a more limited effect on Black participation than did race identification. Blacks who are members of a Black political organization were no more likely to be registered voters, to have voted in 1984, or to be core voters than those who are not members. However, Black organizational membership was

Table 4.4   Social Characteristics of Black Organizational Members and Nonmembers (weighted percentages)

|  | Member (%) | Nonmember (%) |
| --- | --- | --- |
| TOTAL SAMPLE (N = 872) | 23 | 77 |
| GENDER |  |  |
| Male | 26 | 74 |
| Female | 22 | 78 |
| AGE** |  |  |
| 18–24 | 14 | 86 |
| 25–34 | 20 | 80 |
| 35–54 | 33 | 67 |
| 55+ | 23 | 77 |
| EDUCATION** |  |  |
| Less than high school | 10 | 90 |
| High school graduate | 16 | 84 |
| College or more | 37 | 63 |
| HOUSEHOLD INCOME** |  |  |
| Less than $10,000 | 12 | 88 |
| $10–19,999 | 14 | 86 |
| $20–29,999 | 30 | 70 |
| $30,000+ | 46 | 54 |
| HOMEOWNER** |  |  |
| Yes | 32 | 68 |
| No | 14 | 86 |
| REGION |  |  |
| South | 21 | 79 |
| Non-South | 26 | 74 |
| URBANICITY** |  |  |
| Rural | 8 | 92 |
| Small town or city | 24 | 76 |
| Suburb/large city | 26 | 74 |

Source: The 1984 National Black Election Study.
*$p \leq .05$.
**$p \leq .01$.

related to Black campaign activism. Members of Black organizations were more likely to be activists than nonmembers.

The fact that the types of Black organizations named by the NBES were not local but national organizations with largely middle-class membership in part explains this factor's limited effect on Black participation. Today, the Black organizations that are seemingly the most active in political campaigns are not traditional civil rights organizations such as the NAACP but rather ad hoc, grassroots organizations formed solely for the purpose of mobilizing Blacks in the election of a Black candidate. Had a measure of contact by such mobilization organizations been devised, it might have turned out to be powerfully related to all forms of Black participation in the 1984 election.

*Church Membership*

Of the three group-based political measures examined in this analysis, only membership in a politically active church most consistently boosted Blacks' rates of participation. It affected three of the four measures of Black political participation. Thus, Blacks who belonged to activist churches were more likely to vote in the 1984 campaign, to vote regularly, and to participate in campaign activities. This finding powerfully refutes the sociological critiques of the Black church that hold that organized religion works against Black political activism and lends strong support to the arguments of Lincoln and Mamiya (1990).

In general, the overwhelming majority of Blacks can be considered to be quite religious. A full 80 percent of the NBES respondents felt that religion was very important in their lives, while 16 percent felt it was somewhat important. Only 3 percent felt religion was personally not important. While less than one-quarter of the sample belonged to a Black political organization, over 90 percent of the respondents said that they attended some form of church services. Thirty-two percent attended on a weekly basis, 15 percent almost every week, 27 percent once or twice a month, and 20 percent a few times a year, with less than 7 percent never attending church. No other institution possesses such a large and diverse pool of members. Clearly, then, the church, compared to other Black institutions, has the most potential as a mobilizing agent within the Black community.

Both those who argue against the notion of an activist church and those who argue in favor of it have failed to distinguish religiosity from church membership. Gary Marx, in his analysis of Black survey data from 1964, for example, combines both intensity of religious beliefs and church attendance to form a religiosity index. Even if the two are strongly related to each other, church participation and religious beliefs are separate constructs with distinct effects on political participation. Lincoln and Mamiya argue that religion has often served as the primary source of inspiration for those engaged in civil rights militancy. "Other-worldly religious transcendence," they write, "can be related to the motivation, discipline, and courage needed for this-worldly political action" (1990: 234).

However, it is church membership, not necessarily religious beliefs, that actually promotes participation among the ordinary masses of Blacks. Although religion draws people into a church, it is the church that provides an environment that fosters political participation. The church provides a structured setting where Blacks gain important political skills and where political information can be shared.

Not all churches that Blacks attend are activist churches, however. Roughly 60 percent of the NBES respondents in 1984 claimed that their church encourages voting. Slightly over one-third (35 percent) said that there were announcements made about the presidential campaign at their church. This percentage is equal to the percentage of Blacks who reported that elections were discussed in their church in the 1966 study by Matthews and Prothro (1966: 233). Fewer, however, reported having direct contact with the candidates through their church. Only 22 percent said that they attended a service in support of a candidate at their church; 19 percent reported attending a service where there were special collections for candidates during the election year; and 10 percent reported working on behalf of a candidate through the church (see Table 4.5).

The encouragement of voting and the collection of campaign funds for candidates constitute two separate types of political activities that churches apparently engage in.[4] Churches can function as a political clearinghouse where political information is shared, but they can also become directly involved in political campaigns, for example, candidates may be introduced to congregations during

Table 4.5    Measures of Church-Based Political Activism
(weighted percentages)

| | Yes (%) | (N) |
|---|---|---|
| "Have you heard any announcements or talks about the presidential campaign at your church or place of worship so far this year?" | 35 | (1,057) |
| "Has your church or place of worship encouraged members to vote in this election?" | 60 | (1,055) |
| "During this election year, did you attend anything at a church or place of worship in support of a candidate?" | 22 | (851) |
| "Did you do any work for one of the candidates through your church or place of worship?" | 10 | (852) |
| "Did your church or place of worship take up a collection for any candidate during this election year?" | 19 | (851) |

Source: The 1984 National Black Election Study.

prayer meetings. The latter is clearly a more politically aggressive role for the church.

Some church denominations might be more involved in politics than others. Lincoln and Mamiya claim that 80 percent of all Black Christians are members of churches belonging to Baptist, Methodist, and Pentecostal communions (1990: 1). Significant differences between the three main Black denominations include the general autonomy of the Black Baptist minister. Baptist churches are not organized, as are the Black Methodist churches, around a denominational hierarchy, and thus Baptist ministers are presumably more free to engage in social protest. Lincoln and Mamiya note that the majority of ministers involved in the civil rights struggle, including Dr. Martin Luther King, were Baptist (1990: 44). Black Methodist churches, such as the African Methodist Episcopal Zion, are subject to a centralized governmental authority. Furthermore, candidates for ministry in the A.M.E. Church are required to be college graduates (Lincoln and Mamiya, 1990: 71). Founded by former Black slaves in response to the rigid codes of race segregation practiced in the White Methodist Episcopal churches, A.M.E. churches were profoundly anti-slavery and active in the abolitionist movement.

Table 4.6  Church-Based Political Activism by Religious Denomination
(weighted percentages)

| | Political Information? | | | Candidate Contact? | | |
|---|---|---|---|---|---|---|
| Denomination | None (%) | Yes (%) | (N) | None (%) | Yes (%) | (N) |
| Baptist | 29 | 71 | (592) | 61 | 39 | (449) |
| Methodist | 31 | 69 | (79) | 58 | 42 | (58) |
| Pentecostal | 38 | 62 | (75) | 69 | 31 | (54) |
| Catholic/ | 24 | 76 | (68) | 66 | 33 | (53) |
| Episcopalian | | | | | | |
| Jehovah's Witness | 90 | 10 | (21) | 88 | 12 | (18) |

Source: The 1984 National Black Election Study.

Pentecostal churches have grown rapidly during the twentieth century, and one reason for their growth is their adherence to the Black folk religious tradition. The Pentecostal churches' spiritual and emotional styles of worship remain highly attractive to many within the Black community. Given their larger focus on spirituality and other-worldliness, one would expect Black members of Pentecostal churches to be the most politically conservative compared to members of other Black or interracial denominations.

The vast majority of the NBES survey respondents were Baptists— 62 percent—while much smaller percentages of Blacks claimed to be Methodist and African Methodist (10 percent), Catholic (6 percent), or members of fundamentalist churches like Holiness, Pentecostal (Assembly of God), or Church of God (10 percent) assemblies. For the purposes of this analysis, the various denominations were bracketed into the following five general categories: Baptist, Methodist, Pentecostal, Jehovah's Witness, and Catholic;[5] see Table 4.6. All other denominations and churches, for example, Black Muslims (who constituted less than one percent of the sample), were not included in this table.

Although the Baptists and Catholics appear to belong to churches that were the most active in politics in 1984, as shown in the table, large differences among the major denominations did not emerge. Blacks in four of the five church denominations, including Pentecostal churches, were equally active in politics. By contrast, the majority of Blacks who are members of Jehovah's Witness churches were not generally exposed to politics in their churches, most probably because religious doctrines and teachings in the Jehovah's Witness churches strictly prohibit the member's involvement in politics. Only 10 percent (three out of twenty-one) of the Jehovah's Witnesses claimed to have discussed politics in their church, in contrast to 71 percent of the Baptists. The majority of members of Pentecostal denominations were exposed to politics in their church. The number of Pentecostal church members who reported having had contact with candidates through their church was comparable to that of members of other churches, except, again, those who were Jehovah's Witnesses.

The failure to find large denominational differences in the type and degree of political activism among the churches Blacks attend might stem from several reasons. First, the political context in 1984 may have reduced whatever political differences there are between churches like the African Methodist Episcopal church and Pentecostal churches such as the Church of God in Christ. Because of Jesse Jackson's presidential bid, more churches may have become active in voter registration efforts in 1984 than previously. Furthermore, in 1984 a number of national and community-based organizations were involved in massive voter registration drives, making registration a central community concern. Second, as a direct result of the civil rights struggle, Black communions may not differ greatly with respect to their church philosophies on community and political involvement. Pentecostal churches, according to Lincoln and Mamiya (1990), have become more mainstream in terms of church doctrine and teachings. Finally, the social composition of Black churches may have changed. Pentecostal churches no longer cater exclusively to the Black working class and poor, having attracted many new members from the Black middle class. Middle-class Black congregations, as will be shown later, are more likely to be involved in politics.

The fact that the churches Blacks belonged to were active in politics in 1984 suggests that the church continues to serve as a vital conduit to politics within the Black community. Those who are encouraged to vote, made aware of upcoming elections, and given direct access to candidates are more likely to vote and work directly in political campaigns, as Figure 4.1 shows. The percentage

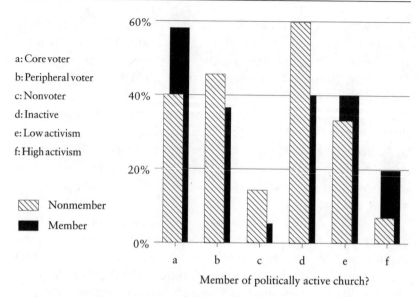

a: Core voter
b: Peripheral voter
c: Nonvoter
d: Inactive
e: Low activism
f: High activism

Nonmember
Member

Member of politically active church?

**Figure 4.1**   Voter Type and Campaign Activism by Membership in a Politically Active Church. (*Source:* 1984 NBES.)

of core voters was far higher among Blacks who belonged to churches where political participation was encouraged (58 percent) than among Blacks at churches where involvement in politics was not stressed (40 percent). Similarly, those at churches where candidate contact was established were more likely to be core voters, while those at churches where candidates were not brought in were slightly more likely to be among the nonvoters. The same relationship holds true for campaign activism. Political information and candidate contact at churches were strongly related to campaign activism. Thus, it is clear that it is not church attendance or religiosity alone that promotes participation among Blacks; rather, activist churches encourage participation. Distinguishing between the two can help explain the mixed history of the church's involvement in the civil rights movement: some churches were politically quiescent, and some were extremely active. The political character of the church, no doubt, depends upon the composition of its members as well as the political orientation of its minister.

As argued earlier, given its large, grassroots membership, the Black church's potential as a political mobilizing force is vast. However, it is not clear that the churches active in politics mobilize Blacks who otherwise would remain outside politics. Recall that although membership in a Black political organization promoted campaign activism, members of such organizations were already more likely to be politically active. Black organization membership, at least in this study, does not appear to reduce significantly the participation gap found between affluent Blacks and poor Blacks or that between well-educated Blacks and less-educated Blacks. Does the Black church, then, diminish or widen the participation gap found in the Black community?

To address this question, one must determine which Blacks are more likely to be exposed to campaign information. Table 4.7 displays the percentages of those reporting having received political information at their church by their social characteristics. The evidence is mixed, even though the differences between Blacks exposed to politics within their church and Blacks who were not are not as striking as in the case of Black organizational membership. Two background variables emerged as significant. First, those who belong to activist churches are more likely to be college-educated. How might this finding be explained? In the Lincoln and Mamiya study of 2,150 Black churches, younger clergy and those with more education were more likely to deliver sermons that were Black-oriented in content than were less-educated, older clergy (1990: 183–85). Furthermore, educated clergy were also more likely to exhibit greater race consciousness than less educated clergy (1990: 175–76). Better-educated congregants may also be more likely to expect that their ministers be involved in local politics.

Second, Black women were more likely to report being members of an activist church than Black men. Here is a clear case of a group that is theoretically less likely to participate in politics whose rates of participation now match Black men's because of their involvement in the church. Black women are more likely to be exposed to politics in their churches because women, in general, are more likely than men to express religious commitments. Furthermore, within the Black community, religion is more important to Black women than to Black men. Black women's involvement in the church can promote greater political activism among their ranks because by being active church members, they can gain skills that can be used in the world

Table 4.7    Social Characteristics of Church-Based Activists
(weighted percentages)

|  | Political Information? | |
|---|---|---|
|  | None (%) | Yes (%) |
| TOTAL SAMPLE (N = 1,150) | 32 | 68 |
| GENDER* | | |
| Male | 35 | 65 |
| Female | 29 | 71 |
| AGE | | |
| 18–24 | 38 | 62 |
| 25–34 | 30 | 70 |
| 35–54 | 29 | 72 |
| 55+ | 35 | 65 |
| EDUCATION** | | |
| Less than high school | 41 | 59 |
| High school graduate | 34 | 66 |
| College or more | 25 | 75 |
| HOUSEHOLD INCOME** | | |
| Less than $10,000 | 37 | 63 |
| $10–19,999 | 35 | 65 |
| $20–29,999 | 24 | 76 |
| $30,000+ | 23 | 77 |
| HOMEOWNER** | | |
| Yes | 26 | 74 |
| No | 36 | 64 |
| REGION | | |
| South | 31 | 69 |
| Non-South | 35 | 65 |
| URBANICITY** | | |
| Rural | 37 | 63 |
| Small town or city | 33 | 67 |
| Suburb/large city | 31 | 69 |

Source: The 1984 National Black Election Study.
*$p \leq .05$.
**$p \leq .01$.

of politics. For example, running for church office, organizing fund-raisers, and coordinating Sunday school or day-care activities help women gain organizational skills that can be used to assist candidates in campaigns.

## Black Officeseeking and Participation

The surge in the number of Black candidates running for office is the single most impressive development in the new stage of Black politics. In general, Blacks seem to participate at higher levels in elections involving Black candidates than in elections where no Black is running. The impact of Jessé Jackson, as a Black seeking the Democratic party's presidential nomination, on Black turnout is addressed in Chapter 5. Black participation also appears to be affected by Black officeseeking at the local and state levels. Can a relationship between Black officeseeking and Black participation be empirically verified, using the NBES data sets?

Unfortunately, the NBES survey lacks an objective measure of the number of Blacks seeking elective office based on the respondent's voting district. Instead, there exists a self-reported measure of Black officeseeking. Respondents were asked if there were any Blacks running for office at the local, state, or national level. Even though 59 percent said that there were Black candidates seeking office in their area, this number should be viewed with extreme caution. Since some Blacks may have missed less visible Black candidates running for office, and others may have included those who were not valid candidates, this measure could be an inaccurate estimate of the actual number of Blacks seeking office in their areas.

Respondents were also asked if they helped campaign for or voted for any Blacks in the November election. These numbers are undoubtedly more reliable than the measure of awareness of Black candidates cited above. Roughly 17 percent said that they helped to campaign for a Black candidate, a figure comparable to the levels of general campaign activism reported in Table 4.1, while 29 percent said that they voted for a Black candidate in the 1984 election.

Black candidates seemingly helped to stimulate Black rates of participation in 1984. Those who campaigned for Black candidates were more likely to be regular voters and campaign activists than

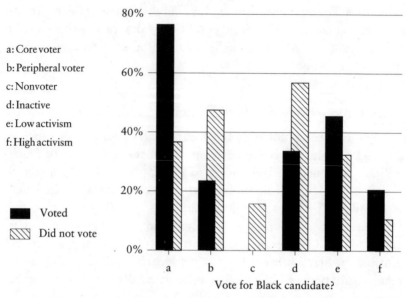

Figure 4.2   Voter Type and Campaign Activism by Vote for Black Candidate. (*Source:* 1984 NBES.)

those who did not. In addition, those who voted for Black candidates were also more likely to participate at higher levels than those who did not vote for a Black candidate. (See Figure 4.2.)

Black candidates can inspire those outside of politics to register and vote. However, in the absence of an objective measure of Black candidate presence, there is no easy way to measure the actual effect of Black candidates on Black rates of political participation. The mobilizing potential of Black candidates, however, can be approximated by examining which Blacks are most likely to vote for Black candidates in principle. In the survey, Blacks were asked if they agreed or disagreed with the statement that "Blacks should always vote for Black candidates when they run." The majority of Blacks disagreed with this statement, with 53 percent disagreeing somewhat and 27 percent disagreeing strongly. Only 6 percent of the sample strongly agreed with this statement, and 13 percent agreed somewhat. Poor, less-educated, and older Blacks are more likely to favor Black candidates when they run. Because these Blacks constitute a segment of the Black community less likely to vote, Black candidates thus have the potential to reduce the participation gap within the Black community. There are examples of this in the elections of big-city Black mayors. In the 1983 Chicago election of Harold Washington, the city's first Black mayor, new Black voters were recruited and mobilized from low-income communities. As a result, registration rates between middle-class, working-class, and poor Black wards were roughly equal (Kleppner, 1985; Preston, 1987). Indeed, with the high turnouts often accompanying precedent-setting candidacies of Blacks, the class-skewed character of Black registration and turnout rates is less pronounced.

## Conclusions

Two important conclusions emerge from the results of the analysis. First, as other research has shown, Black political participation is greatly affected by social position. In general, education divides Blacks on the basis of voting (albeit indirectly, through its effect on factors such as political interest), while income separates those Blacks able to participate on a regular basis in politics and to become active in political campaigns from those not able to participate. Affluent and educated Blacks participate at far greater rates than poor and less-educated Blacks. High school dropouts were three times more likely to be nonvoters than those having a college education. Furthermore, lower-status Blacks tend not to be involved in political campaigns.

Second, even in an environment where race no longer operates as a legal impediment to Black advancement and political participation, group-based resources still carry the potential to offset the disadvantage Blacks have as individual actors and thereby to reduce the racial gap in political participation as well as lessen the class gap in Black participation. However, of the collective resources examined here, Black organizational membership had a very limited effect on Black participation. Blacks who are members of Black political organizations were more likely to be campaign activists, but no more likely to vote than nonmembers. National Black organizations may not be a critical political resource, inasmuch as they do not seemingly recruit or attract members from poorer, less advantaged communities. Presumably, the annual dues and the time commitment constitute barriers that make it difficult for poor Blacks to join. These organizations only serve to enhance the already high rates of Black participation among the advantaged segment. Black political organizations, nevertheless, have the potential for mobilizing a wider cross-section of Blacks. It is quite possible for political organizations operating at the grassroots level to mobilize new Black voters. Such organizations are not likely to be in a position to operate for very long, precisely because their members come from the economically and socially disadvantaged segments of the community. These organizations, therefore, are less able to accumulate the necessary resources to emerge into stable, viable organizations. The study also found that strong race-identifiers were more likely to vote and become active in political campaigns in 1984, but race identification may be more of a contextual variable. Nevertheless, the importance of group consciousness relative to the other group-based resources of Blacks can be overstated since the political context critically influences when and how race identification can stimulate group political activism.

Far from representing an "anti-political agency," the church continues to serve as a vital link to politics within the Black community. Not all churches are involved in electoral politics, however. Although the majority of Blacks said that their churches encourage voting, only one-fifth reported having churches where direct candidate contact was made. These churches were more likely to be found in the South. While its mobilizing potential at the grassroots level within the Black community is unclear, the church appears to mute the participation gap along gender lines. Black women, through their church affiliation, are brought into the political process. This is significant given that of all the gender/race groups, Black women have the worst economic position in American society today. But there is also evidence that suggests that middle-class Blacks are more likely to be members of activist churches; therefore, as with Black organizations, the church may be mobilizing members of the Black community who are already active in politics. Clergy with a strong civil rights and activist orientation tend to be better educated than those weak in such an orientation. Since middle-class Blacks tend to be politically active, they no doubt play a role in transforming their church into an activist church. Alternatively, ministers of middle-class Black churches realize that their congregants are keenly interested in politics, and therefore instinctively cater to that side of their interests. Churches in poor Black communities may be less likely to perceive or feel the need for their involvement in politics.

All in all, only the Black church seemingly has survived intact as a mobilizing vehicle from the past civil rights/Black protest era. Its continued significance may reside in the fact that it not only represents a large constituency base but also has complete financial independence from White-dominated institutions. Lincoln and Mamiya contend that "economic independence appears to be a critical resource for a continuous critical political stance in American society" (1990: 230). The church's involvement in African American politics today may also stem from the fact that although the civil rights struggle provided Blacks access to the political arena and outlawed the practice of racial segregation, it did not liberate Blacks from economic inequality and poverty. Given that Black economic conditions have stagnated and worsened throughout the 1980s, Black ministers and churches have been called upon to work toward solving Black problems. As Lincoln and Mamiya note, "In many Black communities, the people still expect their clergy to exhibit an unmistakable racial consciousness and to speak out on racial matters" (1990: 230). Thus, the Black church's historical involvement in Black political affairs seems not to have been brought about by Blacks' lack of access to the traditional forums of politics. Instead, the status of Blacks as a disadvantaged minority group in American society necessitates its involvement. In this regard, the Black church has not outlived its usefulness in the political arena.

Cases of record-high Black turnouts in response to the candidacies of Blacks abound at the local and state levels. Surely, Blacks' rates of participation are directly related to Black officeseeking. As a political resource, however, the positive effect of Black officeseeking on Black voting behavior appears to be limited. First, the annual percentage of Blacks winning elective office has leveled off. Second, it is far less common for majority-Black districts to have Blacks running for office for the first time. In elections involving incumbent Black officeholders or Blacks succeeding Black elected officials, voter turnout rates are not typically higher than in past elections. On the contrary, in some instances they are substantially lower. Third, once

Blacks are successfully elected to office, Black voter turnouts in urban centers decline substantially (Browning, Marshall, and Tabb, 1979). The newly mobilized urban poor appear to be the first to drop out, and turnout rates subsequently return to normal. Aggregate and opinion polling data at the local level are necessary to assess fully the effects of Black officeseeking on Black voting behavior. Black officeseeking as a political stimulus will be reexamined in Chapter 5, which examines the consequences of Jackson's 1984 and 1988 presidential bids on Black turnout, and again in Chapter 7, which focuses on racial voting in the Black community.

# 5

# Black Turnout in the 1984 and 1988 Presidential Primaries and Elections

While voter participation is generally determined by a set of personal and group characteristics, as discussed in Chapter 4, short-term political forces unique to elections also affect turnout. According to estimates made by the U.S. Census Bureau in the 1984 presidential election, Black participation peaked at 55.8 percent, reversing a trend of almost twenty years of steady decline, only to drop substantially in 1988 to 51.5 percent. White participation in the 1988 presidential election also fell, but less dramatically, dropping by only about two percentage points. What explains the growth and sudden decline in Black voter participation over these past two elections?

One explanation offered for the strong showing of Black voters in 1984 is that Black voter turnout represented a group effort to prevent the reelection of President Ronald Reagan. Black political leaders had been sharply critical of almost all of Reagan's policies: the Reagan budget cuts, his opposition to existing race-specific programs and the legislation commemorating Martin Luther King's birthday as a national holiday, and his foreign policy toward South Africa. Black voters were also strongly critical of President Reagan. Blacks' evaluations of the president were consistently and markedly lower than Whites' evaluations. For almost the complete eight years of his presidency, less than 30 percent of the Black community approved of Reagan's performance in office, in contrast to 70 percent of the White community who approved of the president. Reagan was also perceived as anti-Black by most Blacks. In a 1984 national survey of Americans, 83 percent of Blacks interviewed felt that Reagan's policies had harmed Blacks, and 72 percent of Blacks believed that Reagan was racially prejudiced against Blacks (Williams, 1987: 109). Given their high degree of alienation from Reagan, Blacks were more likely to vote in 1984. A relationship between Reagan and Black registration is revealed in the NBES data set. Fourteen percent of respondents in the NBES sample in 1984 claimed to have been registered for the first time. Blacks who disapproved of Reagan's performance in office were more likely to be new registrants; the survey revealed that nearly a quarter of those who disapproved of Reagan were new registrants, compared to 12 percent of those who expressed approval.

The drop in Black turnout could be related to a number of factors. Perhaps because of disappointment in their ability to affect the outcome of the 1984 presidential election, considerably fewer Blacks made the effort to vote in the 1988 election. Or Black voting may have fallen off simply because Reagan, barred from seeking a third term in office, was not a candidate in the race, and because former Vice-President George Bush, as the Republican presidential nominee, may have appeared less threatening to Blacks.

Of course, Jesse Jackson, as a Democratic presidential contender, also generated intense feelings among Black voters in 1984 and 1988, and his candidacy may be related to Black participation rates during this period. Significantly, Black participation in the Democratic presidential primaries increased for these two elections. In a number of states, Black voter turnout increased from 14 to 87 percent (Cavanagh and Foster, 1984). In the South, especially, Black primary participation rates were well above average. It was reported in 1984 that turnout in predominantly Black districts in Georgia and Alabama was somewhere between 40 and 50 percent, in comparison to the statewide averages of 25 and 28 percent. In 1984, nearly a quarter (22 percent) of those in the NBES sample who voted in the presidential primaries said that their participation was unusual. Given the divisions within the Black community over Walter Mondale and Jesse Jackson, additional interest was generated by Jackson's candidacy. Close to 30 percent of those who said that they were more interested in the presidential election because of

Jackson's candidacy also reported that their participation in the primary was unusual. By comparison, only 14 percent of those who said that their interest in the election had remained the same in spite of Jackson's candidacy said that their participation was unusual.

Thus, the strong appeal of Jackson among Black voters was surely a factor in the high rates of Black participation in the 1984 and 1988 presidential primaries. Those who favored Jackson were more likely to vote. Through the high rates of their participation in the presidential primaries and caucuses, Jackson was able to win the District of Columbia as well as the state of Louisiana in 1984. And in 1988, he was able to win five presidential primary contests (Alabama, Kentucky, Louisiana, Virginia, and the District of Columbia), in addition to a number of caucuses (Alaska, Delaware, Michigan, South Carolina, Texas, and Vermont).

However, assessments regarding the impact of Jackson's 1984 and 1988 candidacies on Black voter turnout in the presidential elections vary. While many of his supporters have claimed that Jackson boosted Black participation in 1984, his detractors have argued that in 1988, Jackson depressed Black participation. Both are highly plausible, considering the different circumstances of the two presidential elections. As the first African American whose candidacy had to be taken seriously, Jackson could very well have brought new Black participants into the political process and boosted Black voter turnout in 1984. As argued in Chapter 4, there is both a historical and an empirical link between Black officeseeking and Black political mobilization. However, it could also be argued that Jackson's second bid for the Democratic presidential nomination was somehow related to the drop in Black turnout in 1988, that Black Jackson supporters stayed home out of frustration over his second failed attempt. Jackson's protracted struggle with the party leadership may have left his supporters angry, both at the party and at its nominee. Dukakis's selection of Lloyd Bentsen as his vice-presidential running mate, in particular, was interpreted by Black progressives as a sign that the party had decided to pursue mainstream White voters, deliberately ignoring their interests. Although George Bush was easily elected, the lower Black turnout in 1988 clearly cost Michael Dukakis and the Democratic party the electoral college vote of several states (California, Maryland, Illinois, and Pennsylvania), where Bush won with less than 51.5 percent of the vote.

In *The Jesse Jackson Phenomenon*, Adolph Reed, Jr., dismisses the claim that Jackson increased Black rates of participation in 1984. In addition to Reagan's reelection bid, he attributes the increase in Black registration in 1984 to several other factors, including the steady pattern of growth in Black registration rates in the South throughout the 1970s and 1980s as well as the national registration drives conducted in the early 1980s. Voter registration efforts were less intensive in 1988 than in 1984, with the major parties as well as private organizations spending significantly less on voter recruitment (Abramson, Aldrich, and Rohde, 1990: 94), and this may have resulted in the drop in Black participation in the 1988 election. Another possible explanation is that because the 1988 turnout was the lowest ever since the 1924 presidential election, Blacks, like Whites, may have stayed home on election day, in a clear demonstration of disapproval for both candidates.

Because Jackson was not on the ballot in either the 1984 or the 1988 presidential election, his candidacy as a primary presidential contender may have had no discernible effect on Black turnout in either of these elections; research has found that prenomination preferences, in general, do not affect turnout in the general election (Stone, 1986; Kinney and Rice, 1988). Voters who supported candidates who lost their party's nomination are no less likely to vote in the general election than those who favored the nominee during the primary season. Prenomination preferences, nevertheless, can affect other forms of voting behavior. Voters whose candidate lost the party's nomination tend to be more critical of their party's nominee and less critical of the opposing party's candidate. They are also less likely to participate in campaign activities such as contributing to the nominee's election funds or campaigning for the nominee.

This chapter will assess the roles that Jackson, Reagan, and Bush may have played in affecting the turnout rates of Blacks in the 1984 and 1988 presidential primaries and elections. I will examine Black rates of participation in the presidential primaries in order to evaluate what impact Jackson's candidacy may have had on stimulating turnout in these contests. I will then assess the effects of Jackson and the Republican presidential contenders on Black participation in the 1984 and 1988 presidential elections.

## Who Voted in the 1984 and 1988 Presidential Primaries?

Although 1984 was a record year for Black participation in the presidential primaries, only 31 percent of those interviewed in the 1984 NBES said that they participated in a presidential primary or caucus. Many simply did not know whether their state held a primary or caucus, with slightly less than half of the sample unable to recall if a primary or caucus was held in their state.

It is clear that participation in presidential primary elections is more difficult than in general presidential elections. Not only is information about the candidates harder to obtain, especially at the start of the nomination contest, but voters must choose from a larger pool of candidates. Furthermore, the rules in primary or caucus elections are more complicated, varying widely by state, and the timing and location of such events frequently change as well. In addition, because primary elections involve only party members, partisanship cannot be used as a basis to select a candidate (Hagen, 1989: 52). As a result, turnout in primary presidential elections is typically much lower than turnout in the presidential elections. Austin Ranney (1972) estimates that between 1948 and 1968 fewer than three out of ten eligible Americans participated in presidential primaries, as compared to the six out of ten who voted in presidential elections during this period.

### Identifying Black Primary Voters

As noted earlier, most political analysts and commentators have attributed the high rates of Black participation in the 1984 and 1988 primary elections to Jackson's candidacies. Doubtless that factor did spur Black rates of participation, because many Blacks, attracted by Jackson's bid for office, decided to support him in the primary election. Presumably, those who favored Jackson would be more likely to vote in the presidential primaries in 1984 and 1988 than those who preferred other presidential contenders, including the party's nominees, former Vice-President Walter Mondale in 1984 and Massachusetts governor Michael Dukakis in 1988.

To see if Jackson's candidacy was indeed related to Black participation in the Democratic presidential primaries, logit models were
devised to estimate the impact of support for Jackson on Black
primary participation. These models included a host of relevant
demographic and attitudinal factors as well.[1] Those who identified
themselves as Republicans or political independents leaning toward
the Republican party were excluded from this analysis, so that only
the primary participation rates of Black Democrats were assessed.
Jackson support was measured according to the standard "feeling
thermometer" of the Center for Political Studies (CPS), which has
a scale of 0 to 100. In general, Blacks rated Jackson very favorably,
giving him a mean score of 75. By comparison, the average rating
for Mondale among Blacks in the sample was 63, and for Reagan,
30. The logit coefficients and their standard errors are shown in
Table 5.1.

Past research has shown that primary voters tend to be older,
better educated, more affluent, and more partisan and issue-oriented
than the population at large (see Hagen, 1989, for summary). This
analysis shows that the same set of relationships holds within the
Black population as well. In general, Black primary voters possess
many of the same characteristics of Black voters and campaign
activists (see Chapter 4). In the 1984 elections, Black primary participants tended to be affluent, older, highly partisan, and more interested in politics than nonparticipants. Moreover, older Blacks were
twice as likely to vote in the 1984 primary as younger Blacks.
Seventy-five percent of those Blacks within the topmost quartile of
political interest voted in the primary, in contrast to 39 percent of
those within the lowest quartile. Black women were no more likely
to be aware of the primary, to participate, or to report that they
usually vote in presidential primaries than Black men. In addition,
strong race-identifiers and those who are members of Black political
organizations were more likely to vote in the 1984 presidential
primary.

No significant relationships were found in the case of Black participation in the 1988 primary election, however.[2] Nevertheless, many
of the important variables identified in the 1984 primary participation model approached statistical significance in this model. The
failure to find statistically significant relationships in 1988 is probably due to the small number of complete cases in the sample.

**Table 5.1** Determinants of Black Electoral Participation in the 1984 and 1988 Presidential Primaries (logit coefficients)

| Independent Variables | Voted in 1984 Primary | | Usually Voted in Primaries (1984) | | Voted in 1988 Primary | |
|---|---|---|---|---|---|---|
| | B | (SE) | B | (SE) | B | (SE) |
| Jackson rating (0–100) | .09 | (.08) | .25 | (.26) | -.01 | (.01) |
| Race identification | .12* | (.05) | .12 | (.10) | .03 | (.11) |
| Black organization (member) | .80** | (.23) | .51 | (.43) | .63 | (.42) |
| Political church (member) | .46** | (.18) | .34 | (.35) | -.38 | (.45) |
| Education | .05 | (.04) | .11 | (.08) | .12 | (.09) |
| Income | .08** | (.03) | .06 | (.06) | .19* | (.08) |
| Age | .02* | (.01) | .04* | (.02) | .02 | (.02) |
| Gender (female) | .17 | (.19) | .27 | (.36) | -.03 | (.39) |
| Region (non-South) | .24 | (.18) | .74* | (.35) | .26 | (.39) |
| System responsiveness (low-high) | .21 | (.08) | .14 | (.14) | -.06 | (.15) |
| Political trust (low-high) | -.05 | (.09) | .17 | (.19) | .07 | (.17) |
| Political interest (low-high) | .17** | (.07) | -.04 | (.14) | .33* | (.16) |
| Partisanship (low-high) | .53** | (.11) | .31 | (.22) | -.17 | (.24) |
| Media use (low-high) | n.a. | n.a. | n.a. | n.a. | .29 | (.23) |
| Home ownership (yes) | .16 | (.20) | .41 | (.39) | -.39 | (.45) |
| Urbanicity (low-high) | .19* | (.07) | .16 | (.14) | .09 | (.13) |
| Constant | -5.45** | (.82) | -6.04** | (1.74) | -3.59 | (1.93) |
| Log likelihood | -399.76 | | -113.58 | | -102.17 | |
| Total cases | 766 | | 255 | | 195 | |
| Predicted correctly | 74% | | 82% | | 74% | |

*Source:* The 1984–1988 National Black Election Study.

*Note:* Black Republicans were excluded from this analysis. Included but not shown as a control variable in the 1988 primary participation model is "Voted in the 1984 Presidential Primary."

*p < .05.

**p < .01.

*The Effect of Jackson*
As shown in Table 5.1, those who rated Jackson favorably were no more likely to vote in the presidential primary, or to report that their participation was unusual, than those whose impressions of Jackson were less favorable. Thus, Jackson support was not related to Black participation in the 1988 primary. Jackson's 1984 campaign may have had an indirect effect on Black primary participation, however, through the Black church's involvement in politics and new rates of participation among southern Blacks. Jackson worked almost exclusively within the Black churches and campaigned extensively within the South. Thus, his campaign appearances may have encouraged the new political participation of Blacks in the South. Blacks who live in the South were more likely to report that their participation in the primary was unusual. In addition, since political interest was strongly related to both primary awareness and primary participation, Jackson's candidacy may have stimulated turnout.

*Some Conclusions*
Broad generalizations about Black primary participation based on these findings are difficult to make, especially since less is known about Black voting behavior in primary elections than in general elections. In *Invisible Politics: Black Political Behavior,* Hanes Walton, Jr., argues that Black rates of participation in primary elections are generally affected by systemic or structural factors that vary across specific campaigns and are not largely determined by such individual-level factors as socioeconomic status or race consciousness (1985: 114). Although the analysis presented here shows Black primary voting to be tied to individual-level factors such as income, age, and even race identification, Walton's argument still holds true: Black primary participation appears to be most responsive to the character, form, and issues in the nominating contest.

For example, given the different nature of the 1976 and 1980 Democratic presidential nominating contests, Walton argues that the turnout of Blacks in the 1976 presidential primary was much higher than their participation in the 1980 presidential primary, estimating that while 30 to 40 percent of Blacks participated in the 1976 primary election, only 20 to 30 percent participated in the 1980 contest. The high rate of Black participation found in 1976,

Walton contends, was a response to Jimmy Carter's candidacy; he writes that "much of the large turnout in 1976 was aided in part by the appearance of the black civil rights leadership from Atlanta, like Andrew Young and the King family which supported Carter" (1985: 96). Four years later, because Carter suffered from low approval ratings within both the Black and White communities as a result of the high rate of inflation and the Iran hostage crisis, Blacks were less motivated to participate in the 1980 presidential primary. However, reliable state-by-state or national estimates of voter participation in primary elections that could be used to support Walton's arguments are difficult to obtain. A 1976 Current Population Survey (CPS), conducted by the U.S. Census Bureau, included a measure of primary participation for the first time, and this remains the most current CPS estimate. In his analysis of seven states from the 1976 CPS data, Michael Hagen (1989) found that approximately 44 percent of Blacks participated in the 1976 presidential primary, an estimate comparable to Walton's.

Of all the contextual variables that can account for variations in Black primary participation over time, it is the individual candidates themselves, Black or White, who can most strongly affect Black rates of participation. However, the candidacies of Blacks do not, *ipso facto,* produce big voter turnouts within the Black community. The power to affect Black turnout rates in presidential primaries does not reside within their candidacies alone. Related political factors such as the extent of the candidates' ties to the Black community, the strength of their political organizations, and the competitive nature of the race determine how many Blacks will turn out and vote in a given primary election.

Jackson, after all, was not the first Black presidential contender in the post–civil rights era of Black politics. In 1972, New York Congresswoman Shirley Chisholm also ran in the Democratic presidential primaries, but she had a less dramatic effect on the participation rates of Black Democratic voters. She competed in only ten state primaries, and for her efforts received only thirty-five delegates, a mere 7 percent of the total number of Black delegates at the 1972 Democratic Party National Convention (Walton, 1985: 93). Chisholm's campaign, by all accounts, including her own,[3] was handicapped by a lack of both funds and a professional campaign organization. Furthermore, Chisholm did not receive the endorse-ments of most Black political leaders or of major feminist organiza-tions like the National Organization for Women. Although Jackson also failed to receive endorsements from most Black political and civil rights leaders for his 1984 campaign (indeed, many Black pro-Mondale leaders actively campaigned against him), he entered the race having the national name recognition that Chisholm lacked. His trip to Syria, which resulted in the freedom of a captured U.S. military serviceman during the early days of his presidential cam-paign, gave him the crucial media coverage that Chisholm was never able to generate. In addition, because Jackson ran in all fifty states, in contrast to Chisholm, he was able to build campaign momentum, gaining more votes in later contests than in earlier ones.

Not only did Jackson reach out to and mobilize additional num-bers of Blacks, but his candidacy also elevated the value of the Black vote. Mondale and Jackson competed fiercely for the Black vote. Consequently, many more Blacks thought it important to participate in this primary election than in past elections; moreover, the media considered the Black vote to be more critical to the outcome of the race, and gave it greater coverage as a result. Jackson also generated new interest in politics among Blacks. More than 45 percent of the respondents claimed that their interest in the 1984 presidential election increased as a result of Jackson's candidacy. Compared to the 51 percent who stated that Jackson had not affected their inter-est, those whose interest peaked because of Jackson were more likely to be interested in politics in general.

## The Impact of Reagan, Bush, and Jackson on Turnout in the Presidential Elections

Black participation in the 1984 presidential election was the highest recorded since the 1964 presidential election, and in the 1984 NBES survey, 15 percent of the respondents claimed to be registered for the first time. There are a number of possible explanations for this. First, while Jackson's candidacy served to encourage additional numbers of Blacks to vote in 1984, Reagan's reelection bid itself could have motivated more Blacks to register and vote. However, the increase in the number of Blacks registered to vote and voting might, instead, have been the product of the voter registration drives conducted by a number of organizations, including the southern-based Voter Education Project (Piven and Cloward, 1988: chap. 6). But because of the decline of these efforts in the 1988 presidential election, Black participation in 1988 fell by four percentage points. Moreover, while many claim that Jackson was responsible for this later low Black turnout, given that his supporters chose not to vote, general voter dissatisfaction with the candidates could have been the real cause of the low Black turnout in 1988.[4]

To determine if Jackson or the Republican presidential contenders (Reagan and Bush) did indeed affect Black turnout in the 1984 and 1988 presidential elections, logit models were constructed, incorporating Reagan, Bush, and Jackson support measures in addition to a number of control variables. The results are shown in Table 5.2. A presidential approval measure for Reagan was used to predict Black participation in the 1984 election. When asked if they approved or disapproved of the way Ronald Reagan was handling his job as president, only 17 percent of the sample approved, with 58 percent disapproving strongly, and 19 percent disapproving somewhat. The Jackson support measure asked whether or not the respondent voted for or *would have voted for* Jackson, or Mondale (Dukakis in 1988), or some other candidate in the presidential primary. It is a dummy variable with three levels: (1) Jackson support; (2) Mondale/Dukakis support; and (3) support for another candidate. In 1988, a Bush evaluation measure was substituted for the Reagan approval measure. Bush was evaluated on a "feeling thermometer" scale that ranged from 0 to 100, where 0 represented cool feelings toward Bush and 100 represented warm feelings. In 1988, Bush received an average rating of 36, somewhat higher than the average rating of 30 that Reagan obtained in the 1984 NBES survey.

The belief that Jackson supporters might fail to show at the polls in 1984 because Jackson was not the nominee was not sustained by this analysis. Jackson primary supporters were in fact more likely to vote than those Blacks who supported Mondale and other candidates. Apparently, the majority of Blacks who were politically active in 1984 were either Mondale or Jackson supporters. At the same time, Reagan had a strong effect on Black participation in

Table 5.2  Determinants of Black Electoral Participation in the 1984 and 1988 Presidential Elections (logit coefficients)

| Independent Variables | Voted in 1984 | | Registered for First Time (1984) | | Voted in 1988 | |
|---|---|---|---|---|---|---|
| | B | (SE) | B | (SE) | B | (SE) |
| Reagan/Bush approval | .22* | (.10) | .14 | (.14) | -.03* | (.02) |
| Primary support (Jackson) | .52* | (.26) | -.48 | (.33) | -1.60* | (.67) |
| Race identification (low-high) | .12 | (.08) | .10 | (.10) | .45* | (.21) |
| Black organization (member) | .49 | (.40) | -1.31* | (.60) | .65 | (.74) |
| Political church (member) | -.17 | (.27) | -.15 | (.35) | 2.79** | (.77) |
| Education | .15* | (.06) | -.36** | (.09) | .21 | (.16) |
| Income | -.03 | (.04) | .04 | (.06) | -.03 | (.12) |
| Age | .02 | (.01) | -.11** | (.02) | .06* | (.03) |
| Gender (female) | .24 | (.26) | -.27 | (.34) | -1.13 | (.73) |
| Region (non-South) | .05 | (.26) | .15 | (.34) | -.57 | (.63) |
| System responsiveness (low-high) | .07 | (.11) | .12 | (.14) | .08 | (.26) |
| Political trust (low-high) | -.06 | (.13) | -.37* | (.18) | .32 | (.32) |
| Political interest (low-high) | .28 | (.09) | .05 | (.12) | .56* | (.26) |
| Partisanship (low-high) | -.44** | (.16) | -.39* | (.20) | .67 | (.41) |
| Media use (low-high) | n.a. | n.a. | n.a. | n.a. | .11 | (.35) |
| Home ownership (yes) | .30 | (.29) | -.51 | (.38) | 1.01 | (.76) |
| Urbanicity (low-high) | .05 | (.10) | -.20 | (.12) | .64* | (.24) |
| Constant | -2.21 | (1.25) | 7.35** | (1.82) | -8.52** | (3.37) |
| Log likelihood | -209.49 | | -129.15 | | -45.64 | |
| Total cases | 524 | | 487 | | 170 | |
| Predicted correctly | 84% | | 89% | | 88% | |

Source: The 1984–1988 National Black Election Study.
Note: Included but not shown as a control variable in the 1988 presidential participation model is "Voted in the 1984 Presidential Election."
*p < .05.
**p < .01.

the general election: Blacks who strongly disapproved of Reagan's performance as president were more likely to vote. All told, Reagan proved to be a strong vote stimulus in the Black community. Neither Reagan nor Jackson was directly related to first-time registration in 1984, however. Those who were not members of a Black political organization were more likely to be first-time registrants.

Prenomination preferences were also significantly related to Black participation in the 1988 presidential election. However, this time Blacks who favored Jackson in the 1988 presidential primary were less likely to vote than those who favored Dukakis or another candidate. Many of the same Jackson supporters who turned out for Mondale in 1984 were apparently unwilling to vote in 1988. Jackson supporters' refusal to go to the polls for Dukakis in the 1988 presidential election may have been a strategic decision stemming from a number of factors. First, Jackson's supporters may have sat out this election out of general disaffection with the Democratic party. The disappointment felt by Blacks over Jackson's second failed attempt may have been much greater than the disappointment felt over his initial failure in 1984, and Democratic leadership may have been held accountable for their disappointment. Given that Jackson supporters were more strongly pro-Democratic and partisan than even Mondale supporters, as shown in Chapter 3, it is unlikely that their nonvoting was an attempt to punish the party. Instead, it is more likely that the nonvoting by Jackson supporters was related to the different nature of the 1988 presidential contest. Mondale was an established political figure within the Black community, while Dukakis was not. Dukakis presented himself not as a liberal (even though the Bush camp effectively labeled him as such), but rather as a political moderate and someone who would more effectively manage government. Dukakis may have been less acceptable to Jackson supporters who desired a more progressive or visionary leader. Furthermore, the drop in White voter turnout in 1988 suggests that neither presidential candidate was especially attractive to the voters.

Thus, even though Jackson supporters were less likely to vote in 1988, the low Black turnout cannot be completely attributed to Jackson. Had a more attractive and dynamic Democratic candidate been nominated, or, conversely, had Bush been perceived by the majority of Blacks to be equally as threatening as Reagan, Blacks might have turned out in greater numbers in 1988.

## Blacks as Strategic Voters

In a classic article originally published in 1960, Angus Campbell argued that the low turnouts observed with regularity in off-year congressional races were largely due to a drop-off in participation among the peripheral voters, those who tend to vote only in presidential elections. Although a segment of the Black electorate was identified as peripheral voters (voting in some, but not all elections), nonvoting in the 1988 presidential election was not solely the act of Black peripheral voters, but of those who favored Jackson in the presidential primary. The nonvoting by Blacks that took place in 1988 was a deliberate effort on the part of Jackson supporters to deny their votes to the Democratic party's presidential nominee, Michael Dukakis. Many, although not all, Black Jackson supporters made a strategic decision not to vote rather than support a candidate they felt did not fully represent their interests.

The 1988 election may not have been the first time in Black electoral history that a minority of Blacks chose not to cast a vote; nor is it likely to be the last. As a political minority, one that is extremely liberal, Blacks must vote in a party system where one party, the Republican party, is virtually closed off to them as an option. As a result, they must frequently decide between supporting a candidate who, they feel, does not adequately represent their interests or not voting at all. In a larger sense, then, the surge and decline captured in the 1984 and 1988 presidential elections illustrate the larger, ongoing electoral trade-off between participation in elections where neither candidate is preferred or nonparticipation (Walters, 1988). In 1988, Jackson supporters made a clear strategic decision not to participate.

Of course, it is risky to label the nonvoting that occurred in 1988 among Blacks as strategic, for this raises certain questions. Could strategic voting—defined as maximizing the effect of one's vote on the desired political outcome (Bartels, 1988: 108–110)—occur among the Jackson voters whose support of Jackson in the Democratic primaries seems to be anything but strategic? No matter how desirable a candidate is perceived to be, strategic voters will not support him or her if the candidate's chances of winning are slim. In Jackson's case, the moment he entered the race as a Democratic presidential contender most political analysts and observers scoffed at his chances of capturing the party's nomination in 1984, and again in 1988. Furthermore, in 1984 many Black leaders counseled Blacks not to support Jackson over Mondale because Jackson, as a Black American, could not win in a race against Reagan or for the presidency. Obviously, Black Jackson supporters ignored this advice, casting a vote that was seen as a "wasted vote" in the eyes of many.

Indeed, current research holds that primary voting, including Black primary voting, is rarely strategic. Larry Bartels argues in *Presidential Primaries* (1988) that strategic voting in multicandidate primaries is unlikely to occur, since it requires that voters attach considerable importance to their vote. Primary voters must believe that they are in a position to swing the outcome of the election in favor of a second-choice candidate, when in fact, writes Bartels, "the actual probability of swinging a statewide election to *any* candidate is . . . infinitesimally small" (1988: 109). Voters, he contends, are unlikely to base their support on such calculations, and instead choose candidates through the advice of friends and families or because of the psychic gratification found in supporting the most appealing and popular candidate (usually the political front-runners). Nonetheless, support for Jackson in the presidential primaries may have been strategic on the part of Blacks if indeed the logic behind their support was to remind the Democratic party of the power of their collective votes. But an answer to the question of what motivated Blacks to support Jackson requires additional research; this issue will be discussed further in the next chapter.

Rational-voter theories assert that when no candidate is favored, the optimal strategy is not to cast a vote (Downs, 1957). To argue that Black Jackson supporters decided against voting in the presidential election as a strategy is then also to suggest that Blacks operate at a level far more politically sophisticated than that of most Americans. Such an argument implies that Blacks are rational voters, when in general American voters are not deemed to be rational voters in much of the research in the field of voting behavior. While these studies do not in fact take American voters to be irrational fools, they imply that voters who face difficult, complex choices with limited information make decisions in far less demanding ways than rational-voter theories demand. Morris Fiorina (1981), for example, in his reappraisal of American voting behavior, argues that voters are more likely to base their evaluations of leaders on policy outcomes than on policy goals or intentions, an act that requires far less of voters.

In spite of the perception that Black voters may be more politically sophisticated than members of other social groups (Lewis and Schneider, 1983), it is not possible to determine through empirical means if, in fact, Black nonvoting in 1988 was a purely rational act or not. The only way one might evaluate the rational grounds for Black nonparticipation in the 1988 presidential election is to ask whether nonvoting would work to the political advantage or disadvantage of Black Democrats. But, of course, an easy answer to such a question does not exist. Through their strategic nonvoting, Black Jackson supporters no doubt hoped to send to the Democratic party a powerful message that they should not and would not be ignored in the next selection of its presidential and vice-presidential candidates. Although their nonvoting this time did not cost the Democratic party the race, it could dramatically affect future presidential races that are close. In the end, only the shape and outcome of future nominating contests will actually reveal if the Democratic party has responded positively to the strong message implicit in Blacks' act of nonvoting (specifically, nominating some other candidate whom Black Jackson supporters would find acceptable), or if a set of Black Democrats will continue to feel ignored by the party in its selection of presidential candidates.

Although nonvoting among Jackson voters might be a politically sophisticated act, it still is a form of nonparticipation. By choosing not to vote, Jackson supporters have intentionally placed themselves outside of politics. But political representation cannot be achieved through nonparticipation. Voting for a second- or third-choice candidate, like Michael Dukakis, who is in the best position to win might be a preferable strategy to nonvoting because if the candidate were elected, some level of political representation would be achieved. As an illustration, consider what the Reverend Calvin O.

Butts of the Abyssinian Baptist Church in Harlem, in a recent *New York Times Magazine* interview, claims to have learned from an encounter with the former mayor of New York City, Edward Koch. According to Butts, in a meeting with a group of Black leaders, Koch said that he "owed them nothing because they had not supported him at the polls."[5] In this interview, Butts is said to have conceded to Koch's "raw logic," stating further that "unless you run against him or support someone against him, you might as well work with him the best you can without compromising your principles." Bayard Rustin makes essentially the same point, but presents it somewhat differently. "The difference," he writes, "between expediency and morality in politics is the difference between selling out a principle and making smaller concessions to win larger ones. The leader who shrinks from this task reveals not his purity but his lack of political sense" (1965: 29). Given that Jackson did not run as a third-party candidate, it might have been better, as an effort to achieve political representation, for Black Jackson supporters to have voted for Dukakis. Indeed, it is likely that many of the Blacks who supported Michael Dukakis in the 1988 presidential election did so in spite of an emotional preference for Jackson. Having grown tired of being out of power during the previous eight years of the Reagan presidency, they wanted to help a Democrat win the White House.

Nevertheless, it is extremely unlikely that, had Jackson supporters turned out and voted in the 1988 presidential election, Bush would have been defeated and Dukakis elected. Betting that the outcomes of voting for Dukakis or not voting at all were identical, Jackson supporters may have felt that their nonparticipation carried with it no loss of representation or other political penalties, as the Butts argument implies.

Clearly, Black Jackson supporters desire presidential candidates who are more progressive than Michael Dukakis. They apparently settled for former Vice-President Walter Mondale as a reasonable substitute for Jesse Jackson in 1984. At the same time, many Democratic party leaders genuinely feel that the party cannot afford to accommodate the preferences of the Jackson wing of the party by nominating someone who would be perceived by the majority of Americans as too liberal to support. But because Black voters are likely to remain to the left of most Americans, the majority of them will continue to campaign for progressive presidential candidates. Given its importance to understanding the future direction and shape of Black electoral politics, the relationship of Blacks with the Democratic party is a critical issue; it will be taken up again in the conclusion of this book.

# 6

# The Black Vote in 1984 and 1988

The most noteworthy feature of the Black vote today is not so much its uniformity as its divergence from the White vote. Prior to 1964, Blacks had displayed greater variation in their voting preferences in presidential elections, but they were part of the voting majority, casting votes for the party whose nominees often won. Blacks' preferences for Democratic presidential candidates, however, are no longer in line with the preferences of the voting majority. In five of the last six presidential elections, Blacks, by huge margins, voted for the presidential candidate who lost. In the 1984–1988 NBES, nine out of ten Blacks who reported having voted in the presidential election supported Mondale in 1984 and Dukakis in 1988—both Democratic candidates who were defeated by their Republican opponents.[1] This chapter explores the reasons why Democratic candidates continue to receive such strong support in the Black community, and shows how economic conditions as much as partisan preference affected the Black vote in the 1984 and 1988 presidential elections. Finally, this chapter examines the factors that contributed to Jesse Jackson's success in the Black community in the 1984 and 1988 presidential primaries.

## Blacks' Evaluations of Presidential Nominees and Presidents

Since 1964, public ratings of Democratic presidential contenders have declined. With the exception of Barry Goldwater, Republican

Table 6.1   Mean Feeling Thermometer Ratings of Democratic and
Republican Presidential Candidates by Race and Party,
1972–1988 (standard deviations in parentheses)

|  | 1972 | 1976 | 1980 | 1984 | 1988 |
|---|---|---|---|---|---|
|  | McGovern | Carter | Carter | Mondale | Dukakis |
| Blacks | 76 (19) | 80 (19) | 76 (20) | 76 (28) | 69 (21) |
| Whites | 46 (28) | 60 (26) | 54 (27) | 55 (25) | 54 (27) |
|  | DEMOCRATS ONLY | | | | |
|  | McGovern | Carter | Carter | Mondale | Dukakis |
| Blacks | 82 (14) | 84 (16) | 79 (16) | 81 (16) | 73 (20) |
| Whites | 55 (28) | 73 (21) | 68 (22) | 70 (21) | 70 (23) |
|  | Nixon | Ford | Reagan | Reagan | Bush |
| Blacks | 49 (29) | 47 (24) | 42 (26) | 38 (28) | 46 (26) |
| Whites | 67 (26) | 62 (23) | 57 (25) | 64 (27) | 63 (27) |

Source: The American National Election Studies Cumulative File, 1952–1988.
Note: In the cumulative data file, the feeling thermometer ratings range from 0 to
97; values of 97 to 100 have been coded 97.

presidential candidates now receive more consistently favorable
evaluations from the general public than Democratic presidential
candidates (Asher, 1988: 126). Blacks' evaluations of Democratic
presidential contenders, by contrast, have remained uniformly high.
As Table 6.1 shows, from 1972 to 1988, Democratic presidential
candidates have received average "feeling thermometer" ratings
between 76 and 80 from Blacks, but ratings that average below 60
from Whites. Even taking into account party preference, there are
still large differences between the ratings that Blacks and Whites
give to Democratic candidates. Over the sixteen-year period, Black
Democrats rated Democratic candidates ten points higher on average than did White Democrats.

The 1972 election is viewed by many as marking the end of
the Democratic party's advantage over the Republican party in
presidential races. George McGovern, the party's nominee, received
the lowest average evaluation (46) by Whites of all the Democratic
candidates since 1972. Intraparty cleavages over the Vietnam war
as well as race, gender, and generational conflict which culminated
in the riot at the 1968 Democratic party's national convention had

left the party in a shambles; four years later, the party had not recovered. In 1972, Richard Nixon was reelected by a landslide, with most Democrats defecting from the party; Jewish and Black voters were the only groups to stick by McGovern (Asher, 1988: 169). The huge loss suffered by McGovern was due, in part, to poor campaign management. His campaign staff had leaked discrediting and conflicting stories to the press, giving the public the impression that McGovern's organization was "fragmented" (Asher, 1988: 163–164). Also, after it was revealed that McGovern's running mate, Missouri Senator Thomas Eagleton, had received shock treatment for depression, McGovern dropped him suddenly from the ticket, although he had initially indicated full confidence in his choice. Compounding these problems was the public's perception that McGovern was too liberal. Countless surveys revealed that on the majority of issues of the day, the public was more comfortable with the policies that Nixon stood for than the ones McGovern represented (Asher, 1988: 165; Miller et al., 1976; but see also Popkin et al., 1976).

As the candidate evaluations in Table 6.1 suggest, Blacks' evaluations of the candidates are not merely reflections of their partisan preferences, but are based on racial and policy considerations as well. Democratic nominees are strongly favored both because of the civil rights legacy of the Kennedy-Johnson era, and because of the general liberal image of the party and its candidates. However, Blacks' ratings of Democratic presidential contenders are not necessarily uniformly high. As Mondale's chief rival and alternative to Jackson, Gary Hart fared less well among Black voters in 1984. In the 1984 National Election Study, Blacks rated Hart less positively at 60 than they rated Mondale at 73. But other potential presidential contenders in the 1984 nominating race, such as Senator Ted Kennedy and former 1972 presidential nominee George McGovern, earned high marks of 80 and 73, respectively. Hart, perhaps, was received less strongly in the Black community than Mondale, Kennedy, and McGovern because he was less well known, not having campaigned especially for Black votes in 1984 or 1988. Research on voter perceptions of the candidates suggests that voters are generally "risk averse," rating lower those candidates they know less about (Bartels, 1988). Similarly, in 1988, New York governor Mario

Cuomo, another possible candidate, did not receive especially high marks (53) from the Black respondents in the National Election Study, even though, like Kennedy, he was recognized as having strong liberal credentials. However, Cuomo's policy record as governor was not widely established, especially since, in the end, he chose not to run for president in 1988.

As the party's choice to head the presidential ticket, Michael Dukakis was an established figure in national politics. Yet, in 1988, as the party's nominee, Dukakis earned the lowest rating (73) from Black Democrats since 1972 and the lowest (69) among Blacks in general, and for the first time, the ten-point difference between how Black Democrats rated the Democratic candidates and how White Democrats rated them disappeared. It is too soon to interpret this drop as an indication that Blacks are becoming cooler toward Democratic presidential nominees,[2] since thus far there has been no real slippage in the percentage of Blacks who identify with the Democratic party; nor did George Bush benefit from the dampened enthusiasm Blacks had for the 1988 Democratic presidential contender in terms of votes. Blacks may have been less supportive of Dukakis than of past Democratic presidential nominees in light of their perception that he was indifferent to Black political concerns and favored the strategy of moving away from the party's liberal base, which included the majority of Black Democrats. In addition, Dukakis, unlike Walter Mondale, appeared to have conceded the Black primary vote to Jesse Jackson, even though he still needed unified Black support to win the general election. Obviously, as a campaign strategy, this hurt him in the Black community, and it may not have helped him much in the White community. His evaluation from Whites, which was in the mid-50s, was comparable to those that past Democratic candidates had received, yet his election returns were higher than those for Walter Mondale in 1984.

As one of four Republican presidential nominees, Ronald Reagan earned the two lowest ratings from Blacks in the sixteen-year period examined here. Blacks' impressions of Reagan were even less favorable in 1984 than in 1980, even though Whites' ratings of Reagan in 1984 were slightly higher than four years earlier. Blacks' negative ratings of Reagan are based not only on his conservative and Republican policy positions, but also on their perceptions of his performance as president. As Table 6.2 reveals, a large majority of Blacks were strongly critical of Reagan, generally disapproving of him, but also disapproving of his management of the economy, his attempt to balance the federal budget, and his foreign policies. Less than a quarter of the Black community expressed approval of President Reagan. In contrast, the majority of White Americans approved of Reagan's policies and conduct, except in the case of the federal budget. In this area, 58 percent of Whites disapproved of Reagan's management of the budget, while only 41 percent approved.

Longitudinal surveys also show that Black approval ratings of Reagan remained extremely low throughout his two terms in office. Fewer than 20 to 30 percent of those in the Black community approved of the president. Reagan never obtained a 40 percent approval rating from Blacks. In contrast, White approval ratings never dipped below 50 percent, peaking in January 1986 at 70 percent (see Figure 6.1).

As the former vice-president, George Bush received the cool evaluation from Blacks that Republican nominees since 1972 had received. In 1988, Blacks rated him at 46. Blacks' evaluations of Bush's performance as president, however, were initially more favorable than the ones Reagan received. However, as shown in Figure 6.2, Blacks have become more critical of Bush. Bush's veto of the 1990 civil rights bill caused ill feelings in the Black community, and Blacks' attitudes toward the Gulf War were also related to Bush's low ratings. While 70 to 80 percent of the general public solidly supported U.S. military intervention in the Gulf, Blacks were evenly divided over the war. Toward the final months of the war, only 33 percent of Blacks surveyed felt that the U.S. "did the right thing in starting military actions against Iraq," while the majority felt that the U.S. should have "waited longer to see if the trade embargo and other economic sanctions worked."[3]

## Economic Conditions and the Black Presidential Vote

In 1980, Ronald Reagan became one of the few challengers in U.S. history to defeat a sitting president.[4] He was able to win not because his conservative rhetoric appealed to the majority of voters but because voters had been dissatisfied with the way the incumbent

Table 6.2  Blacks' and Whites' Evaluations of Reagan's Performance in 1984 (percentages)

| Do you approve or disapprove of the way Ronald Reagan: | | Strongly Approve (%) | Somewhat Approve (%) | Somewhat Disapprove (%) | Strongly Disapprove (%) | (N) |
|---|---|---|---|---|---|---|
| Is handling his job as president? | Blacks | 8 | 15 | 24 | 53 | (221) |
| | Whites | 39 | 29 | 14 | 18 | (1,808) |
| Is handling the economy? | Blacks | 8 | 15 | 20 | 58 | (221) |
| | Whites | 34 | 28 | 14 | 23 | (1,807) |
| Is handling balancing the budget? | Blacks | 4 | 10 | 19 | 67 | (210) |
| | Whites | 17 | 25 | 19 | 39 | (1,689) |
| Is handling foreign relations? | Blacks | 10 | 10 | 16 | 63 | (214) |
| | Whites | 29 | 27 | 15 | 29 | (1,800) |

Source: The 1984 American National Election Study.

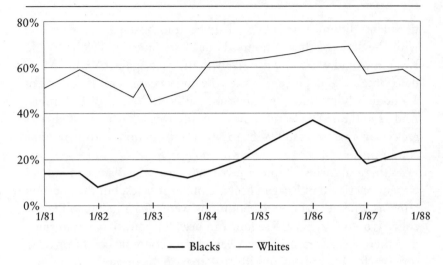

Figure 6.1   Percentage Approval for Reagan by Race, 1981–1988.
(*Source:* CBS/*New York Times* surveys.)

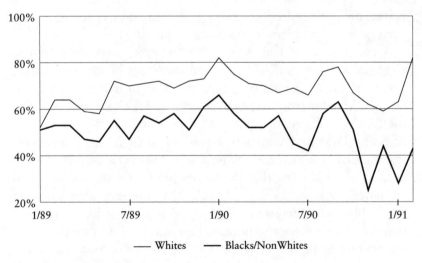

Figure 6.2   Percentage Approval for Bush by Race, 1989–1991.
(*Source:* Gallup Organization.)

president, Jimmy Carter, handled the Iran-hostage situation and with the state of the economy. Four years later, in 1984, Ronald Reagan would win more decisively in the race against Walter Mondale, obtaining 59 percent of the vote and sweeping all states except Mondale's home state of Minnesota and the District of Columbia. And as in the 1980 election, the economy was a key issue: Reagan's reelection mainly resulted from voter satisfaction with economic conditions.

As this and earlier chapters have made clear, the Black community was more critical of Reagan because of his policies, but the question remains whether economic conditions were also a factor in Blacks' collective vote against Reagan. Empirical studies have confirmed that there is a relationship between macroeconomic conditions and support for incumbent presidents—that the economy largely predicts the outcome of presidential elections (for a summary, see Fiorina, 1991, and Hibbs, 1987). Put simply, incumbent presidents are rewarded in economic good times and punished in economic bad times. As discussed in Chapter 1, Blacks had suffered the most in the early 1980s, especially as a result of the 1982 recession. Poverty and unemployment had increased in the Black community under the Reagan administration. The number of Black families living below the poverty line increased during this period, and even though real earning power dropped throughout the nation, economic conditions were more severe in the Black community.

A comparison of Blacks' and Whites' perceptions of economic conditions, shown in Table 6.3, indicates that Blacks and Whites perceived their personal economic situation in like terms, even as they disagreed sharply in their assessments of the economic situation for Blacks and that of the national economy. Large percentages of both Blacks and Whites reported that their personal economic situation had improved in the past year. However, even though 46 percent of Blacks felt that their personal economic situation had improved, only 28 percent thought that the economic situation facing Blacks had improved. In fact, 35 percent of Blacks thought that the group's economic position had worsened over the past year. By contrast, 83 percent of Whites felt that Blacks' economic situation had either improved or stayed the same over the past year. Racial differences were also striking with respect to the assessments of the

Table 6.3    Blacks' and Whites' Economic Assessments from One Year Ago in 1984: Personal, Blacks', and National

| From one year ago: | Gotten Better (%) | Stayed the Same (%) | Gotten Worse (%) | (N) |
|---|---|---|---|---|
| PERSONAL ECONOMIC SITUATION | | | | |
| Blacks | 46 | 21 | 33 | (1,136) |
| Whites | 45 | 29 | 26 | (1,913) |
| BLACKS' ECONOMIC SITUATION | | | | |
| Blacks | 28 | 37 | 35 | (1,099) |
| Whites | 39 | 44 | 17 | (1,671) |
| NATIONAL ECONOMY | | | | |
| Blacks | 20 | 32 | 48 | (1,127) |
| Whites | 46 | 33 | 21 | (1,883) |

Source: The 1984 National Black Election Study (Black sample, weighted percentages); the 1984 American National Election Study (Whites only).

state of the national economy: 46 percent of Whites felt that the nation's economy had improved over the prior year, while 48 percent of Blacks claimed that the economy had worsened during that period. Only 20 percent of Blacks felt that economic conditions had improved nationally. Based on their different characterizations of the national economy, many Blacks and Whites were effectively living and working in two different countries.

Do Blacks' economic judgments matter politically? Studies based on survey data have shown that voters' evaluations of their own personal economic situation explain little about their voting preferences, while their perceptions of the health of the general economy explain a great deal. To a lesser extent, the economic situation of the groups with which voters choose to identify also affects their political calculations, albeit *indirectly,* in that voters' assessment of the economic status of their group affects their view of the state of the economy in general, which, in turn, determines whom they will vote for (Kinder, Adams, and Gronke, 1989). The NBES uses the same set of questions about the economy, as shown in Table 6.3, thereby permitting an analysis of their relative effects on Blacks' vote choices. Table 6.4 displays the results of logit analysis used to estimate the Black presidential vote. This analysis includes both those who reported voting in the presidential election and those who

Table 6.4    Economic Determinants of the Black Presidential Vote in 1984 and 1988 (logit coefficients)

| Independent Variables | Voted for Mondale (1984) | | Voted for Dukakis (1988) | |
|---|---|---|---|---|
| | B | (SE) | B | (SE) |
| Personal economic situation (better-worse) | −.01 | (.14) | .39 | (.28) |
| Group economic situation (better-worse) | .51** | (.15) | .58* | (.29) |
| National economy (better-worse) | .55** | (.13) | −.17 | (.24) |
| Party identification (Republican-Democrat) | .55** | (.09) | .63** | (.15) |
| Ideological identification (conservative-liberal) | .06 | (.07) | .25* | (.13) |
| Constant | −.19 | (.66) | 1.92 | (1.31) |
| Log likelihood | −163.05 | | −62.008 | |
| Total cases | 573 | | 264 | |
| Predicted correctly | 88% | | 91% | |

*Source:* The 1984–1988 National Black Election Study.

*Note:* Both voters and nonvoters are included in this analysis. Also, the following variables were dropped from the models because of their nonsignificance: race identification, income, gender, region, and urbanicity.

*p < .05.
**p < .01.

did not. Party identification, race identification, liberal/conservative identification, family income, gender, region, and urbanicity were introduced as control variables in the model.

Both Blacks' assessments of the economy and assessments of their racial group were directly related to the Black vote in 1984. Blacks who felt that the economic position of Blacks had worsened over the past year and those who felt that the nation's economy had worsened were more likely to vote for Mondale. However, in 1988, only group economic judgments affected the voting decisions of Blacks. Blacks who reported that their group's position became worse over the past year were more likely to cast votes for Dukakis. However, the Black vote in 1984 and 1988 was not entirely based on Blacks' judgments about the health of the economy and the economic status of their group. Party identification strongly predicted vote choice in 1984 and 1988. Predictably, Blacks who identified strongly with the Democratic party were more likely to vote Democratic than Black political independents and Republicans. Ideological identification also affected the 1984 Black vote, such that self-identified Black liberals were also more likely to support Mondale over Reagan. Nevertheless, the Black vote was differentiated by little else. Family income had no independent effect on the Black vote. Coupled with the results of Chapter 3, this finding should put to rest speculation concerning increased support for the GOP among affluent Blacks. Apparently, exit polls from the 1990 midterm elections revealed that 22 percent of Blacks had voted Republican (see Welch and Foster, 1992)—a level double that of the Black Republican vote in the 1988 presidential election. Presumably, this support for the GOP would come from affluent Blacks, since affluent Whites are more likely to vote Republican in a given election. However, as Chapter 3 established, middle-income to wealthier Blacks were no more likely to identify with the Republican party than were poor Blacks. Nor did income affect the Black vote in this analysis (see also Welch and Foster, 1992). The potential for increasing Black support for the GOP exists in poor Black areas as much as it does in affluent ones. Race identification, gender, region, and urbanicity also had no independent effect on the Black vote in 1984 and 1988.

## Black Support for Jesse Jackson

The Jackson candidacies in 1984 and 1988 represented a test for the Democratic party and for Blacks. On the one hand, leaders and representatives of the Democratic party struggled with the dilemma of maintaining their biracial coalition of liberal Blacks and conservative White southerners while dealing effectively with Jackson. The party had to find a way of accommodating Jackson without appearing to have slighted him or to have caved in to his demands. On the other hand, Black Democrats struggled with their clear preference for Jackson and the pragmatic decision to fully support the party's nominee in the interest of party unity. Jackson was clearly the favorite among Blacks. In spite of the fact that Blacks overwhelmingly voted Democratic in the 1984 and 1988 presidential elections, both the party and Blacks have charged each other with failing the test that Jackson represented. Indeed, the party still does not know whether it can count on the Black vote in presidential elections in the future. Similarly, many Black Democrats still feel that the party does not take them or their representatives seriously enough.

In the 1984 NBES, the overwhelming majority of Blacks (88 percent) thought that Jesse Jackson's candidacy for president in 1984 was a good idea (see also Gurin, Hatchett, and Jackson, 1989: 151). NBES Blacks rated Jackson highly at 74. Whites in the 1984 National Election Study, by contrast, felt decidedly cool toward Jackson; he was rated at 40. Despite this strong level of support for his campaign from Blacks, Jackson still did not receive a unanimous endorsement from Blacks in 1984. He was, however, the first choice of the majority of Blacks to head the Democratic party's presidential ticket. Combining primary voters with the nonvoters, Jackson received about 57 percent of the Black primary vote, while Walter Mondale managed to get a 27 percent share of Black primary support. Counting only those who voted in their state's primary or caucus (about 31 percent of the sample), Jackson received only a slightly smaller margin of support, about 55 percent. Blacks were asked whom they supported in the primary, and also whether they would vote for Jackson, Mondale, or Reagan in the general election if Jackson ran as an independent. This was an important political matter for Jackson, since he could use his campaign as a bargaining vehicle only insofar as he could capture the majority of the Black primary vote and, if necessary, deny this Black vote to the eventual Democratic presidential nominee. Slightly more than half (53 percent) claimed that they would vote for Jackson, while only 32 percent expressed support for Mondale. Eleven percent of the respondents were unsure of whom they would support in such an event.

Table 6.5 displays the determinants of both Jackson primary support and support for Jackson as an independent in 1984. A number of demographic and attitudinal variables were associated with support for Jackson in the presidential primary. Black primary supporters of Jackson were younger, better educated, and more affluent, as well as strong race and liberal identifiers. Surprisingly,

Table 6.5    Determinants of Jackson Support as a Democratic Presidential Primary Contender and as an Independent Candidate for President (logit coefficients)

| Independent Variables | Jackson as Primary Contender | | Jackson as Independent Candidate | |
|---|---|---|---|---|
| | B | (SE) | B | (SE) |
| Gender (female) | .16 | (.19) | −.14 | (.19) |
| Age | −.02* | (.01) | −.02** | (.01) |
| Education | .12** | (.04) | .03 | (.04) |
| Urbanicity (low-high) | −.00 | (.07) | −.14 | (.07) |
| Income | .07* | (.03) | −.07* | (.03) |
| Race identification (low-high) | .17** | (.05) | .23** | (.06) |
| Region (non-South) | .14 | (.19) | .00 | (.20) |
| Party strength | −.21 | (.12) | .19 | (.12) |
| Ideological identification (liberal-conservative) | .09* | (.05) | .00 | (.04) |
| Constant | −2.55** | (.78) | .45 | (.75) |
| Log likelihood | −341.44 | | −329.9 | |
| Total cases | 537 | | 525 | |
| Predicted correctly | 64% | | 64% | |

Source: The 1984 National Black Election Study.
Note: Republicans and independents leaning toward the Republican party were excluded from analysis.
*p < .05.
**p < .01.

partisanship had no direct effect on support for Jackson in the 1984 Democratic primary. Blacks who considered themselves "strong Democrats" were just as likely to vote for Jackson in the primaries as those who identified themselves as "weak Democrats" or "nonpartisans." However, as Michael Preston (1989) argues, partisanship was perhaps indirectly related to Jackson support in 1984, in that older Blacks, who tend to be the most partisan (as shown in Chapter 3), were less supportive of Jackson's presidential bid. Preston, in his analysis of the 1984 NBES, shows that within different age groups of strong Democrats, support for Mondale increased as age increased: from 14 percent in the 18 to 26 age category, to 22 percent in the 27 to 44 age category, to 42 percent in the 45 to 64 age category (1989: 141). Preston notes that older Black Democrats, whom he labels the "Black establishment type," may have been less supportive of Jackson because of their perception that he would never win the Democratic party's nomination and because of their desire that Walter Mondale beat Gary Hart, who was a less established political figure in the Black community (1989: 142). It is also possible that some Blacks were not willing to risk their standing in the party's ranks to support a candidate that many felt had no chance of winning.

Even though Jackson had campaigned on behalf of the "disinherited" and the "disfranchised," poor and less-educated Blacks were not as likely to express support for Jackson or to have voted for him in the primary. This finding supports one of Adolph Reed's (1986) claims that educated and affluent Blacks were more likely to support Jackson, and that Jackson failed to win over Blacks at "the grass roots," as Jackson supporters had publicly maintained. The social class difference in primary support for Jackson is a bit surprising, since Black political elites had endorsed Mondale for president in 1984. However, the social class difference in Jackson support might be based on the different set of political calculations made by affluent and poor Blacks. On the one hand, it is possible that higher-status Blacks valued Jackson's candidacy for its symbolic importance, and for its potential to open doors for Blacks at the national level of politics, particularly since middle-class Blacks are more likely to benefit from their greater access to and representation in the Democratic party. On the other hand, poor Blacks, who had suffered the most economically under the Reagan administration, might have felt it most important to support the candidate whom they perceived to be in the best position to win against Reagan in the general election—in this case, Walter Mondale. Poor Blacks may have also perceived Mondale as more likely than Jackson to deliver tangible policy benefits to them.

Self-identified Black liberals and strong race-identifiers were also more supportive of Jackson's candidacy in the presidential primary election. Clearly, Jackson's liberal policy views account for the higher levels of support he received among these two groups in the Black community. In the 1984 pre-election survey, Blacks were asked to place themselves, Reagan, Mondale, and Jackson on a policy scale on two issues, defense spending and government assistance to Blacks and minorities. Blacks' self-placement and their perceptions of where Jackson stood on these two issues were virtually identical. On defense spending, Blacks placed themselves at 0.58 on a scale from 0 (conservative) to 1 (liberal) and Jackson at 0.57; on federal programs to assist minority groups, the average self-placement was 0.67, while for Jackson it was 0.68. Mondale, in contrast, was placed closer to the midpoint, receiving a score of 0.49 on defense spending and 0.53 on minority assistance. Also, in 1984 Jackson focused on a number of issues important to Blacks, namely, registration requirements and run-off primaries. In light of these issues, strong race-identifiers were attracted to Jackson's candidacy because of his promotion of civil rights and racial equality and fairness.

An entirely different pattern emerges between the demographic variables and support for Jackson as a political independent (see Table 6.5). Education is no longer related to Jackson support, while the relationship between income and Jackson support is reversed. College-educated Blacks were not more likely to support Jackson as an independent candidate, and affluent Blacks, who were more supportive of Jackson as a primary contender, were actually more likely to oppose an independent bid by Jackson. Only the young were as likely to favor an independent Jackson bid as they were to favor his bid for the party's nomination. Moreover, other social background determinants—region, gender, urbanicity, partisanship, race and ideological identification—were all found to be unrelated to support for Jackson as an independent candidate.

The contrasting pair of relationships between income and support for Jackson as a primary contender and income and support for Jackson as an independent candidate held important implications for Jackson if he had chosen to run as a third party candidate in 1984 or 1988. Third party candidates rarely do well in presidential races for a number of reasons. First, the party system works against them because state requirements for placement on the general election ballot are especially burdensome, and many independents fail to obtain ballot access in all fifty states. Second, third party candidates often lack the resources to compete effectively against major party candidates. Third, the majority of Americans, having identified with one of the two major parties, are less inclined to support minor parties and their candidates. For American voters, support for third party candidates is the "path of last resort" (Rosenstone, Behr, and Lazarus, 1984). Thus, despite the fact that more than half of the sample claimed allegiance to Jackson as an independent, it is doubtful that he would have earned half of the Black vote in the general election, since those Blacks who tend to vote, that is, middle- to upper-income Blacks, were less inclined to support him as a political independent in 1984.

In their analysis of third parties in American presidential elections, Rosenstone, Behr, and Lazarus (1984) maintain that "major party failure" rather than "political alienation" lies behind major party defections or disloyalty. Nevertheless, it is possible that poor Blacks were especially attracted to an independent Jackson bid for president because they are usually not involved in partisan electoral politics, while middle- to upper-income Blacks tend to be active members of the Democratic party. Moreover, poor Blacks are more likely to express cynical views about partisan politics than affluent Blacks. For example, in the 1984 NBES, a full 60 percent of those earning less than $10,000 annually voiced agreement with the statement that "public officials don't care much about what people like me think," in contrast to 34 percent of those making annual salaries of $30,000 or more. It is possible that the economically advantaged segment of the Black community, while critical of the current status of Blacks in the Democratic party, still saw themselves as able to participate in party politics and felt that Jackson's bid for the party's presidential nomination would help advance their interests within the party. At the same time, poor Blacks, who cannot envision themselves as playing a major role in partisan politics even with someone like Jackson as a major party contender, are more attracted to political alternatives outside the major party system, such as the one found in an independent Jackson bid for president. Thus, support for Jackson's independent bid in future elections might come from the more politically alienated and locked-out segment of the Black community.

Rosenstone, Behr, and Lazarus also contend that because presidential candidates are well aware of the odds facing them as a third party candidate in presidential races, such candidates will often not attempt a third party bid unless the major party compels them to

(1984: 194). They maintain that the "larger the losing faction at the major party convention, the more likely it is that a nationally prestigious politician will mount a third party campaign" (1984: 194). In 1988, Jackson won a larger share of the party's primary vote than in 1984, but it seemed that he was less poised to run as an independent in 1988. In 1984, Jackson had formed his own organization, the Rainbow Coalition, which could have been the base for an independent candidacy. In 1988, it seemed as if Jackson chose to put more of his energies into regular party activities than into strengthening his own independent organization. Furthermore, friction between Jackson supporters and party regulars appears to have been less in 1988 than in 1984, and it appears that the party was more willing to accommodate Jackson than it had been in 1984. Thus Jackson had less cause to declare himself independent of the party and a contender in the general election.[5] Unlike Walter Mondale and his supporters in 1984, the Dukakis camp made a number of concessions to Jackson before the national party convention took place.

In 1988, Jackson won the majority endorsement of Blacks as a primary contestant, polling in most states more than 90 percent of the Black vote. Exit-poll data revealed no significant demographic differences in Black support for Jackson in 1988. Jackson did better in 1988 by winning over the Black "establishment types"—older Blacks who had been skeptical about his chances for securing the nomination and his place within the party, and who felt that Walter Mondale not only had a better chance of winning but was equally supportive of Black interests. Witnessing Jackson's limited successes in 1984 and having no strong liberal alternative in the field of seven Democratic contenders, the majority of Blacks who had supported Mondale in 1984 became Jackson supporters in 1988.

The 1988 NBES reinterview, however, is not a representative sample of Blacks and their political views in 1988. In the 1988 survey, only 60 percent of those reinterviewed supported Jackson as a primary contender, in contrast to the 90 percent of Blacks estimated by exit polls. The exit polls leave the impression that Jackson only gained support and lost no Black support. But exit polls survey only those who participated in their state's primary or caucus, while the 1988 reinterview includes primary voters and nonvoters alike. While Jackson gained new support among NBES respondents in 1988, he also lost a share of his original support. As the numbers show in Table 6.6, of those reinterviewed in 1988, 15 percent had supported Jackson as a primary contender in 1984, but did not in 1988, while 20 percent of those who had not supported him during the primary season in 1984 supported him in 1988. Similarly, 11 percent would have supported him as an independent candidate in the general election in 1984, but not in 1988, and 18 percent of those who said that they would not support him as an independent candidate in 1984 would have supported him as such in the general election against Dukakis and Bush. Jackson also had his most solid supporters and detractors in the Black community. About 38 percent of those reinterviewed in 1988 had supported him in both 1984 and 1988, and roughly 50 percent of those would have voted for him as an independent candidate in 1984 and 1988. Twenty-seven percent of those reinterviewed in 1988 had not supported Jackson in the primary election in 1984 or 1988, while 22 percent would not have supported him as an independent candidate in both election years.

Predictably, those less positive about Jackson were less likely to support him as a primary or an independent presidential contender in either 1984 or 1988. Still, Jackson managed to earn quite high average ratings from Blacks who did not support him in 1984 and 1988. Blacks who chose not to support him in either year rated him at 70 on a scale from 0 to 100, a rating comparable to what Michael Dukakis earned from Blacks, while Blacks who supported Jackson in both 1984 and 1988 rated him at 87. In fact, only a quarter of those who did not support Jackson in either year felt that Jackson's candidacy was a "bad idea," while 75 percent still felt it was a "good idea." A number of Blacks who had chosen to support Mondale in 1984 and Dukakis in 1988 tended to express support for Jackson and even to take pride in his campaign, but still considered a vote for Jackson to be wasted. Nevertheless, virtually 100 percent of those who had supported Jackson in both years felt that his candidacy was a "good idea."

Few differences emerged between those Blacks who had solidly backed Jackson in the 1984 and 1988 presidential primaries and those who had not. Middle-aged and college-educated Blacks tended to be the strongest Jackson supporters, while the Black elderly and those without a high school diploma were less likely to support Jackson as a primary contender. Of those 55 years of age and older, 42 percent of the 1988 respondents did not support Jackson in either 1984 or 1988, compared to 22 percent of those 18 to 34 years of age. Similarly, 38 percent of those without a high school diploma did not support Jackson in either of his two bids, compared to the 43 percent of college-educated Blacks who supported Jackson both times.

No intragroup differences emerged that account for patterns of support for Jackson as an independent presidential contender in 1984 and 1988. Roughly half of the sample, men and women, young and old, affluent and poor, endorsed an independent Jackson bid in both 1984 and 1988.

After managing two credible campaigns for the Democratic party's presidential nomination, Jackson has emerged as a national leader of the Black community. However, Jackson's base of political support in the Black community depends on whether he chooses to run as a political insider or as an outsider. As a Democratic primary contender in 1984, Jackson did especially well among younger, college-educated, affluent, liberal, and race-conscious Blacks. If he had run as a political independent, he would have been supported by younger but poor Blacks. The class schism that exists in the Black community over the two types of Jackson campaign strategies is based on a deeper schism that exists among Blacks regarding political strategies and tactics generally; this topic will be explored further in the next chapter.

Jackson, in fact, presented himself as both an insider and an outsider, especially in his 1988 campaign, and this was critical to his broad appeal among Black voters. As an insider, he ran as a Democrat and chose not to become a political independent. As an outsider, he challenged party rules and disregarded party norms. For example, after winning the Michigan caucus and doing well in the Illinois primary, he then lost badly to Michael Dukakis in Wisconsin and New York, but chose to continue running. Apparently, the political norm, however, is that losers step aside, especially in the latter months of the primary season, in order to allow the front-runner to sweep victoriously into the national conference,

**Table 6.6** Change and Continuity in Black Support for Jackson by Jackson Rating and Social Characteristics in 1984 and 1988 (weighted percentages and means)

| Rating and Social Characteristics in 1988 | Jackson as Primary Contender | | | | | Jackson as Independent Candidate | | | | |
|---|---|---|---|---|---|---|---|---|---|---|
| | Neither Year | 1984 Only | 1988 Only | Both Years | (N) | Neither Year | 1984 Only | 1988 Only | Both Years | (N) |
| TOTAL SAMPLE | 27% | 15 | 20 | 38 | (338) | 22% | 11 | 18 | 50 | (353) |
| MEAN JACKSON RATING (0–100) | 70 | 70 | 78 | 87** | (336) | 72 | 73 | 80 | 86** | (340) |
| GENDER | | | | | | | | | | |
| Male | 29% | 16 | 18 | 37 | (136) | 27% | 15 | 18 | 41 | (141) |
| Female | 25 | 15 | 21 | 39 | (202) | 19 | 8 | 17 | 56 | (199) |
| AGE | | | | | | | | | | |
| 18–34 | 22% | 8 | 23 | 46** | (100) | 19% | 12 | 20 | 50 | (111) |
| 35–54 | 21 | 20 | 16 | 43 | (134) | 24 | 10 | 14 | 51 | (124) |
| 55+ | 42 | 18 | 19 | 20 | (103) | 25 | 10 | 19 | 45 | (104) |

| | | | | | | | | | |
|---|---|---|---|---|---|---|---|---|---|
| **EDUCATION** | | | | | | | | | |
| 0–12 years | 38% | 10 | 22 | 30* | (61) | 17% | 10 | 19 | 55 | (67) |
| High school graduate | 25 | 18 | 22 | 35 | (93) | 25 | 13 | 20 | 42 | (104) |
| College | 24 | 17 | 17 | 43 | (172) | 25 | 10 | 16 | 49 | (162) |
| **FAMILY INCOME** | | | | | | | | | |
| $10–19,999 | 32% | 13 | 21 | 34 | (126) | 24% | 11 | 16 | 49 | (141) |
| $20–29,999 | 11 | 20 | 33 | 36 | (52) | 21 | 13 | 19 | 47 | (50) |
| $30,000+ | 28 | 15 | 14 | 43 | (122) | 27 | 10 | 20 | 43 | (115) |
| **REGION** | | | | | | | | | |
| South | 22% | 17 | 24 | 37 | (158) | 20% | 11 | 16 | 53 | (168) |
| Non-South | 30 | 14 | 16 | 39 | (180) | 26 | 10 | 18 | 46 | (172) |
| **URBANICITY** | | | | | | | | | |
| Rural | 25% | 9 | 27 | 39 | (36) | 26% | 14 | 11 | 49* | (36) |
| Small town/city | 26 | 11 | 17 | 46 | (88) | 11 | 15 | 15 | 59 | (101) |
| Suburb/large city | 28 | 20 | 19 | 33 | (204) | 30 | 8 | 22 | 41 | (196) |

*Source:* The 1984–1988 National Black Election Study.

*p < .05.

**p < .01.

enabling the nominee to prepare his attack against his Republican competitor. Jackson's refusal to "step aside" led to a storm of criticism.[6] Most political analysts were baffled by Jackson's behavior at this point. The political journalists Jack Germond and Jules Witcover, for example, write that "Jackson's decision to press on in the trappings of a serious contender marked the evolution of the Jackson adventure from a predominantly electoral exercise to more a politico-sociological one—from a campaign for the presidential nomination to a crusade to move Dukakis on policy matters important to Jackson and his cohorts, and to make a statement for history" (1989: 321). To those not in Jackson's camp, they add, it also appeared as if Jackson was "on a power trip, driven by the emotion of his own campaign and the adulation directed toward him by his followers and even some young reporters in his traveling entourage" (1989: 321). However, Jackson's behavior at this point corresponded perfectly with Ronald Walters's (1988) strategic plan that Black presidential contenders must aggregate the Black vote and espouse Black interests up to the time of the convention. Even though he would not be able to overtake Dukakis, Jackson still needed the additional delegates he might pick up, especially in the populous state of California, in order to develop an organization that could wrest concessions from the party and its nominee. The Democratic party's rules make it extremely difficult for the winner of a state's primary or caucus to win all of the state's delegates. Thus, Jackson was assured of winning delegates even in the contests where he consistently lost to Dukakis. Although the insider/outsider Jackson may have perplexed political analysts, it was consistent with Blacks' self-image that, even with access to the political arena, they must still fight for inclusion. Jackson fully symbolizes this dual identity of Blacks.

## Conclusions

Although Democratic presidential contenders are less popular today, having sustained a series of losses, Black Americans rate Democrats seeking the presidency quite positively, and far above their Republican competitors. Even while Democrats generally receive better ratings from Blacks than from Whites because the overwhelming majority of Blacks are Democrats, Black Democrats rate Democratic presidential candidates more positively than do White Democrats. One reason for this is the party's liberal image relative to the Republican party's image in the Black community. But as Democratic leaders attempt to move the party closer to the center as a means of regaining White support lost during the Reagan years, Blacks' ratings of Democratic candidates will no doubt decline. In 1988, as the Democratic presidential nominee, Michael Dukakis received roughly equal evaluations from Black and White Democrats—the first time this had occurred since 1972—which suggests that Blacks are less supportive of moderates than they are of progressives.

Even as Democratic party leaders bemoan their string of losses and debate how they might recapture and hold onto the White House, it is clear that presidential elections are not simply popularity contests between presidential candidates but are referenda on the economy. Sound economies favor the party in power, while failing ones help the party out of power. As popular as Ronald Reagan was during his eight years as president, his approval ratings were nevertheless sensitive to the performance of the general economy, even while they appeared impervious to everything else, including the deaths of Marines in Beirut. The 1982 recession caused a serious drop in Reagan's approval ratings. Black voters behave no differently from White voters in this regard, except that, along with their impressions of how well the general economy is performing, the group's economic position is reflected in their voting decisions. The steadfast loyalty to the Democratic party shown by Blacks in presidential elections reflects the fact that a large minority of Blacks feel that their group has not benefited economically under past Republican administrations. Thus, underlying Blacks' support for the Democratic party and its candidates is the belief that their collective economic interests are best supported by Democratic presidents. Blacks' concern for the group's economic well-being in addition to the nation's economic health makes it more difficult for GOP presidents and challengers to recruit additional Black voters, since their party must show itself to be responsive to both national economic conditions and those for Blacks as a group.

Finally, although Jackson was popular in the Black community, he did not win the unanimous endorsement of Black voters in 1984.

Most resistant to Jackson's 1984 campaign were older, less educated, poor Blacks and Blacks who were weak race-identifiers and
self-identified conservatives. These Blacks were more likely to support Walter Mondale's bid, perhaps because they felt it was more
critical to support the candidate in the better position to win in a
race against Ronald Reagan. Younger, highly educated, and middle-
to-upper-income Blacks may have supported Jackson because they
thought it important to send a "protest vote" to the party, in an
effort to force the party to become more responsive to their interests
and needs.

However, Blacks who had backed Mondale in 1984 supported
Jackson in 1988 largely because Jackson had shown voters in 1984
that he could run a credible campaign for the party's nomination.
His campaign differed from those of past Black presidential aspirants, who had often staged a more symbolic bid for president. To
earn majority-Black support, Black presidential aspirants, therefore,
must prove themselves to be capable of running a viable campaign
for the presidency. This fact alone may prove to be too great a
barrier for Black presidential candidates to overcome, since surveys
show that large majorities of Americans, both Black and White,
believe that America is not ready to elect a Black president.

# 7

# Black Power and Electoral Politics

A persistent theme in Black politics is political independence (Walters, 1988; Gurin, Hatchett, and Jackson, 1989). Whether at the local or national level of politics, Black leaders have debated whether Blacks should remain politically independent or join coalitions. The conflict among Black leaders over ways to achieve greater political power is not new, however; it is rooted in a century-old debate among Black political leaders and intellectuals that includes Frederick Douglass, Marcus Garvey, W. E. B. Du Bois, and Harold Cruse. It has complicated almost every Black policy issue, leading to such questions as whether Blacks should work to integrate public schools or concentrate their efforts on improving Black community schools, and whether Blacks should work within the Democratic party or form an all-Black political organization. Support for Black political independence peaked during the late 1960s and mid-1970s but declined by the 1980s. Nonetheless, the notion of Black political independence still appeals to a certain segment in the Black community. This chapter will describe how the Black power movement helped promote the idea of Black political independence during the early electoral phase of Black politics, but how and why it failed to be endorsed as a political agenda by most Black elected officials. In addition, this chapter will examine who within the Black community traditionally supports Black nationalist ideologies and why such support appears to be growing.

## The Black Power Movement

The Black power slogan was first used in June 1966 during James Meredith's march through the South. It represented a controversial turn in the direction of the Black civil rights struggle. Black organizations such as the Student Nonviolent Coordinating Committee (SNCC) and the Congress of Racial Equality (CORE) became advocates of Black political independence as the avenue for Black advancement, while more mainstream organizations like the National Association for the Advancement of Colored People (NAACP) and the Southern Christian Leadership Conference (SCLC) continued to preach interracial cooperation and unity. In *Black Power* (1967), Stokely Carmichael and Charles V. Hamilton put forth the rationale behind the Black political independence movement, contending that Blacks first had to develop autonomous political organizations before pursuing political coalitions with Whites. The authors argued that without their own political base, Blacks would have to rely on the "goodwill" of White liberals to achieve their political goals, and, in the event that their interests conflicted with those of White liberals, Black interests could be easily abandoned. And indeed, as the militants bitterly pointed out, White support for the movement had declined as Blacks moved away from a focus on legal rights to pursue social and economic justice.

The Black power movement[1] profoundly affected Black politics. It led to a proliferation of Black community-based political organizations, all with the larger, expressed goal of expanding Black political power. These organizations, working at the grassroots level, did not operate under a single umbrella organization. Lacking the strong church network that had greatly facilitated the civil rights movement in the South, Black community activists in the North were more critically dependent upon outside financial support, including federal funds for such programs as the Community Action Program. As federal monies disappeared under Richard Nixon's second term in office, so, too, did many of these community agencies. However, these organizations did serve a critical role in increasing Black rates of voter participation, in the election of new Black representatives in urban centers, and more broadly, in facilitating the transfer of

Black political activities from protest to electoral politics (Smith, 1981; see also Greenstone and Peterson, 1973; Browning, Marshall, and Tabb, 1984; Morone, 1990: 220–252, for a general description of their impact).

Although Black power brought new energies, constituents, and fresh resolve to the decade-old civil rights struggle, it set Black political leaders against each other. Established, mainstream Black leaders, like Dr. King, had distanced themselves from it, reaffirming in the process their commitment to interracial cooperation and non-violence. Bayard Rustin, a King tactician, was ardently opposed to the Black power initiative. He believed that because Blacks were a numerical minority, they could not progress without the support of White liberals. Furthermore, he argued that Black power isolated Blacks and encouraged "anti-Negro forces" (1969: 253). Moreover, newly elected Black leaders repudiated much of the Black power agenda because it contradicted their political reality. More often than not, these politicians had won with the critical support of White liberals as well as the unified support of Blacks. Charles Bullock maintains that Black candidates "unacceptable to Whites have difficulty in getting elected" (1984: 249), and he estimates that even in majority-Black districts, most Black candidates need at least 22 percent of the White vote to win (1984: 251). In their award-winning study of ten northern California cities, Rufus Browning, Dale Rogers Marshall, and David Tabb show that Black empowerment was achieved more readily through coalitions, not separatism. In cities like Oakland where Black activists had pursued a separatist strategy, Black empowerment had only been achieved when Blacks became a voting majority. Furthermore, they argue, in order to secure and maintain their support from Whites, Black politicians need to be seen as political moderates. They need "dual legitimacy" to maintain unified Black support and to attract a critical share of White support (Button and Scher, 1989). In contrast, those who preached "Black power" have been seen by the public, and portrayed by the media, as radicals. Thus, although Black power clearly facilitated the transfer from protest to electoral politics, many Black politicians, like many of the civil rights activists, shunned its goals as impractical and divisive. The Black power slogan became the discordant note in the new Black politics.

The turning away from Black power by Black politicians can best be seen in the history of the Congressional Black Caucus (CBC). Having twice been denied access to the president by Nixon's assistant, John D. Ehrlichman, when they were seeking to discuss the effects of the administration's policies on Black Americans, Black House members formed the CBC in 1971 to maximize their collective influence in Congress (Brisbane, 1974: 262–263). The CBC was viewed by many "as a concrete manifestation of black political power" (Barnett, 1982: 28). Yet in a relatively short time, many Black legislators, including some of the CBC's original founders, became critical of the organization, viewing it as "ineffectual and floundering" (Barnett, 1982: 37). By the 1980s, the number of Black House members totaled more than twenty, half of whom had been elected in majority-White districts. Increasingly, these Black representatives would view and present themselves as legislators and representatives of their districts, not as spokespersons for "the 20 million Black people at-large." Furthermore, as Black legislators gained greater seniority and stature in the House, the perceived need for the organization was reduced. In the end, the symbolic importance of the CBC as an independent Black operation could not cloak the emerging differences among Black House members' priorities, management styles, and self-images. With the defection of the White southern vote to the GOP in national elections, southern control of the Democratic party was broken. Black Democratic legislators now found the party much more responsive to their needs, even while Black Democratic voters remained frustrated with the party's responsiveness.

Independent Black organizations were also weakened by a lack of support from Black political elites, evident in the debate for a national Black political party. Local all-Black parties had managed to mobilize Black voters and elect some Blacks to office. For example, in South Carolina's 1970 state races, three United Citizens party candidates were elected as the state's first Black legislators since Reconstruction (Walton, 1972b: 124). Local Black activists felt that they could greatly improve their chances for electoral success with a nationally based operation. However, many senior Black leaders were opposed to the idea, both as representatives of the Democratic party and on pragmatic grounds: third-party candidates seldom won. Efforts to start the process of organizing such a party invariably fell apart, as in the 1972 Gary, Indiana Convention that Manning Marable described as the "high point of Black nationalist agitation in the post–World War II period" (1985: 187). At the start of this convention, there was considerable friction between Black nationalist groups and professional politicians. In the end, however, the Black nationalists' policy statements prevailed over the more temperate agenda of the Black leadership elite on such issues as busing and U.S. support of Israel. The nationalists' policy statements greatly embarrassed many of the national Black leaders who had participated in the conference (Walters, 1988: 86–89). Many of these leaders later publicly repudiated the policy statements issued from the convention, and a few condemned the convention itself.

## Black Political Independence and Racial Voting

Traditionally, within the Black community, Black nationalist leaders like Marcus Garvey have been able to attract only a margin of support. Yet mainstream Black political leaders often have incorporated Black nationalist ideas into their thinking, and it would be incorrect to describe the majority of Blacks as opposed in principle to Black nationalism. Published analyses of Black nationalism, which peaked during the early 1970s only to disappear in the 1980s, have been limited and inconsistent. In addition, research on Black nationalism, perhaps more than other topics in Afro-American studies, has tended to suffer from the methodological and political prejudices of researchers. The 1984 NBES itself contains a limited set of questions designed to measure Black support for Black nationalism. It would be wrong, however, to classify those respondents who concur with this set of measures as representing "Black nationalists." Black nationalists hold a number of divergent and conflicting views on class, socialism, Africa, and other issues which are not captured in these measures.

As shown in Table 7.1, Black support for Black nationalist ideas varies considerably. "Buy Black" is a concept still favored by the majority in the Black community. More than half (56 percent) of the NBES respondents in 1984 supported the idea of "shopping in Black-owned stores whenever possible." Moreover, cultural Black

Table 7.1    Level of Support for Black Nationalism in 1984 (weighted percentages)

| Question Wording | In Agreement/Yes (%) | (N) |
|---|---|---|
| "Black people should shop in Black-owned stores whenever possible" | 56 | (852) |
| "Black children should learn an African language" | 36 | (851) |
| "Do you think Blacks should form their own political party?" | 28 | (1,135) |
| "Blacks should always vote for Black candidates when they run" | 19 | (852) |
| "Blacks should not have anything to do with Whites if they can help it" | 4 | (852) |

Source: The 1984 National Black Election Study.

nationalism continues to receive support from Blacks today; 36 percent in the sample felt that Black children should learn "an African language." However, lower levels of support were found for the idea of Black political independence and racial voting. Fewer than 30 percent of the respondents thought that Blacks should form their own political party, and only 19 percent felt that Blacks should always vote for Black candidates when they run for political office. The idea of racial separatism, a controversial but recurring theme of Black nationalism, received the lowest margin of support among Blacks; only 4 percent of the sample voiced agreement with the statement "Blacks should not have anything to do with Whites if they can help it." Indeed, the Black majority's resistance to Black nationalism is explicitly linked to its strong objection to racial separatism.

Those in favor of an independent Black party are somewhat more likely to endorse racial voting. One-third of Black party supporters favored the idea of always supporting Black candidates, in contrast to the 12 percent of those opposed to an independent Black party. Both Black party and Black candidate supporters tended to be devoted supporters of Jesse Jackson in 1984; 72 percent of those who favored an independent Black party said that they would vote for Jackson as an independent presidential candidate, in comparison to 50 percent of those who opposed the notion of an all-Black party. But, like support for Jackson as a political independent, partisanship was not related to support for a Black political party or racial voting. Strong and weak partisans as well as political independents were equally opposed to a Black party and unlikely to give unconditional support to Black candidates.

According to the historian Wilson Moses, Black nationalism initially received strong support from the Black upper classes during the mid-1800s to early 1900s because, like all Blacks of that period, they were "denied access to the mainstream institutions in American cultural and intellectual life" (1978: 29). However, upper- and middle-class Blacks gradually rejected the concept as social institutions became more open. Black nationalism became largely the refuge of poor and working-class Blacks, who saw it as a means of escape from their circumstances. Traditionally, support for Black nationalism swells as conditions among the Black population deteriorate and as increasing numbers come to believe that better relations between the races are unlikely. The significant factors related to support for a Black party and racial voting are shown in Table 7.2. In general, those favoring a Black independent party and who give unconditional support to Black candidates are younger, poorer, and less educated. Those residing in the South were more likely to give preference to Black candidates in principle, although the results of this analysis do not support the belief that Black political nationalism is exclusively an urban phenomenon. Strong racial identifiers within the Black community were more likely to express support for the idea of a Black political party, but were no more likely than weak racial identifiers to endorse racial voting. Significantly, both Black party supporters and racial voters perceived race relations as generally poor. Blacks who agreed with the statement "Whites generally want to keep Blacks down" (38 percent of the sample), and not with the statements "Whites today give Blacks a better break" or "don't care one way or another," tended to support Black political independence and racial voting.

The problem of inaccessibility is also a factor in explaining why support for Black political independence splits along class lines in the Black community. The Black poor and those with less education

**Table 7.2**    Determinants of Black Party and Black Candidate Supporters (logit coefficients)

| Independent Variables | Support Black Political Party | | Always Support Black Candidates | |
|---|---|---|---|---|
| | B | (SE) | B | (SE) |
| Gender (female) | .00 | (.17) | −.02 | (.23) |
| Age | −.03** | (.01) | .03** | (.01) |
| Education | −.18** | (.04) | −.02 | (.04) |
| Income | −.10** | (.03) | −.14** | (.04) |
| Region (non-South) | .09 | (.17) | −.46* | (.23) |
| Urbanicity (low-high) | −.02 | (.06) | −.15 | (.08) |
| Race identification | .09* | (.05) | .08 | (.06) |
| Race relations (poor) | .45** | (.10) | .43** | (.14) |
| Constant | 1.46* | (.64) | −2.40* | (.81) |
| Log likelihood | −459.89 | | −282.36 | |
| Total cases | 850 | | 674 | |
| Predicted correctly | 72% | | 82% | |

*Source:* The 1984 National Black Election Study.
*$p < .05$.
**$p < .01$.

are less likely to be involved in electoral and party politics because they often lack the political skills, time, and money necessary to participate fully. However, in order to be viable, Black parties are dependent upon the full support of the Black community, and such parties might deliberately work to be more accessible to the Black poor. Certainly, independent Black parties historically have a better record of mobilizing the Black poor than the major parties. Moreover, because Black parties have tended to field Black candidates, they may be better able to generate new and stronger interest in politics among the politically inactive in the Black community. In addition, because these smaller parties are not loose coalitions of multiple and competing interests, as is the Democratic party, the interests of the Black poor are less likely to be ignored. Thus, poor Blacks might view Black party organizations as more responsive to their needs than the major parties. Yet, because there is no strong support from the Black middle class and the Black political elite, the emergence of a nationally based Black third party is highly unlikely.

In general, race can provide important political cues for voters, and the belief that Black parties may better represent Black interests also extends to Black candidates. On one hand, those who are poorly informed about their political choices often assume that Black candidates are more liberal than other candidates. Williams (1989) reports that 22 percent of Whites surveyed in 1987 perceived Black candidates to be more liberal than White candidates, with an even higher percentage of Blacks believing them to be more liberal as well. On the other hand, even those who are well informed may support the candidate of their racial group when political differences between the set of candidates are not strong. In the latter case, racial voting may be, as Bullock writes, "the product of racism, or it may be the result of reliance on a simply, readily available cue, much as a candidate's last name prompts some ethnically oriented voters to forsake party identification and support a fellow ethnic" (1984: 240). Nevertheless, the majority of Blacks eschew racial voting even if it may be motivated by group loyalty and pride; fewer than one in five endorsed it in the NBES survey. Moreover, those Black candidates who do not represent the majority's liberal policy interests have tended to do poorly within the Black community. For example, Black Republicans have managed to obtain no more than a quarter share of the Black vote in such campaigns as Bill Lucas's 1986 bid for the governor's seat in Michigan. President Reagan had made a political appearance on Lucas's behalf, and Lucas also ran ads on Black radio stations announcing, "Vote for the Man, not the Party!" Yet only 21 percent of the Blacks who turned out supported Lucas, and the incumbent Democratic governor won in a landslide, obtaining the highest percentage of the vote for a Michigan governor since 1928. In 1988, a Black Republican, Alan Keyes, ran for the Senate. Like Lucas, he received visible support from President Reagan. While Keyes did noticeably better than Bush in the majority-Black city of Baltimore, receiving 41 percent compared to Bush's 25 percent, he received virtually the identical percentage of the vote as Bush did (30 percent) in Prince George's county, a suburb of Washington that is half Black.[2] Finally, in Virginia, another Black Republican, Maurice Dawkins, was unable to receive significant support from the Black community for his Senate bid. Dawkins's campaign had been generally disastrous; it was revealed that Dawkins had lied on his résumé, and he also had difficulties generating funds and ideas for his campaign. Still, his opponent, Charles Robb, did not do as well among Black voters as Michael Dukakis did. The *Richmond-Times Dispatch*, in its analysis of Black support for Robb and Dukakis, reported that falloff for Senate candidates was customary, but the paper also noted that Robb's snub of Jesse Jackson may have been a contributing factor as well.

## The Resurgence of Black Nationalism

There are a few Black elected officials who continue to solidify their support in the Black community by casting political issues as a power conflict between Blacks and Whites. Gus Savage, for example, in his most recent reelection bid successfully marshaled his dwindling Black support by running an aggressively pro-Black campaign. Savage had been elected to the second congressional district of Illinois in 1980; his standing in his majority-Black district had fallen because of reports of a congressional investigation of his sexual harassment of a Peace Corps student in Africa and his abysmally low attendance record in Congress. He narrowly held onto his seat against machine-sponsored challengers, but by the mid-1980s he faced relatively weak opponents. In 1990, however, he faced a strong challenge in the Democratic primary from Mel Reynolds, a Black political newcomer who nevertheless had strong credentials as a Rhodes Scholar and was endorsed by the city's two newspapers. Reynolds accepted PAC money for his campaign from a Jewish organization, and Savage was able to label him effectively a "puppet of White interests" and win the primary race with 52 percent of the vote.[3] In Washington, D.C., Marion Barry supporters also attempted to win back the Black community by claiming that his drug bust had been part of "the Plan" by Whites to take back political control of the nation's capital.

However, other political ideas developed by Black nationalists have found new credibility and support within the Black community and have earned a measure of support among Whites as well. For example, community-controlled, majority-Black schools had been a Black nationalist idea long scorned by Black and White liberals who advocated busing as the principal means of improving the quality of public education for Blacks. Yet faced with the seeming intractability of school segregation and alarmingly high attrition rates among Black teens, school boards in both Detroit and Milwaukee have recently approved plans to create separate public schools for Black boys that cater exclusively to their needs.[4] In Boston, such a Black nationalist program did not meet with success, however. A group of Black professionals attempted to turn Roxbury, the largely Black community in Boston, into a separate and autonomous city called Mandela. Mandela advocates argued that the Black and minority community in Boston would be able to achieve greater political and economic power through its secession from Boston. But their plan divided the Black leadership in Boston and failed to pass in two referenda (Travis, 1990: 117). Yet other Black nationalist ideals have returned to have a larger, broader-based impact on American society. African-influenced dress and music have become extremely popular with Black youth, and with American youth more generally. The strong Black nationalist messages contained in most rap music may, in fact, have considerable influence on the political consciousness of the Black youth of today, who will become the voters of tomorrow.

Black nationalism continues to flourish, of course, in the practices and teachings of the Black Muslims. Black Muslims suffered major setbacks in the scandal surrounding Malcolm X's assassination and their split into factions in the aftermath of the death of Elijiah Muhammad, their prophet. But, under the leadership of Louis Farrakhan, the Nation of Islam appears to be rebounding, finding new support through its recent activities. The patrol groups that Black Muslims have organized in high-crime, inner-city housing developments appear to have been successful in pushing out the drug dealers who had taken over these communities and whose drug-related violence had turned these areas into miniature war zones. Some, in fact, credit the Muslims as being perhaps the only Black organization that has attempted to deal realistically with the growing crime problem in Black communities. Furthermore, the polite, articulate, and well-dressed Black Muslim guardsmen (known collectively as the Fruit of Islam) have gained new respect among members of the Black community, especially among those who had been the most skeptical—the Black elderly.

Black Muslims have also sought new political legitimacy as elected officials; recently, and for the first time ever, they fielded three of their own in the Washington, D.C. area. None of the three Muslim candidates won office. The organization had attempted to win electoral support from the Black community by using traditional political tactics: fundraising and local canvassing. Moreover, the candidates stressed that they were seeking the support of everyone, Whites as well as Blacks. The Muslims' entry into politics was no doubt encouraged by the 1984 presidential bid of Jesse Jackson. Louis Farrakhan had openly urged his followers to support Jackson, breaking from the Nation's traditional policy of noninvolvement in politics. Nonetheless, the Muslims appear to have found a new critical source of support among Blacks who have become dissatisfied with their current set of Black elected representatives. In a speech given at a housing complex in Washington, Farrakhan reportedly said that the "current crop of leaders, black and white, have been ineffective in purging black communities of drugs, crime and other social ills," adding that these politicians "used the people to get what they want then forget to serve the people."[5] Speaking in the aftermath of former Washington Mayor Marion Barry's drug bust, Farrakhan promised that Black Muslim politicians would be "upright alternatives."

Conflict between Black nationalists and Black elected officials appears to be intensifying. In New York City, for example, Black nationalist organizations supported the election of David Dinkins as the city's first Black mayor, yet they have threatened to withdraw their support from Dinkins in 1993 unless he supports more of their political agenda. Dinkins won with less than 51 percent of the vote in 1989; thus, he can ill afford to alienate any group from his original electoral coalition. Nevertheless, political threats by Black nationalists may not be truly credible. Black nationalist groups have managed to attract many thousands of Blacks for rallies and protests, but, given their limited financial base, they have difficulties in getting their supporters to the polls. Blacks most supportive of Black nationalist principles are those least likely to vote—the young, the poor, and the least educated. The Blacks who do vote have tended not to support Black nationalist candidates and causes in the voting booth. For example, in the most recent New York City council primary elections, the majority of Blacks voting in majority-Black districts favored two White incumbents over two very well known, but controversial, local Black activists, C. Vernon Mason and Colin E. Moore.

Nevertheless, the challenge to Black mayors from Black nationalists and their supporters must be viewed as very real, whether Black Muslims and nationalists are elected to office or remain positioned as political gadflies. Black nationalists have clearly found a new and productive political niche in challenging the established Black leadership, confirming once more their adaptability to changing political climates. Furthermore, if Black nationalism is indeed borne of racial despair, as the analysis presented here suggests, then it seems certain that its ranks will increase, especially among the unemployed Black male youth and those who consider government's response to their community's worsening economic and social problems to be wholly inadequate, if not openly hostile.

# 8

# Black Electoral Politics and Beyond

The incorporation of Blacks into mainstream politics represents one of the most important outcomes of the civil rights struggle.
But even as Blacks have emerged in the 1970s and 1980s as important players in American politics, they still face considerable challenges in the electoral arena that threaten to diminish their political
gains. These challenges include their political isolation in the 1980s,
both within the national policy arena and within the Democratic
party, and their desire to fulfill a political agenda that the White
majority finds unacceptable. This chapter returns to the central
themes raised in the book's introductory chapter: Are Blacks
engaged in a political movement? How might Black voters, confronted by a national political environment that currently does not
favor Black policy objectives, increase their political effectiveness?
Finally, what potential direction might the "new Black politics"
take?

## Group-Oriented Politics or a Movement?

A critical finding emerging from this book is that the transformation
from protest to politics has had little effect on Blacks' group loyalties:
most Black Americans today remain strongly group-oriented. Not
only does a majority (75 percent) feel that their lives are affected
by what happens to Blacks as a group, but many also think about
what it means to be Black today. Together, the centrality and salience

of racial group membership among Blacks account for much of their liberal policy profiles and political identities as Democrats. Race identification also significantly shapes Black political behavior. Strong race-identifiers were more likely to participate in electoral politics and to support Jesse Jackson's presidential bids than weak race-identifiers. In addition, concern for the group's economic situation accounted for the pro-Democratic direction of the Black vote in 1984 and 1988. This book has also revealed the extent to which Blacks continue to utilize in electoral politics collective resources that were critical to the emergence of the civil rights struggle. Along with group consciousness, Black political organizations and institutions such as the Black church play important roles in the political mobilization of the Black community today. The crucial involvement of the Black church can best be seen in Jesse Jackson's presidential bids. But he is only one of a number of such Black officeseekers who have relied on community resources to win office. The prominence of race in the political attitudes and actions of Black Americans strongly rebuts the pluralist point of view that Blacks' integration into the political system and their social and economic advancement would weaken their group orientation toward politics.[1]

Having intact both a strong racial group orientation toward politics as well as functioning indigenous political resources, can Black voters be characterized as the participants in a Black political movement? A critical and necessary component of a political movement is its functioning ideology: members must share a common political identity and self-awareness of a particular concern (Freeman, 1983: 2). Even though Black politics has shifted its focus away from a purely civil rights agenda, Blacks possess this common identity and remain focused on a primary objective: group empowerment. Still, differences between the protest and electoral phases of Black politics remain that strongly contradict the characterization of the new Black politics as a political movement. First, as this book shows, electoral politics, unlike protest politics, is limited to a class-restricted segment of the Black community. The new Black politics mobilizes a smaller pool of Black participants than did the Black protest movement. Even Jackson's presidential bid failed to mobilize more than one-third of the Black community in 1984. Second, the transformation from protest to politics has led to the bureaucratization and greater oligarchization (the concentration of power in the hands of a minority) of the original movement structure. Blacks today experience politics as members of the Democratic party organization. Moreover, as the eminent political sociologists Max Weber and Robert Michels have each argued, over time, radical movements inevitably become "routinized," their leaders more accommodationist, hence conservative, and their structure less open and less responsive to their mass membership base.[2] Such a process was evident even in Jackson's presidential bids; while his 1984 campaign had struck many as a grassroots political movement, his 1988 campaign appeared strikingly less so. As Robert C. Smith writes of Jackson's 1988 presidential campaign relative to his 1984 campaign: "One observes evidence of the incipient institutionalization of the 'campaign movement'; less insurgency, more inclusion; less protest, more working within the system; less movement, more traditional campaign" (1990: 230).

To assess fully the question of the "new Black politics" as a political movement, it is necessary to review the literature on movement formation. For the civil rights movement, a critical factor was the development of Black indigenous political resources. Although Blacks possess important political resources, including group consciousness, such resources, in and of themselves, do not make a political movement. Movements need favorable political conditions to develop; they also require leadership. Blacks currently lack both. First, the political environment that helped make possible Blacks' efforts to organize for and to realize political and social change during the civil rights era is today far less open to such efforts. The political doors to Blacks began to close as the principal policy objective of Blacks was transformed from civil rights to economic justice. According to the conservative political historian Hugh Davis Graham, Lyndon Johnson presided over this change, asserting in a 1965 commencement address to Howard University graduates that it was not enough for government to "just open the gates of opportunity" to Blacks, but that government must "seek not just freedom [for Blacks] but opportunity—not just legal equity but human ability—not just equality as a right and a theory but equality as a fact and as a result" (Graham, 1990: 174). Graham also credits Richard Nixon with helping to implement the second phase of the civil rights policy revolution. As the presidential architect of the Philadelphia Plan, a program that guaranteed a proportion of funds to minority federal contractors, Nixon was, according to Graham, an unlikely proponent of "proportional hiring" and received little credit in the civil rights establishment for his program (1990: 344–345).

It was this shift from "equal opportunity to equality of fact" that led to the erosion of White support for Black civil rights initiatives. The civil rights era indeed ushered in a new climate of racial tolerance in the United States. But while a nearly absolute majority of White Americans came to favor the dismantling of "separate but equal," the extension of the franchise to southern Blacks, and equal access for Blacks in employment and education opportunities, many still reject the current civil rights policies aimed at reducing racial inequality in schools, in the workplace, and, more broadly, in society. Countless studies have shown that although most Whites now support the principle of racial equality, most contest the steps to implement racial equality (Schuman, Steeh, and Bobo, 1985; Kluegel and Smith, 1986). Consequently, support for affirmative action among political elites has begun to wane.

Not only has national leadership started to back away from this issue, but the Supreme Court, which had narrowly accepted affirmative action in its 1978 and 1979 *Bakke* and *Weber* decisions, has also become critical of it. By the late 1980s, the composition of the Court was such that a majority was positioned against race-preferential remedies on behalf of Blacks. Thus, in a 1989 ruling, a 6 to 3 majority held that a minority contract set-aside program that had been voluntarily established by the city of Richmond, Virginia, was unconstitutional. And it is very likely that the Court will continue to restrict further, if not overturn completely, its earlier judicial decisions favoring race-based remedies for past discrimination.

While political opportunities for Blacks contracted as the Republican party ascended to power in national politics, new tensions between Blacks and their traditional liberal allies also escalated. Thomas Edsall and Mary Edsall (1991) argue that affirmative action, in particular, has pitted Blacks against Whites in a climate of declining job opportunities and job security. They contend that this conflict has placed the Democratic party at a competitive disadvantage against the GOP in the last five presidential elections, and that it will continue to do so as long as the party supports policies that the electorate does not support. Moreover, Blacks' efforts to protect their voting rights and to increase the number of Black officeholders through government and court enforcement of Section 5 of the Voting Rights Act have increasingly come under attack. Critics contend that the court rulings favoring the establishment of majority-Black districts represent an unjustified, race-based entitlement (see Thernstrom, 1987). While Whites' opposition to the enforcement of Section 5 of the Voting Rights Act is not as extreme as their opposition to other federally mandated civil rights programs, such as affirmative action in employment and higher education, redistricting has recently pitted Blacks against the Democratic party. The creation of majority-Black congressional districts has increased the number of safe districts for Republicans, a development that the Democratic party opposes. Nonetheless, it was Section 5 of the Voting Rights Act that made it possible for Black voters to elect their own state legislators in the South (Grofman and Handley, 1991; Parker, 1990). Even today, legal action in this matter continues to produce the largest net gains in the number of Black elected officials. For example, 63 percent of the 397 Black officials elected between January 1988 and January 1989 were elected in Alabama, after a judge ordered the state to abandon its at-large election system for 180 municipal and county jurisdictions (Barnes, 1990: 263). Presently, there are only five Black congressional legislators from the South. However, the redistricting and reapportioning taking place could ultimately more than double the number of Black House members from the South, resulting in new Black legislators in Alabama, North Carolina, South Carolina, and Virginia, where there are currently no Black legislators.

Not only is the political climate unfavorable to the emergence of a Black political movement, but Blacks also lack the leadership necessary to direct such a movement. Some have suggested that Jesse Jackson, having won majority-Black support for his 1984 and 1988 presidential bids, has effectively filled the leadership void created by the assassination of Dr. Martin Luther King in 1968. Jackson, while indisputably a charismatic speaker, nevertheless has failed to earn the level of support by the Black civil rights establishment necessary to guide a movement like the one King had. Jackson's announcement in 1983 to seek the presidency had met with open skepticism and even derision by many Black political leaders, who maintained that Walter Mondale was in a better position to successfully challenge incumbent President Reagan. In stark contrast to 1984, however, and with few exceptions, most national Black elected officials supported Jackson's 1988 bid. Black leaders supported Jackson's second bid because his Democratic opponents lacked the political stature and civil rights record that Mondale had had in 1984. Moreover, Black leaders felt pressured by Jackson's strong popularity among Black voters. But Jackson also was less threatening to the Black leadership establishment in 1988 than he had been as a political newcomer in 1984. In fact, Robert Smith maintains that "given [Jackson's] success in 1984, many of these [Black] leaders probably saw a Jackson campaign as a viable vehicle to enhance their own leverage and bargaining power in national as well as state and local Democratic party politics" (1990: 216). But having won the Black political establishment's endorsement in 1988 by no means guarantees Jackson future such endorsements.[3] And it is precisely because Black leaders are unable or unwilling to coalesce around Jackson or any other Black leader that the potential for a new movement remains sharply limited.

Related to this leadership problem (see also Marable, 1990: 223–227) are the severe political divisions that exist within the Black leadership community. In part, this conflict extends back to the fierce but still unresolved ideological battles over strategies and goals that so crippled the civil rights movement in its latter stages (McAdam, 1982). The conflict also stems from the sheer difficulty inherent in formulating and reaching consensus on public policies to help solve the mammoth social and economic problems many Blacks are confronted by today, including welfare dependency, drug addiction, teenage delinquency, and AIDS. At present, it appears that most Black political activists and their allies are committed to only one civil rights objective, that is, the goal of increasing Black political representation. However, even this issue has become increasingly problematic for Blacks in the post–civil rights environment. Not only have Blacks and Democratic party leaders become divided over the matter of drawing new majority-Black districts to increase Black representation, as noted earlier, but Blacks themselves have been caught in "internecine warfare" over which Black candidates Blacks should collectively support (Morris, 1992). Black versus Black political races in near-majority or majority-Black jurisdictions, which have increased in frequency over time, have occasionally left Blacks in political disarray, and in some cases, out of power altogether. Furthermore, in 1991, Black national leaders clashed over the matter of President Bush's nomination of a Black conservative to the Supreme Court, Clarence Thomas. Thomas, the former head of the Equal Employment Opportunity Commission under the Reagan administration, had made clear in published articles and public forums his opposition to affirmative action. However, the Southern Christian Leadership Conference still favored his confirmation, while the National Urban League remained neutral. That left the NAACP as the only major civil rights group to oppose him. In the end, the Senate confirmed Thomas to the Supreme Court by a margin of 52 to 48. A number of his swing southern Democratic backers in the Senate, in fact, attributed much of their decision to Thomas's strong support in the Black community. Early opinion polls had showed Blacks uncharacteristically divided in the beginning, although at the end of the proceedings, surveys showed 70 percent Black support in Thomas's favor.[4] As a new associate justice, Thomas is expected to help the Court's majority conservative bloc overturn its 1978 *Bakke* decision upholding affirmative action at public institutions.

Finally, if one accepts the definition of political movements as those that attempt to radically change individuals, societal institutions, or the structure of society, the new Black politics cannot adequately function as a political movement. In taking up electoral politics, Blacks and their leaders have implicitly embraced strategies that preclude the possibility of radical goals. As a number of studies have shown, at most, the elections of Black mayors and city council members have led to large increases in Black municipal employment (Karnig and Welch, 1980; Eisinger, 1982; Browning, Marshall, and Tabb, 1984; Mlandenka, 1989), improvements in city services for Blacks (Button, 1989), and limited increases in expenditures for social services (Karnig and Welch, 1980). Such elections have not produced the radical and profound changes envisioned by the civil rights activists of the 1960s. The Jim Crow system was legally abolished, but Black and White majorities still, on the whole, live separately. Politics has had no effect on the economic inequalities that persist between the races. The general conclusion reached by analysts in this area remains not far from that of William Keech, a pioneering analyst of the impact of the Black vote in the South, a few years after the passage of the Voting Rights Act. "The vote," he wrote, "is most useful for the least important gains" (1968: 94).

Black elected leaders cannot be faulted for the failure of Blacks to realize their civil rights objectives through traditional politics since, as a class, they face certain powerful constraints that limit their policymaking effectiveness (Reed, 1988; Button and Scher, 1989: 210; Bush, 1984; Karnig and Welch, 1980: 150–151). Democracies favor majorities, not minorities. However, Black elected officials represent fewer than 2 percent of the total number of elected officials in this country, and to work in a legislative body, Black policymakers must often moderate their positions. Indeed, empirical analyses of the linkages between public opinion and public policies have found that once in office, Democratic and Republican legislators often move toward the center of public opinion (Erikson, Wright, and McIver, 1989). Lack of cooperation is also a problem for some local Black policymakers who must contend with majorities in city councils that are hostile to their interests. Form of government also matters, since Black city legislators have considerably less influence in at-large electoral systems than in single-member district systems (Mlandenka, 1989). And in general, Black politicians find their political effectiveness enhanced greatly when they belong to a majority in the city council or are members of the dominant political coalition (Browning, Marshall, and Tabb, 1984). But still, even in local governments where Black legislators and their allies constitute a political majority, Black politicians have been unable to implement the sweeping new policies that their constituents demand. Because local governments are essentially the "creatures of the state" (Karnig and Welch, 1980: 151), the fiscal problems of local and state governments have limited the abilities of Black politicians to implement policies that can help alleviate the multiple and complex set of social and economic problems facing the Black poor. Because of their cities' financial crises, Black mayors in general have opted for traditional business-oriented development policies, rather than community-based redistributive programs (Reed, 1988; Stone, 1989). These policies have helped revitalize the central business districts in cities like Atlanta, Oakland, Detroit, and Newark and have benefited the Black business elite, even while the conditions of the Black poor have deteriorated (for example, see Orfield and Ashkinaze, 1991). Finally, in light of the division between legislative, executive, and judicial powers, as well as state and federal authority, policy change proceeds slowly in the United States. Because the policymaking environment favors incrementalism, policies that are implemented are almost always modest in scope.

To conclude, although traditional politics is a limited vehicle for pursuing radical change, Black egalitarian objectives are still radical insofar as racial equality will necessitate the implementation of radical social programs that address class inequalities as well as racial inequalities. Such policies, because they go well beyond the scope of the types of public policies currently under debate, are highly unlikely to materialize, nor will they materialize through the application of Black voting alone. The new Black politics, while not a functional movement, may, in fact, represent the "dormant stage" of a long-term struggle waged by Blacks to achieve racial equality. Still, it is not reasonable to expect that such a movement will emerge in the near future, given the lack of adequate leadership and the bleak political opportunities for economic and social change.

## Black Alternatives to the Ballot

The continued commitment shown by Blacks to the goal of racial equality suggests that new Black political initiatives to promote greater racial equality and racial justice through political means, as evident in Jackson's 1984 and 1988 presidential campaigns, are likely to emerge. However, given the structural constraints to the policymaking effectiveness of the Black vote, the general unresponsiveness of Republican administrations to Blacks' social and economic problems, and the growing isolation of Blacks within the Democratic party, what initiatives might Blacks pursue to increase their political effectiveness? Ronald Walters, a political scientist at Howard University, argues that the current period closely resembles the first quarter of this century, when Blacks were rejected by both major parties (1988: 198). Walters does point out, however, that a critical difference between then and now is that Black voters today constitute an electoral force of over ten million. Thus, he argues that Blacks should pursue alternatives to the Democratic party in order to achieve their political objectives. One of the number of alternatives to major-party involvement that he proposes is the development of a third party organization. But the barriers to the development of such a third party, briefly discussed in Chapter 6, are formidable. The American party system works against the emergence of third parties, and third party candidates rarely possess the financial resources to compete effectively against major-party candidates (Rosenstone, Behr, and Lazarus, 1984). Furthermore, as shown in Chapter 7, the idea of a Black third party carries only weak support in the Black community. Four out of every five Black potential voters oppose the idea of an independent Black party, and most Black elected officials are flatly against the idea as well. Walters does not necessarily endorse an all-Black party but, rather, raises the possibility of a *multiracial* one. Clearly, a multiracial third party is more viable in national elections than an all-Black party, since Blacks are a voting minority. However, multiracial coalitions have their own set of special problems. It is estimated that Jesse Jackson received only about one-third of the Hispanic vote (excluding Cuban-Americans) in his 1984 bid for the Democratic party's nomination (Gutteriez, 1989: 123). Although Blacks have successfully combined their voting strength with Hispanics to elect Black mayors in such cities as Chicago and New York, coalitions between the two groups nevertheless tend to be fragile and rarely sustainable. Discord between Latinos and Blacks is often centered around questions of leadership rather than policy objectives. Blacks and Latinos do share a number of political concerns, including improving the public school system and reducing the unemployment rate. But the redistricting taking place today has intensified conflict between the two groups in areas such as New York City and Texas, where Black and Hispanic leaders have clashed over the vote-dilution of Hispanics in efforts to create new majority-Black districts.

A second political option for Blacks that Walters presents is what he calls a "Black presidential strategy." Black voters, he argues, should field a Black candidate for president, not particularly to gain the office, but to achieve their policy objectives. Jesse Jackson's

1984 and 1988 presidential bids are representative of this strategy. However, as Chapter 1 makes clear, Jackson's presidential bid as a bargaining vehicle actually achieved very few concessions for Blacks from the Democratic party. In 1984, the absence of full Black support for Jackson in the primaries and his failure to win support from the Black political elite deflated his campaign. In 1988, however, Jackson's placement as second runner-up no doubt led to the Democratic party's decision to appoint its first Black national chairman and to revise party nominating rules that worked against minority candidates. In both 1984 and 1988, Jackson powerfully spoke for many Black Americans. Furthermore, as the analyses presented in this book have revealed, his candidacy was linked to the massive mobilization of Blacks in the 1984 and 1988 presidential primary elections and the 1984 general election. Finally, Jackson's candidacies broke new ground for future Black presidential aspirants, including Virginia's Governor Douglas Wilder, and, ultimately, may encourage the candidacies of political progressives. Several of the candidates in the 1992 race expressed some of the policy concerns raised by Jackson in 1984 and 1988 and adopted his dramatic, grassroots-oriented campaign style (notably, former California governor Edmund G. "Jerry" Brown, Jr.). Jackson ruled out a third bid for the party's presidential nomination in 1992, but he has indicated that he will continue to speak on behalf of Black Democrats even though he is not a presidential candidate. In the end, however, the merits of a Black presidential strategy need to be evaluated through an analysis of presidential bids by other Black candidates, since there are some who would argue that the alienation of White Democrats generated by Jackson's candidacies outweighed any of the net benefits they produced for Blacks.

As an alternative to Walters's set of proposals, Blacks might improve their situation through their participation in issue-oriented coalitions rather than electoral coalitions.[5] In such a scenario, Blacks could concentrate their political activities on the direct attainment of their policy objectives, in contrast to their current strategy of working to elect candidates in the hope that a few of their policy goals might be realized. It was, in fact, precisely this type of activity that led to the passage of the 1991 Civil Rights Act, which, among other things, required employers to show that personnel policies having a discriminatory effect on minorities and women were substantially and demonstratively related to job performance.

In practice, however, issue coalitions might prove to be more difficult to direct effectively. Single-issue coalitions are more difficult to form and manage than electoral coalitions. The time frames involved are radically different, with electoral coalitions working intensively during most of a given election year, while interest groups must operate every day over a span of many years. In addition, members of electoral coalitions are rewarded for their efforts on a more regular basis and more concretely, depending on how often they get their candidates elected. In contrast, interest organizations achieve their objectives far less frequently and far less decisively. Often, it is only after years of lobbying efforts that an interest group might win a significant piece of legislation. Finally, issue-oriented organizations require more commitment, time, and interest from their members than electoral coalitions, and, as a consequence, they tend to attract the membership of those in the middle and upper-middle classes. Moreover, these organizations could also contribute to the political fragmentation of the Black community. James Button, in fact, contends that voting as a group activity was more effective for Blacks in the post–civil rights South than organizational activity (1989: 224–225).

Protest, of course, continues to serve as the ultimate alternative to all electoral strategies. Two distinguished social scientists, Frances Fox Piven and Richard Cloward (1977), have argued that, historically, the economically disadvantaged and politically powerless have benefited more through protest than through voting. Historians of the civil rights era have explicitly linked Black protest and grassroots activism to congressional action on civil rights (see, for example, Graham, 1990). Congress was greatly influenced by the dramatic events that took place in Selma and Birmingham, and pushed accordingly for the end of the Jim Crow system and of the denial of the franchise to Blacks in the South. In addition, Black rioting in the inner cities resulted in significant increases in federal expenditures on social welfare (Button, 1978) and can be linked to congressional support for the fair housing bill of 1968. Thus, the landmark civil rights legislation seemingly only came about as a result of Black political agitation.

Yet, protest undeniably also contributed a great deal to the loss of White support for Blacks' struggle for racial equality. Black militancy has been linked to the rise of White Republicanism and to the internal divisions found today between Black progressives and White moderates within the Democratic party (see Edsalls, 1991). James Button, contrasting conventional politics with unconventional political strategies, contends that political violence is a "double-edged sword" (1989: 232). It powerfully illustrates Black grievances but can heighten White hostility toward Blacks and lead to a political backlash against them. Nevertheless, in later work, he concedes that Black protest was essential for the social and political change that took place in the South (1989: 237).

Recently, Aldon Morris (1992), a sociologist at Northwestern University, has argued that Blacks must continue to utilize protest if they hope to produce significant change in the near future. Addressing the paradoxical relationship between the large-scale increase in the number of Black elected officials and the group's high level of poverty, he advocates combining political protest with electoral politics to augment the limited political power of Black elected officials. Community-based Black protest, he writes, could "counter the conservative tendencies inherent in electoral politics" and help keep Black politicians "honest and focused on the goal of black empowerment" (1992: 173). Morris views Black protest politics and electoral politics as the "twin cornerstones necessary in the empowerment of the African-American community" (1992: 173).

It is highly doubtful that the masses of Blacks will organize through their own efforts to protest as they did during the civil rights era, since the majority strongly believe in the efficacy of voting over protest, as noted in Chapter 4. Black elected officials are also unlikely to aid Blacks' efforts in developing stable protest organizations. As argued in Chapter 7, Black politicians generally eschew the idea of Black militancy. Those politicians who engage in protest very often are portrayed negatively by the media and viewed negatively by the White community, and most Black officeholders require a certain level of White support to stay in office. Black politicians would also likely view such organizations as a real threat to their political standing. Mobilized groups of Black protesters representing a broader base of the community could always turn against certain

Black elected officials, especially since an increasing number of Black protest leaders have become as critical of Black elected leadership as they are of White elected leadership.

Still, if protest erupts, it is likely to erupt once again in the inner cities, where Blacks are heavily concentrated and where the plight of the Black urban poor has worsened dramatically. Although race differences in educational attainment and earnings have declined steadily since World War II, the incidence of poverty in the Black community is three times higher than among Whites, and, in spite of the general decline in Black poverty (with its increase in the 1980s), this ratio has remained constant over the last three decades (Cotton, 1989). Furthermore, the small but steady improvements seen in Black male wage differentials are greatly overshadowed by the fact that a growing group of Black males have not found employment. Particularly distressing are the economic indicators for Black male teenagers. This group has nearly closed the racial gap in educational attainment, but its rate of unemployment is twice that of its White counterpart. Some economists maintain that wages for Black males have increased since World War II because low-skilled, low-paid Black males are dropping out of the employment sector, causing the wages of employed Black males to rise (see Cotton, 1989). Even the bleak picture seen in these economic indicators cannot adequately capture the current state of hopelessness found in urban Black America. In *The Truly Disadvantaged* (1987), William J. Wilson maintains that conditions in the ghettos have worsened and that life for the Blacks at the bottom has become significantly less secure and more violent. The *New York Times* recently reported that the life expectancy of the average Black male in Harlem is significantly lower than that of those living in Third World countries. Others have described what is taking place in the inner cities as a "quiet riot"—unnoticed and unthreatening to most Americans but "even more destructive of human life than the violent riots of twenty years ago" (Harris and Rogers, 1988: 182).

## Conclusion

It is risky to project the future. However, the 1970s and early 1980s may represent the peak period in the growth of the number of Black elected officials. The percentage increase in the number of Black elected officials has dropped considerably, from an average yearly increase of 14 percent between 1971 and 1979 to 5 percent between 1980 and 1988.[6] Unless redistricting and reapportionment lead to new majority-Black districts, the yearly increase in the number of Black elected officials in the 1990s is expected to be considerably lower than 5 percent. Nearly all majority-Black districts today have Black representatives; thus, most expect future Black politicians to emerge from districts where Blacks are only a minority of the voters. While the elections of David Dinkins in New York and Douglas Wilder in Virginia were widely hailed as political breakthroughs for Blacks, other Black candidates have been unable to duplicate these victories. In 1990, two popular and strongly backed Black candidates lost their bids for statewide positions. In North Carolina, Harvey Gantt failed to unseat the conservative Republican incumbent, Jesse Helms, for the Senate, despite strong party backing and considerable financial support. Moreover, Andrew Young was unable to win the governor's seat in Georgia in spite of having won over many White Democrats during his service as mayor of Atlanta. Also a subject of some controversy is whether these new Black politicians elected in majority-White districts are adequate spokespersons for Blacks. Some have argued that if in campaigning for office, these Black politicians downplay Black concerns about civil rights and poverty, then their elections are "almost superfluous and meaningless" (Barnes, 1990: 262). Still, the presumed differences in policy preferences and political style between Black politicians from majority-Black districts and the so-called "new breed of Black politicians" from majority-White areas have not been adequately researched and remain, at this point, wholly speculative.[7]

Black political leaders will continue to advocate renewed federal efforts to combat poverty and unemployment in the Black community. These programs should extend well beyond what was attempted under the Johnson administration; John Jacob, head of the National Urban League, has likened such an undertaking on behalf of Blacks to the Marshall Plan for Western Europe after World War II.[8] However, aggressive new economic programs to boost employment and counteract poverty are unlikely to be undertaken by the current Republican administration. Given the current political climate, together with the structural constraints that limit

Black elected officials' policy effectiveness, Black voters are likely to experience diminished expectations concerning their vote. Most Blacks believe that they have benefited as a group from electoral politics. In a 1980 national face-to-face survey of Black Americans,[9] 72 percent said that the elections of Blacks to political office have helped the cause of Blacks, while only 2 percent said that such elections have hurt. One quarter of the Blacks in the 1980 survey, nevertheless, felt that the elections of Blacks have had no impact. According to these respondents, not enough Blacks had been elected to office to make a difference, and Black elected officials were, on the whole, politically ineffective, or, at the least, no different from the White elected officials whom they had replaced. A few expressed the view that, in spite of these elections, Whites still controlled the country.

It is possible that the percentage of those who view the elections of Blacks as having made no impact on their lives will grow. There are signs that Black expectations have declined, and increasing numbers of Blacks are dropping out of local politics. Voter turnout in large U.S. cities has generally declined over the years, suggesting that support for Black mayors has diminished, chiefly among the least critical members of their electoral coalitions, that is, mainly the poor. But although Black criticism of Black mayoral administrations apparently has grown, Black mayors have been remarkably successful in staying in office, and, on the whole, they remain fairly popular with their constituents. Coleman Young of Detroit and Tom Bradley of Los Angeles, for example, have both served their cities' longest consecutive terms as mayors, while Maynard Jackson, limited to two consecutive terms as mayor by city charter, has recently been reelected to the mayor's post in Atlanta, eight years after leaving office. Black mayors elected in cities with Black voting majorities have the double advantage of being able to pursue business-oriented politics, thereby winning financial support for their reelection bids, and also being able to rely on the loyalty of Black voters to forestall challenges from White opponents.

Unless the federal government becomes more responsive, Black rates of participation at the national level may decline as well. And, indeed, the U.S. Census's Current Population Survey data show that Black participation in the 1990 midterm elections fell from its level in the 1986 midterm elections. Given that participation is strongly tied to policy outputs, any falloff in Black participation in the future will probably occur among those who have benefited least from the new Black politics.

The merits of full participation have been strongly debated, nevertheless. Some argue that the current high levels of nonvoting in the United States represent a failure of democracy, while others maintain that those who fail to participate are generally satisfied with their lot.[10] There is some empirical work suggesting that while nonvoters do not hold significantly different policy attitudes from voters, they are somewhat more likely to favor Democratic candidates (Wolfinger and Rosenstone, 1980). Since on issues such as welfare spending, affluent Blacks are more conservative than poor Blacks, who constitute a large share of the Black nonvoters, it is possible that higher levels of Black nonvoting could have policy consequences. Such consequences, however, may not have much impact on public policy. Affluent Blacks are remarkably more progressive than their White counterparts (Gilliam and Whitby, 1989), because, as shown in Chapter 2, their conservatism is often counterbalanced by their race consciousness. Most important, since there is not a wide range of social policies under debate in the United States, the class cleavage found in the Black community may not greatly affect the spending levels on current social welfare programs. The class division would have far greater significance if radical, redistributive policies were under consideration, since affluent Blacks, as well as many mainstream Black political leaders, reject them.

Any falloff in Black rates of participation should not, however, be interpreted as a withdrawal. Having finally become political insiders in American politics, the new Black voters are highly unlikely to relinquish this position. But the scope and direction of their involvement in politics in the future will critically depend on the emergence of new leaders, who, like Jesse Jackson, espouse "ballot box" methods, but who also prove to be more effective in delivering political programs aimed at achieving the community's long-elusive dream of racial equality.

# 9

# A Show of Loyalty:
# Black Voters in the 1992 Elections

In breaking the Republican party's twelve-year hold on the White House, Arkansas governor Bill Clinton did what many had begun to think politically impossible: he fashioned a winning coalition out of traditionally Democratic groups, including urban voters, labor, Catholics, Jews, Blacks, and those voting Republican since 1980—self-identified political independents, White suburbanites, and the young. Clinton won the lion's share of the Black vote despite having made no aggressive effort toward its securement. As a matter of fact, during his campaign for the party's nomination he made several political gaffes that alienated many in the Black community.[1] First, in what appeared to be a calculated attempt at signaling to conservative Whites that he was not "in the Jackson camp," he attacked the rap artist Sister Souljah while at Jesse Jackson's side moments after a reconciliatory meeting between the two men. As an invited guest at a June 1992 meeting of Jackson's political organization, the Rainbow Coalition, Sister Souljah reportedly had told the audience that "if Black people kill Black people every day, why not have a week and kill White people?"[2] Some months earlier, it had been reported that Clinton had accused Jesse Jackson of "backstabbing" after he was told mistakenly that Jackson had endorsed a rival Democrat, Tom Harkin, for the party's nomination. Finally, there had been photographs taken (and used against him by Jerry Brown, another rival for the party's nomination) of Clinton playing golf at a segregated Little Rock country club. (Arkansas, along with Alabama, has the dubious distinction of being one of two states without a civil rights law barring job discrimination and is one of nine states that does not bar housing discrimination.) Still, support for Clinton among Blacks in Arkansas was strong. Most important, in the end, none of these events seemingly mattered to the majority of Black voters: telephone polls conducted by the major media organizations taken one month prior to the November election revealed solid Black support for Bill Clinton.

In retrospect, Bill Clinton's getting the Black vote was most remarkable for the apparent ease with which he won it. After nearly a decade of discord and complaint by Black Democrats that the party took their vote for granted and the party had turned to the right, a number of analysts speculated that Blacks would remain cool toward this moderate Southern Democrat. Yet Clinton took two-thirds of the Black primary vote against more liberal party rivals, such as Jerry Brown and Tom Harkin (although Harkin, dropping out just prior to the Super Tuesday elections, endorsed Clinton). Moreover, in 1992 the majority of Blacks cast Democratic ballots, despite having for the first time in twelve years an alternative to the major parties: third-party candidate H. Ross Perot. While Perot won 19 percent of the popular vote, he obtained only 7 percent of the Black vote.

Why did the overwhelming majority of Blacks turn out in higher numbers and vote for this moderate Arkansas governor?[3] And what was the impact of the 1992 congressional elections on Black politics at the national level? Not only did the party preferred by African Americans finally gain control of the White House in 1992, but, through implementation of the 1982-amended Voting Rights Act, a record number of Blacks were elected to Congress as well. The growth in Black elected officials at the national level corresponds to the two-pronged political strategy of Blacks that involves increasing Black political representation in order to maximize their influence over the national policymaking process. While it is too soon to predict if this aggregation of Black electoral power will bring about a more responsive national government, recent events affecting Blacks' level of influence in national government, and in particular the Supreme Court's 1993 ruling in *Shaw v. Reno,* are part of the story.

## Explaining Black Party Loyalty in 1992

The 1992 Democratic primary contest initially began like the 1984 and 1988 primary seasons, having, once more, a Black candidate aspiring to win the Democratic party's presidential nomination and make history. This candidate was not the Reverend Jesse Jackson, as many had anticipated given his successful second run for the nomination in 1988, but Virginia's Governor L. Douglas Wilder. (After keeping many guessing about his plans for 1992, Jackson had announced one year in advance of the November election that he would not seek the Democratic party's nomination a third time.) Wilder had already made history by becoming the nation's first elected Black governor since Reconstruction. In spite of his early entry into the presidential race, however, or perhaps because of it, Wilder pulled out of the contest well before any primaries. He had become embroiled in a highly publicized and poisonous political battle with one of his state's senators, Charles S. Robb, and because of this, together with the fact that Jackson made no secret of his dislike of the governor, Wilder was having trouble raising campaign funds. Wilder's dropping out left the Black primary vote wide open to a field of Democratic hopefuls, all of whom were making their first presidential bids.

Coming from states having few Blacks, both Iowa's Tom Harkin and Nebraska's Bob Kerrey ended their bids with little or no Black support. Similarly, Paul Tsongas, no longer a U.S. Senator, ended his campaign in mid-March, having exhausted his campaign funds. Perhaps the most conservative of the five contenders, he, too, had won over few Blacks. In spite of the fact that Jesse Jackson had garnered over 90 percent of the Black primary vote in 1988, none of these candidates, except Edmund "Jerry" Brown, Jr. (and only later on in his campaign), laid claims to Jackson's large base of support. Jackson, furthermore, did not choose to endorse publicly any of the candidates, despite some polls indicating that his endorsement would greatly influence Black voting. In a last-minute effort to generate momentum for his campaign in New York, after a surprise victory in Connecticut, Brown pledged that if nominated, he would choose Jesse Jackson to be his running mate. Jackson still did not choose this moment for public endorsement of Brown, who

Table 9.1    Voting and Registration by Race in Presidential Elections, 1964–1992

| | 1964[a] | 1968 | 1972 | 1976 | 1980 | 1984 | 1988 | 1992 |
|---|---|---|---|---|---|---|---|---|
| PERCENT REPORTED VOTING | | | | | | | | |
| Black | 58.5[a] | 57.6 | 52.1 | 48.7 | 50.5 | 55.8 | 51.5 | 54 |
| White | 70.7 | 69.1 | 64.5 | 60.9 | 60.9 | 61.4 | 59.1 | 63.6 |
| Gap | −12.2 | −11.5 | −12.4 | −12.2 | −10.4 | −5.6 | −7.6 | −9.6 |
| PERCENT REPORTED REGISTERED | | | | | | | | |
| Black | | 66.2 | 65.5 | 58.5 | 60 | 66.3 | 64.5 | 63.9 |
| White | | 75.4 | 73.4 | 68.3 | 68.4 | 69.6 | 67.9 | 70.1 |
| Gap | | −9.2 | −7.9 | −9.8 | −8.4 | −3.3 | −3.4 | −6.2 |

Source: Current Population Reports, P20-466 (Nov. 1992), Tables A and B.
a. Includes Blacks and other races in 1964.

hung on—in Jackson-like fashion—until the primary in his home state of California, which was the last. Although he lost New York's primary to Clinton, Brown's direct appeal to Blacks worked, if only modestly: Clinton took less of the Black vote in New York, 52 percent, while Brown won 39 percent, according to exit polls. Bill Clinton, claiming to be running a "unifying campaign" that appealed to everyone, made, in fact, few highly publicized campaign stops in Black areas. One reporter labeled the Clinton campaign in the Black community a "stealth campaign." However, in the end Clinton accrued the majority share of the Black primary vote. Notably, Black participation in many state presidential primaries fell substantially in 1992 from its high levels in 1988 and 1984, when Jackson was on the ticket.

Although turnout among Black voters increased in 1992, it did not return to the 1984 level. Overall voter turnout, however, peaked in 1992, reversing a nearly thirty-year record of general decline (see Table 9.1). Yet the 1984 presidential election remains the high water mark of Black voter turnout. Even though some have interpreted the peak turnout rate for the 1992 election as a sign that voter confidence and trust might be rebounding, this does not appear to be the case for Black Americans. Despite the dramatic rise in voter participation in 1992 over 1988, the gap between Whites and Blacks in political participation increased from 7.6 percent in 1988 to 9.6 percent. Thus, although many Whites apparently returned to the voting booths in 1992, many Blacks still stayed home.

Table 9.2    Percentage of Registered Voters Who Did Not Vote, by Race and Hispanic Origin, 1968–1992

| Year | Blacks (%) | Whites (%) | Hispanics (%) |
|---|---|---|---|
| 1968 | 13.0[a] | 8.4[a] | n.a. |
| 1972 | 20.4 | 12.2 | 15.7 |
| 1976 | 16.7 | 10.8 | 16.7 |
| 1980 | 15.9 | 10.9 | 17.8 |
| 1984 | 15.8 | 11.8 | 18.5 |
| 1988 | 20.1 | 13.0 | 18.9 |
| 1992 | 15.4 | 9.3 | 17.5 |

Source: Calculated from Tables 1 and 2 in the Current Population Reports, P-20, No. 192, 253, 322, 370, 405, 440, 466.

a. Number of registered voters was estimated by adding to the total number who voted those registrants who did not vote in the 1968 presidential election.

The large jump in overall voter participation in 1992 was primarily due to increases in turnout among registrants rather than to increases in registration. Yet among Blacks, voting rebounded less dramatically than among Whites both because of the decline in Black voter registration and because of Black registrants' lower rates of turnout. Since 1968, voting among registrants has been substantially lower among Blacks than among Whites and Hispanics (see Table 9.2). In fact, among the Black registrants, 15.4 percent reported not having voted in the 1992 election. In contrast, only 9.3 percent of the White registrants reported not having voted in this election. Nonvoting among Black registrants was particularly pronounced during the 1972 and 1988 presidential elections, as was the nonvoting among Whites. These two elections were similar insofar as the Democrats were organizationally weak and divided in their effort to unseat incumbent Republican presidents. Nevertheless, indifference to presidential politics ran especially high in the 1988 presidential election among Black voters because many of these nonvoting Black registrants were those who had solidly backed Jesse Jackson in the Democratic presidential primaries and caucuses (see Chapter 5). Black registrants' nonvoting in this election, in fact, exceeded 20 percent. The rate of nonvoting among Black registrants in the 1992 race was consistent with other presidential elections— around 15 percent.

The reemerging racial gap in voter participation may signal Black dissatisfaction with national politics, and lends strong support to Hirschman's (1970) concept of "exit" as it applies to the post–civil rights era of Black politics. There appears to be a substantial minority of Blacks who are indifferent to presidential election outcomes and who choose not to vote on election day. Who are these nonvoting Black voters? Black registrants under 35 are less likely to vote than older Blacks; in particular, young Black male registrants are less likely to vote. More than 30 percent of Black men 18 to 24 years of age reported not having voted in the 1992 presidential election, in contrast to 21 percent of Black women in the same age category. Black registrants over the age of 34, of both genders, are more inclined to vote. Fewer than 13 percent of the Black male and female registrants over the age of 34 failed to vote in the 1992 presidential election. One reason why young Black males are less likely to turn up at the polls is that they are, in general, less attached to the Democratic party than are women and older Blacks (see Chapter 3). Their lower levels of attachment to the Democratic party are expressed through their higher rates of nonparticipation.

Still, turnout among Blacks in 1992 rose, indicating that presidential politics in 1992 was different from the situation in 1988. What had changed? First and foremost, Jackson's absence and general detachment from the primary race produced a different atmosphere. Although there was definite friction between Jackson and Clinton, the latter's securing the Black vote depended on the goodwill of Jackson. If Jackson had endorsed Jerry Brown or any other candidate, or, what would have been even more threatening, had declared his own campaign for president, Clinton probably would have lost his hold over the Black vote. Moreover, Blacks had become even more critical of President Bush than they had been in 1988. Bush's low standing among Blacks in 1992 was comparable to that of Ronald Reagan in 1984. This erosion of Bush's rating alone probably prompted more Blacks to go to the polls.

Securing 83 percent of the Black vote, Clinton managed to win the largest plurality of the White vote as well (42 percent versus 39 percent for George Bush, according to the exit polls conducted by Voter Research & Surveys), the first time this had happened for a Democrat since Lyndon Johnson's victory in 1964. Clinton's dual

Table 9.3   Blacks' and Whites' Economic Assessments from One Year Ago in 1992: Personal and National

| From one year ago: | Got Better (%) | Stayed the Same (%) | Got Worse (%) | (N) |
|---|---|---|---|---|
| PERSONAL ECONOMIC SITUATION | | | | |
| Blacks | 26 | 33.5 | 41 | 316 |
| Whites | 31 | 36 | 34 | 2,066 |
| NATIONAL ECONOMY | | | | |
| Blacks | 3 | 18 | 79.5 | 310 |
| Whites | 5 | 24 | 72 | 2,052 |
| LEVEL OF UNEMPLOYMENT | | | | |
| Blacks | 5 | 11 | 84 | 316 |
| Whites | 2 | 17.5 | 80 | 2,048 |
| INFLATION | | | | |
| Blacks | 3 | 20 | 76 | 315 |
| Whites | 7 | 42 | 51 | 2,041 |

Source: The 1992 American National Election Study.

success with Blacks and Whites owed much to the fact that not only did increasing percentages of both groups feel that their own economic situation had deteriorated over the past year, but also—and even more remarkably—both groups this time were in relative agreement about the state of the nation's economy. Compared to 1984, fewer Americans, Black or White, saw improvements in their family's economic situation in 1992 over previous years. Although 46 percent of Blacks and 45 percent of Whites felt that their personal economic situation had gotten better from one year earlier in 1984, only 26 percent of Blacks and 31 percent of Whites thought in 1992 that their finances had improved over the past year (see Table 9.3). More striking are the extremely small numbers of respondents found in the 1992 National Election Study who felt that the economy had improved over the past year. A mere 3 percent of Blacks and a scant 5 percent of Whites thought that the economy had gotten better. On the contrary, most Blacks and Whites considered the economy to have gotten worse, with Blacks (as was the case in 1984) far more likely than Whites to say—by a margin of about 15 percent in both election years—that the economy was *much* worse off. This unfavorable view of the nation's economy was a much more radical shift in perspective for White voters, since large pluralities of Blacks had always considered the 1980s to be tough economically. With exit surveys indicating that the economy was a top concern among the largest plurality of voters, this more negative view of the economy by Whites was a prime reason why many more voted Democratic in 1992.

Although George Bush had enjoyed some of the highest approval ratings ever recorded for an American president during his four years in office, as the presidential election approached his standing fell markedly among White and Black voters alike. Bush's "feeling thermometer" rating declined from an average of 63 in 1988 to 53.5 four years later among Whites. Blacks, who had been somewhat warmer toward Bush in 1988 compared to Ronald Reagan in 1984, also cooled appreciably toward him in 1992; his rating dipped to 38 from 46 over the same four-year period. Given Blacks' negative view of the nation's economy and Bush's diminished standing, it was practically impossible for the Republicans to make new inroads into the Black vote in 1992.

While Whites' grim appraisals of their economic situation and of the economy made them more critical of Bush, they did not lead to significantly higher assessments of Bill Clinton. In 1992 Whites gave Clinton an average rating of 53, which was no better than their 1988 rating of Michael Dukakis (see Table 6.1). Likewise, Blacks' mean score assessment of Clinton at 68 was no higher than the one they had given Dukakis. Even self-identified Black Democrats expressed no greater warmth for Clinton than they had for Dukakis, giving Clinton an average rating of 72. What these numbers indicate, in fact, is that Blacks expressed less enthusiasm for the Democratic party's last two presidential nominees today than they had from 1972 to 1984.

Even though Blacks have cooled somewhat toward the Democratic party's presidential nominees, most remain firmly convinced that the party does a better job of representing their policy interests. When asked in the 1992 National Election Study which party they thought would do a better job of handling the nation's economy, foreign affairs, the problem of poverty, and health care, Blacks, by overwhelming percentages, named the Democratic party. In fact, as Table 9.4 shows, near-unanimous percentages of Blacks felt that

Table 9.4    Percentage Who Favored the Democrats on Policy among Those
Who See Party Difference by Race (total numbers in parentheses)

|  | The Democrats | |
|---|---|---|
|  | Blacks (%) | Whites (%) |
| Which party do you think would do a better job of: | | |
| Handling the nation's economy? | 94 | 60 |
|  | (203) | (1,149) |
| Handling foreign affairs? | 61.5 | 28 |
|  | (200) | (1,377) |
| Solving the problem of poverty? | 94 | 80 |
|  | (226) | (1,253) |
| Making health care more affordable? | 96 | 80 |
|  | (237) | (1,330) |
| Which party is more likely to: | | |
| Cut social security? | 12 | 23 |
|  | (192) | (1,011) |
| Raise taxes? | 27 | 69.5 |
|  | (164) | (1,124) |

Source: 1992 NES.

the Democrats would, in general, perform better on this set of policy matters. Ninety-five percent felt that the Democrats would handle the nation's economy better than the Republicans, handle foreign affairs better, and make health care more affordable. Blacks were somewhat less uniform in feeling that Democrats are superior to Republicans in handling foreign relations and in not raising taxes. About one in four of the Black respondents felt that the Democrats were more likely than the Republicans to raise taxes, and a full 39 percent felt that the Republicans would perform better than the Democrats in foreign affairs. The majority of White respondents (about 80 percent) felt that the Democrats would perform better than the Republicans on social welfare matters: poverty, health care, and social security. But, unlike Blacks, Whites were divided in their assessments of whether the Democrats or Republicans were better equipped to handle the economy, foreign affairs, and likely to not raise taxes. In the area of foreign affairs, in fact, a majority of the White respondents felt that Republicans, by and large, would likely do a better job than the Democrats.

Table 9.5    Percentage Who Said Neither Party or Had No Opinion
on Major Party Policy Performance by Race (total numbers
in parentheses)

| | Neither Party/ Don't Know | |
|---|---|---|
| | Blacks (%) | Whites (%) |
| Which party do you think would do a better job of: | | |
| Handling the nation's economy? | 36 | 44 |
| | (317) | (2,067) |
| Handling foreign affairs? | 37 | 33 |
| | (317) | (2,068) |
| Solving the problem of poverty? | 29 | 39 |
| | (317) | (2,066) |
| Making health care more affordable? | 25 | 36 |
| | (317) | (2,064) |
| Which party is more likely to: | | |
| Cut social security? | 40 | 51 |
| | (318) | (2,068) |
| Raise taxes? | 48 | 46 |
| | (318) | (2,070) |

Source: 1992 NES.

While an overwhelming majority of Blacks were of the opinion
that the Democrats perform better than the Republicans across a
number of policy domains, a substantial minority, nevertheless,
failed to see any difference between the Republicans and the Democrats on such matters. Table 9.5 shows the percentages of respondents by race who voluntarily stated that neither party would do a
better job or who had no opinion on this matter. As the table
indicates, although fewer Blacks than Whites thought that neither
party's performance was better, 25 to 37 percent of Blacks held
such views. Similarly, 40 percent of the Black respondents thought
that both parties were likely to cut social security, and about half
felt that both parties were likely to raise taxes. Thus, although
Blacks uniformly rejected the Republican party on policy matters
in favor of the Democratic party, a sizable minority felt, as did
Whites, that on these five policies, differences between the two major
parties were trivial. Blacks, in other words, while overwhelmingly

pro-Democratic in their party preference, may still be no more partisan in their political orientation than Whites.

To assess more formally the issue of the degree of Black partisanship, the perceptions of major party difference items were regressed on a set of social demographic and attitudinal variables, including racial group membership. Those who identify with a party are defined as partisans and are expected to see large differences between the parties, as well as those who have experienced politics longer (older Americans) and those better informed about politics (better educated Americans). Income might or might not have an independent impact on such perceptions. Finally, gender was included in the model because since 1980 significant gender differences in party preferences have emerged. Because the measure of party difference is a dummy variable, logit analysis was performed. The results are reported in Table 9.6.

While partisanship was consistently related to the perception of party difference, as predicted, racial group membership had an independent effect on four of the six items only, mostly on the three social welfare items: poverty, health care, and social security.[4] Blacks were also more likely to recognize party differences on their economic record. Interestingly, gender mattered for four of the six items as well. Women were more likely than men to recognize differences between the two major parties in handling the nation's economy, on foreign affairs, on health care, and in raising taxes. No consistent patterns were found for age and income, while better educated respondents were more likely to discern party differences on the six policy items than less educated respondents.

Blacks' perception that the Democratic party is substantively different from the Republican party in the areas of the economy and social welfare is a central factor that explains why most Blacks remain loyal Democrats. Although I have stressed the Democratic party's championship of landmark civil rights legislation as central to the new surge in Black identification with the Democrats, President Johnson's "War on Poverty" legislation also boosted their rates of Democratic identification. Given the absence of a direct question on the performance of the parties in addressing racial inequalities in the 1992 National Election Study, it is not possible to determine whether Blacks continue to see substantial differences between the

**Table 9.6** Logit Analysis of Perception of Major Party Policy Performance

| | Nation's Economy | | Foreign Affairs | | Solve Poverty | | Health Care | | Social Security | | Raise Taxes | |
|---|---|---|---|---|---|---|---|---|---|---|---|---|
| Intercept | -.61* | (.25) | .12 | (.26) | -.13 | (.25) | -.09 | (.26) | .46 | (.24) | .41 | (.24) |
| Gender (Male) | -.22* | (.09) | -.23* | (.10) | -.11 | (.09) | -.22* | (.10) | .02 | (.09) | -.45** | (.09) |
| Race (Black) | .29* | (.14) | -.10 | (.14) | .47** | (.15) | .54** | (.15) | .42** | (.14) | -.05 | (.13) |
| Partisan (Yes) | 1.09** | (.09) | .72** | (.10) | .85** | (.09) | .75** | (.10) | .27** | (.09) | .43** | (.09) |
| Age | .00 | (.00) | .00 | (.00) | .00 | (.00) | .00 | (.00) | -.01** | (.003) | .00 | (.00) |
| Education | .15** | (.03) | .10** | (.03) | .14** | (.03) | .10** | (.03) | -.03 | (.03) | .11** | (.03) |
| Income | -.01 | (.01) | .01 | (.01) | -.01 | (.01) | -.01 | (.01) | -.00 | (.01) | .00 | (.01) |
| Total cases | 2,130 | | 2,132 | | 2,129 | | 2,127 | | 2,131 | | 2,134 | |
| Log likelihood | -1363.8 | | -1310.8 | | -1340.7 | | -1305.4 | | -1457.7 | | -1432.8 | |
| % Correct | 64.5 | | 68.2 | | 65 | | 67.2 | | 53.7 | | 58.5 | |

*Source:* 1992 NES.
* $p < .05$; ** $p < .01$.

parties on racial issues or to determine if race policies are strongly linked to the party's record on social welfare policies. Given the rising tide of racial conservatism within the Republican party that emerged in 1964 with Barry Goldwater's nomination and possibly ended with George Bush's signature on the 1991 Civil Rights Act, both racial issues and social welfare policies explain the preponderance and strength of Blacks' pro-Democratic preferences. But it is possible that in the weighting of these two factors, the party's performance on social welfare policy matters more to Black Democrats today than it does on race.

President Clinton's domestic policy performance will likely determine how many Blacks go to the polls in 1996 and how many will vote Democratic. Clinton's proposed universal health insurance plan, considered to be the centerpiece of his domestic agenda, already has wide support among Blacks and Whites. Most Americans, as the surveys indicate, while uncertain about how the President's plan should work, are adamant in their view that the federal government should pass legislation guaranteeing Americans adequate and cost-effective health coverage (Bowman and Ladd, 1993b). In addition to health care, in focusing on crime and reform of the welfare system Clinton has identified issues that disproportionately affect African Americans. While research on race and public opinion has shown that on a number of political matters Blacks and Whites express wholly divergent opinions, few such racial divisions exist in the broad outlines of the President's proposed measures to fight crime and reform welfare. Even though substantial numbers of Blacks remain divided over and mostly opposed to the death penalty (see Table 2.5), increasing numbers now support mandatory sentencing for certain classes of criminals. One survey conducted by the Joint Center for Political and Economic Studies of 750 Blacks found that 73 percent favored imposing mandatory sentences for drug dealers (Dionne, 1992). Most Blacks, like Whites, also favor the President's "three strikes" mandatory sentencing policy that imposes a life sentence for criminals convicted of three violent felonies (Brownstein, 1994). Gun control has also become a policy which the majority of Americans now favor.

Although Blacks remain more liberal than Whites in their support of the welfare system, most Blacks, like Whites, feel that this system should be changed (Bowman and Ladd, 1993a). Large majorities among both racial groups hold the view that the welfare system discourages those on it from working. In fact, 81 percent of Blacks and 83 percent of Whites felt that the "current welfare system discourages poor people from finding work." Few Americans (6 percent), however, wanted to scrap the American welfare system altogether. Nor, contrary to popular belief, did many Americans think that welfare payments should be cut back. About 20 percent (both Black and White) of those surveyed favored cutting the amount of money given to all people on welfare.[5] In reforming the system, nearly all of the respondents (over 90 percent) endorsed the goal of changing the system to make welfare recipients more self-sufficient.

While consensus views exist among Blacks and Whites, the form of the proposed legislation will definitely affect the level of Blacks' support for Clinton's domestic agenda. Blacks are likely to reject any health insurance program that is not universal, that is, one that does not extend to every American the opportunity to participate in some form of the health coverage program. A vote on health care legislation is not expected until 1995. At this point, however, the President has vowed not to compromise on the principle of the policy's universality. Equally important to Blacks will be the form that Clinton's welfare reform initiatives take. Even though most Blacks believe in the need for reform, there are gaps in Blacks' and Whites' attitudes on some of the proposed steps that could be taken to make welfare recipients more self-sufficient. While nearly everyone favors the government's adopting sterner measures to make fathers support their children, fewer than one-half of those surveyed, with more Black and self-identified liberals likely in favor, supported the notion of a public child support system, in other words, paying child support "directly out of public funds" to mothers if the government cannot make the father pay. In addition, according to the results of a survey conducted by the Los Angeles Times, fewer Blacks than Whites endorsed the mandatory work requirement for welfare recipients, although majorities in both groups were in favor of a work requirement—73 percent among Blacks versus 90 percent among Whites (Brownstein, 1994). Finally, although most Blacks want new laws imposing tougher penalties for criminals, many remain skeptical that such laws will be applied fairly. A Los Angeles

*Times* survey found that Blacks felt that anti-crime laws, if passed, would likely discriminate against them—43 percent versus only 18 percent among Whites (Brownstein, 1994). Black House legislators and Jesse Jackson have already expressed criticism of the President's anti-crime bill. They want more crime prevention measures included in the bill, including federal funding for drug rehabilitation, and are vowing to block passage of the bill if such measures are not added. There will also likely be a fight over welfare between the President and Black legislators if the reform proposals are more punitive than inducement-oriented.

Overall, the results from the 1992 presidential election indicate that despite Blacks' having become somewhat less enamored of the party's nominees, there remains the perception that substantive differences exist between the two parties. These perceptions of party difference nurture and sustain the strong Democratic voting patterns of Blacks. On this basis, Clinton, as the first Democratic president since 1976, has a tremendous opportunity to strengthen Blacks' links to the party. Although nothing in my analysis suggests that there is any movement away from the Democrats by Blacks, the emerging racial gap in voter participation represents a disturbing sign that Blacks are becoming increasingly disenchanted with their role in presidential politics. A large minority of Blacks, including even those registered to vote, feel that their vote doesn't matter in presidential elections and are staying away from the polls.

### Blacks and Third-Party Candidate Ross Perot

The 1992 presidential election presented voters with a third political option. Instead of voting for the Democrat or the Republican, Black voters could have cast ballots for Texas billionaire Ross Perot, as 19 percent of all the voters did. Instead, exit polling revealed that Perot won a scant 7 percent share of the Black vote.[6] Perot, in fact, did worse among Black voters than among all other social groups (with the possible exception of Jewish voters; see Pomper, 1993). Perot's inability to win over Black voters was partly a reflection of his message as much as it was their rejection of the messenger. Perot's chief campaign theme of deficit reduction is an inherently conservative one, in contrast to Clinton's message of stimulating the economy and of job creation. Being largely liberal in their policy orientation, Blacks preferred Clinton's campaign message over Perot's. Perot also was largely unknown to most Black voters, who, for the reasons identified above, chose to stick with the Democratic party.

Perot, however, had not entirely ignored Black voters in his off-again, on-again quest for the presidency. Some, in fact, have suggested that Perot's disastrous speech to the NAACP on July 11, 1992, hopelessly soured Blacks on his bid. Perot's speech, in which he talked about job creation and reviving the economy, nevertheless had offended his audience. Perot's use of "you people" in reference to Blacks along with his story about his parents' record of generosity toward poor Blacks in Texas during the Depression years (for example, his father "always" paid his Black employees, and his mother gave food to hobos, "many of them Black," who came by the house) was seen as patronizing. Perot later apologized for his remarks, stating that he did not mean to offend anyone by them. Actually, data from the National Election Study show that Blacks were no cooler toward this third-party candidate than Whites; neither group rated him above the midpoint of 50. Black and White feeling thermometer ratings of Ross Perot were 41 and 46, respectively.

Although Perot garnered few Black votes, which Blacks were more likely to support him? Is there any evidence that those Blacks who supported Jesse Jackson's bids in 1984 and 1988 (see Table 6.5) were also those who cast ballots for Ross Perot? To determine if certain types of Black voters were more likely to support Perot's candidacy over Bill Clinton's, or Perot's over George Bush's, as well as identifying the Black voters who voted for Bush over Clinton, three logit models using the exit poll data collected by Voter Research & Surveys were estimated.[7] Partisanship, as one might expect, had the largest impact on the Black vote in 1992. Blacks who identified themselves as Democrats cast Democratic ballots, while those who identified with the Republican party voted for George Bush over Clinton (see the first column of Table 9.7). Black Republicans as well as self-declared political independents were also more likely to have voted for Ross Perot over Clinton (see the second column of Table 9.7) . With Black independents favoring Clinton over Bush, however, if 1992 had simply been a two-way race, then

Table 9.7    Logit Analysis of the Black Presidential Vote in 1992 (weighted data)

| Independent Variables | Bush v. Clinton | | Clinton v. Perot | | Perot v. Bush | |
|---|---|---|---|---|---|---|
| | B | (SE) | B | (SE) | B | (SE) |
| Female | −.218 | (.348) | .996* | (.397) | −.799 | (.570) |
| South | .052 | (.366) | .685 | (.413) | −.845 | (.565) |
| Urban/Suburban | −.596 | (.399) | .935* | (.465) | .281 | (.559) |
| Income (low-high) | .316* | (.165) | −.161 | (.193) | −.247 | (.250) |
| Age | .090 | (.094) | .138 | (.102) | −.260 | (.150) |
| Republican | 3.635** | (.437) | −3.574** | (.596) | .130 | (.679) |
| Independent | 1.308** | (.420) | −2.789** | (.438) | 1.258* | (.628) |
| Ideology (lib-con) | .689** | (.258) | .106 | (.306) | −.627 | (.356) |
| Education (low-high) | −.004 | (.174) | .410* | (.199) | −.257 | (.267) |
| Constant | −4.909** | (1.184) | −.171 | (1.159) | 4.228* | (1.753) |
| Log likelihood | −128.228 | | −101.916 | | −50.567 | |
| Total cases | 574 | | 560 | | 92 | |
| Pseudo R-squared | .31 | | .29 | | .18 | |

Source: The 1992 Exit Polls, Voter Research & Surveys.
Note: Democratic party affiliation is the base category for the two party identification dummy variables (Republican and Independent).
*p < .05; **p < .01.

Clinton probably would have secured almost all of the Black vote minus the votes of Black Republicans. Blacks' political ideology mattered as well in this election. Self-identified Black conservatives, even taking partisanship into account, were more likely to have voted for George Bush.

While region had no effect on the Black vote, gender and income did. Black men were more likely than Black women to have voted for Perot over Clinton, although when the choice was between Perot and Bush, they were no more likely than Black women to have voted for Perot. Income, though it did not have a separate impact on the Black vote in 1984 or 1988 (according to the analysis of the National Black Election Study), did in 1992. Affluent Blacks were somewhat more likely to have voted for George Bush over Bill Clinton. It may be that high-income Blacks were more likely to vote Republican in this election given the absence of race from the 1992 presidential campaign. There were no furloughed Black rapists ("Willie Horton" tactics) or "welfare queen" stories exploited by the Republicans in 1992. Race issues were largely absent, as all three presidential candidates pledged their support to protecting Blacks' civil rights.

Since Perot's Black supporters were more likely to be self-identified independents or Republicans, and male, it appears that even in the Black community Perot was more effective in stealing votes away from George Bush than he was in stealing them from Bill Clinton. Obviously, to have done better in the Black community, Perot would have needed to reach out more effectively to Clinton's most fervent supporters: Black Democrats. Since Perot did somewhat better than Clinton among political independents, less educated Blacks, and those residing in rural areas, the groups most supportive of Perot were actually quite different from Jackson's base of support. Blacks who voted for Perot are more detached from the Democratic party than are Jackson's supporters. They are also more ideologically diverse, leaning toward conservative, whereas Jackson's strongest level of support came from those Blacks who identify themselves as liberal and are strongly race-conscious. Like Jackson's Black supporters, Black Perot voters, nevertheless, appear to be searching for an alternative to the Democratic party. If Perot chooses to run again in 1996, he will likely direct much of his campaign against the incumbent President as he did in 1992. In this case, however, the President is a Democrat. Perot's ability to build stronger support in the Black community for his candidacy will depend on Clinton's domestic policy record, and on Perot's ability to present his bid as a better alternative to either the Democratic or the Republican party.

### A Record Expansion of Blacks' Legislative Power

The 1992 House elections, which brought 110 new faces to Congress—the most since 1948—also added 13 new Black lawmakers to the House. Including the District of Columbia's nonvoting elected House representative, Eleanor Norton Holmes, these elections brought the total number of African Americans in the U.S. House of Representatives to a record 39. At the same time, in Illinois, Carol Moseley Braun made history by becoming the nation's first Black female U.S. Senator.[8] Braun's bid, prompted by her outrage over how the Senate had handled the Clarence Thomas–Anita Hill affair, began with her surprise victory over incumbent Senator Alan Dixon in the Democratic primary. Senator Dixon had cast one of the pivotal votes for Thomas. After defeating Dixon, Braun went on to win against her Republican opponent in the general election by a comfortable margin of 10 percent.

Until Braun's nomination victory, no Black woman with major party backing had ever competed for the U.S. Senate. Since 1968, fewer than a dozen White women and only a few Black men have run for the Senate as major party candidates; fewer still have actually won. In 1988, for example, two Black candidates, both Republicans, ran for the Senate; they lost. As the lone Black senatorial candidate in 1990, Harvey Gantt, a former Democratic mayor of North Carolina's largest city, Charlotte, also lost, despite having strong party support and substantial funding. In 1984 ten women ran for the U.S. Senate, but only one won. In 1990 eight women ran, but only one—the same one who originally won in 1984, an incumbent senator from Kansas, Nancy Kassebaum—won her election. The fact that the 1992 elections added four women to the Senate, in addition to the record number elected to the House, made 1992 the "Year of the Woman." Prior to Braun's election, no Blacks and only two women were serving in the U.S. Senate. In winning her seat, Braun became one of seven women now serving in the Senate.

Winning simultaneously the feminist vote and the Black vote, Braun also owed much of her primary victory over Dixon to the anti-incumbency mood of voters that erupted in 1992 over the House banking scandal.[9] Nearly all Illinois incumbents fared badly in their March primaries. Along with Dixon, two senior Black House representatives, five-term representative Charles Hayes, and six-term representative Gus Savage were defeated by their younger Black opponents.[10] Except for the retirement of Representative Mervyn Dymally of California and the defeat of Hayes and Savage, all other Black House members were returned to office. Only two Black House incumbents had faced serious challenges in their reelection bids: the lone Black Republican in the House, Gary Franks, and New York Democrat Ed Towns, who had run in a redrawn Brooklyn district.

Of the thirteen new Black lawmakers now in the House of Representatives, all were elected in newly drawn majority-Black or minority districts in the South under the 1982 extension of the Voting Rights Act. During the 1980s only four new Black districts were created, and none existed at all in five southern states: Alabama, Florida, North Carolina, South Carolina, and Virginia. Only through implementation of the 1982 Voting Rights Act did these states in their 1990 redistricting process create their first majority-Black (or minority) congressional districts. Several states had required prodding by the Justice Department to construct these new minority districts. Georgia's initial redistricting plan, for example, which had only two Black districts, had twice been rejected by the Justice Department under the preclearance provision of the Voting Rights Act before state legislators finally ratified a plan that included a third Black congressional seat.  North Carolina's Democratic-controlled state legislature initially submitted a plan that had only one majority-Black district, which the Justice Department also rejected. The legislature then submitted a redistricting plan in which two majority-minority districts were constructed and in which two Blacks won. North Carolina's plan was successfully challenged in the Supreme Court by White plaintiffs as an infringement of the Constitution's Fourteenth Amendment.

Many political analysts believe that the Republican-controlled Justice Department's insistence that southern states draw a maximum number of Black and Latino-majority districts was politically motivated. Aggregating Black voters into a majority-Black district then reduces the percentage of Blacks—mostly Democrats—in adjacent districts, enhancing Republican odds of victory there. In Alabama, for example, after the percentage of Ben Erdreich's Black district population was cut from 32 to 10 percent to create the state's first majority-Black district, he lost his reelection bid to a Republican. In the nine states with new Black districts, the number of Black congressional representatives increased from four to seventeen, but the Republicans also picked up nine new seats as well (Lublin, 1994).[11] These GOP victories occurred only in the states where the Democrats did not have firm control of the remapping process; in the states that ratified Democratic-proposed plans, the GOP made no gains (Lublin, 1994). These GOP victories came at a price. Bush narrowly lost to Clinton in those states such as Georgia where new Black districts had been drawn and where the turnout among Blacks had been markedly higher than in 1988 (Meacham,

1993). But African Americans may have paid a price as well: because the Republicans had a net gain of ten seats in the House, the GOP victories have increased the overall conservatism of the House. These gains will likely diminish the overall prospects for congressional support of African American–backed legislation (Lublin, 1994).

Georgia, Louisiana, Maryland, and Texas added additional majority-Black districts in the 1990 remapping process. Georgia, having created its first majority-Black district after the 1980 census, in which the former civil rights activist John Lewis was elected in 1982, created two additional majority-Black districts, in which Blacks were elected. One of these new districts, located in the southwestern part of the state, is only 50 percent Black. In this district Sanford Bishop, a Black state senator, defeated incumbent representative Charles Hatcher in the runoff by 53 to 47 percent. Black suburbanization during the 1980s prompted the creation of a second majority-Black congressional seat in Maryland.

The 1992 elections increased Black representation in the House by 50 percent—from 26 to 39. Black legislators now constitute nearly 15 percent of the Democratic legislators in the House. Currently, African Americans also chair three of the House's 23 committees (the Armed Services, Government Operations, and Post Office and Civil Service Committees) and 14 of its 117 subcommittees. In addition, Black House members are poised to take over the ultra-important Ways and Means Committee and Judiciary Committee in the coming years.[12] With all but three of the 16 new Black House legislators having won in the South, some analysts speculate that this change may minimize the overarching liberal character of the Congressional Black Caucus (CBC). Whether this happens or not, members of the CBC have not modified their desire to remain the chief lobbying group for African Americans at large. Maryland's representative Kweisi Mfume's election as the CBC's chairman symbolizes the new readiness of the CBC to flex its larger political muscles, since Mfume has remarked on a number of occasions his willingness to block Clinton-sponsored legislation that is perceived by the organization as contrary to Blacks' collective interests. While this is a critical issue, it is too soon to predict what impact, if any, this expansion in Black legislative power will have on the new Democratic administration.

Toward this end, however, Black leaders at the national level have undertaken new efforts at fostering greater organizational unity. As discussed in Chapter 8, the serious ideological divisions among Black leaders that had emerged during the last years of the civil rights struggle were not resolved in the 1980s. Moreover, new divisions arose over Jesse Jackson's entry into presidential politics in 1984 (Reed, 1986). In September of 1993 the NAACP and CBC, under their new leadership by Benjamin Chavis and Kweisi Mfume, announced their plans to work with other national Black leaders, including Jesse Jackson and Louis Farrakhan of the Nation of Islam, to promote programs that would aid Blacks. In particular, Black leaders sought to address the spiraling murder rate of inner-city Black males. This new united effort, however, has already been undermined by an incident involving the Nation of Islam. In a November 1993 speech at Kean College in New Jersey, Khalid Abdul Muhammad, a senior aide of Louis Farrakhan, gave a bigoted speech directed against Catholics, Whites, and Jews. The speech revived the longstanding conflict between the Black Muslim leader and Jewish organizations; the Anti-Defamation League of the B'nai B'rith took out a full-page ad in the *New York Times* calling attention to the speech. CBC members, Jackson, and other Black leaders quickly denounced the speech, but Farrakhan initially did not. Although Farrakhan has since fired this aide, the incident in renewing Whites' suspicions of the Nation of Islam has jeopardized the efforts by Black leaders to work together with the controversial Black Muslim organization. Organizational unity may be difficult to achieve, and not only because of the problem of anti-Semitism within the Nation of Islam. The CBC, NAACP, CORE, and SCLC had all taken different positions on the matter of Clarence Thomas's confirmation to the Supreme Court (Pinderhughes, 1992; Marable, 1992). Unity among the national Black political organizations may prove to be elusive given their differences in ideology and the existing potential for their interests to clash. But unity is essential if these organizations hope to enhance their effectiveness as lobbying agencies for African Americans.

African Americans' record political gains in 1992 come at a time when the principal mechanism for increasing Black officeholding— federal enforcement of the Voting Rights Act—has come under attack by both conservatives and the courts. Since the Democratic party's crushing defeat in the 1984 presidential election, conservative party members have alleged that the party's embrace of Blacks' racial and civil rights agenda has caused moderate Whites to abandon the party (see Edsall and Edsall, 1991). At the center of this intra-party debate is not only Blacks' advocacy of affirmative action initiatives to ameliorate racial inequality, but their support of the Voting Rights Act. For critics such as Abigail Thernstrom (1987), the Voting Rights Act is no longer an instrument to restore voting rights to Southern Blacks, but in its 1982 extension became a "quota mechanism" for Blacks, "mandating" that districts be drawn to "guarantee" the election of a Black.[13]

The controversy over the Voting Rights Act came to a head when, in June 1993, the President, voicing agreement with her critics, withdrew his nomination of Lani Guinier, a Black law professor, to head the Civil Rights Division of the Justice Department. Although the President has since nominated another African American with strong voting rights credentials to fill the Justice Department's civil rights post,[14] the storm over Lani Guinier remains significant because it reveals the depth of the rift between Black liberals and White moderates within the Democratic party over the Voting Rights Act. Guinier's nomination was objected to by a number of prominent Democrats on both ideological and political grounds. Those hostile to Guinier portrayed her as a "radical," even "anti-democratic." Formerly a voting rights lawyer, Guinier had written several articles in which she advocated alternative voting schemes, such as cumulative voting, and restructuring electoral laws in ways that would compel White legislative majorities to take into account the interests of the Black minority. Guinier's main critics, in fact, in having labeled her a "quota queen," had wrongly characterized her views as favoring a route that would lead to further expansion of majority-Black voting districts.[15] While Guinier did not oppose the Voting Rights Act, she argued that as the only road toward Black political empowerment, it was severely limited.

What infuriated Guinier's Black supporters was that after she had been savagely attacked and mischaracterized by her opponents in the media, the President withdrew her nomination before giving her the chance to defend herself and her views before the Senate. Guinier's experience, as some have observed, was not unlike the experience of minority plaintiffs she had defended in voting rights suits, instances in which the racial minority in a given jurisdiction had been silenced and excluded in what was ostensibly an open, democratic system. In addition to provoking an angry reaction from Black House legislators and other prominent Black leaders, the President's desertion of Guinier left many Black voters feeling betrayed. According to a survey conducted by the Gallup Organization of 322 Blacks, more than half (55 percent) of those surveyed disapproved of Clinton's decision to drop Guinier in comparison to only 31 percent of Whites. About one-quarter of Blacks in this survey approved of her withdrawal, in contrast to 48 percent of Whites.[16] Moreover, her "dis-appointment," as Guinier now refers to the President's withdrawal of her nomination (Russakoff, 1993), caused the President's approval ratings among Blacks to drop. Clinton's approval rating in June fell fourteen points to 61 from 75 percent in May.

Shortly after the controversy over Guinier, the Supreme Court ruled narrowly by a 5 to 4 margin that North Carolina's new congressional redistricting plan constituted a racial gerrymander and violated the constitutional rights of the White plaintiffs who had objected to it. In *Shaw v. Reno*, writing for the majority, Justice Sandra Day O'Connor maintained that the plan, which resembled in her words "the most egregious racial gerrymanders of the past," violated the constitutional right of all voters to participate in a "color-blind process." The district, connecting Black populations in Charlotte and Durham, was 160 miles long, intersected other districts, and had the width of the state's I-85 highway at some points. O'Connor argued that redistricting plans such as North Carolina's could "balkanize" American politics "into competing racial factions," and were, therefore, unconstitutional even when "done for remedial purposes." The Court's *Shaw* decision comes at a time when the potential for creating additional majority-Black congressional districts is practically exhausted—existing at this point, perhaps, in two states alone (Pennsylvania and New York).[17]

*Shaw v. Reno* did not explicitly claim racial gerrymandering under the Voting Rights Act to be unconstitutional, as conservative critics had hoped. Thus the ideological controversy surrounding the Voting Rights Act remains wholly unresolved, as does the debate over results-oriented affirmative action policies more broadly. Although the Supreme Court did not object to the creation of majority-Black or majority-minority districts, the decision is likely to result in the invalidation of the new maps that led to the record gains by African Americans in 1992 in the House elections. The ruling has clearly introduced new uncertainty as to the electoral fate of Eva Clayton and Mel Watt, who, having won in the two new majority-minority districts, became the first Blacks elected in North Carolina since the end of Reconstruction.[18] Moreover, lower courts' interpretations of *Shaw* could go further in objecting to the designation of minority districts altogether, as did a federal court decision, *Hays v. Louisiana,* that invalidated Louisiana's plan. Ruling that the plan was now "null and void," the three-judge panel stated that Louisiana was not obligated under the Voting Rights Act's Section 2 to draw a second Black district that was not geographically compact. There are also court challenges pending for other newly constructed Black districts in the South, including those in Florida, Georgia, and Texas. In fact, the challenged new Black districts in Georgia and Florida, over 200 miles long, stretch well beyond North Carolina's unconstitutionally gerrymandered 12th district.

While the majority decision in *Shaw v. Reno* corresponds to a deeply felt public longing for the "de-racialization" of American politics, it may also unintentionally deepen the rancorous political battles that have emerged between Blacks and Democratic state legislators in the redistricting process. State legislators drew the oddly shaped Black-and-Native-American seat in North Carolina not simply to win preclearance from the Justice Department, but to preserve the seats of their White Democratic incumbents.[19] Toward that end, the Democrats in North Carolina (and in Texas) were remarkably successful, while their counterparts in Georgia were not. Not only did the number of GOP-held districts remain unchanged in the states where Democratic gerrymanders were put in place, but in North Carolina's case, in addition to electing two new Black House members, the plan allowed the Democrats to win the additional seat that the state had gained because of population growth. New computer technology has enabled state legislators to better protect their incumbents while carving out new—albeit oddly shaped—majority-Black districts. The *Shaw* decision, however, in prohibiting "creative cartography," will undoubtedly limit the Democrats' use of such technology to keep their White incumbents safe and increase Black representation at the same time.

Future decisions by the courts on minority voting rights following *Shaw* are likely to reduce the number of Black legislators in Congress. However, because Black state legislators today play a more central role in the redistricting process, it is doubtful that the 1992 political gains of Blacks will be severely rolled back as a result of *Shaw,* as many liberals fear. Some of the new Black House members won in districts that they drew as state legislators. Eddie Bernice Johnson, for example, chaired the redistricting subcommittee in Texas as a second-term state senator, winning an astonishing 92 percent of the vote in her primary. Cleo Fields, whose Z-shaped district was successfully challenged by White plaintiffs in federal court, also chaired his state's redistricting committee. These Black legislators are likely to fight for the maintenance of Black districts. But if the Democratic party, in striving to meet the murky new "bizarreness" standard set forth in *Shaw,* favors incumbency over increasing minority representation, the temporary odd-couple alliances between Black state legislators and state GOP leaders on redistricting matters are likely to flourish. In the immediate future, the Republicans will be the chief beneficiaries of *Shaw.*

While centrists may have welcomed *Shaw* as signaling an end to an era of "racial spoils system" for Blacks, Black representation will remain a critical issue within the Democratic party for some time to come. As the 1990s unfold, the demand for representation within the Democratic party is likely to intensify. In addition to the more powerful role played by Blacks within the party, there have been other changes taking place that have substantially transformed the party. Latinos have become increasingly more influential within the Democratic party's rank. The percentage of Democratic identifiers who are Latinos doubled from 5 percent in 1980 to 10 percent by 1992 (Stanley and Niemi, 1994). Given that Latinos are likely to surpass African Americans in population growth to become the largest minority group in the United States, it is likely that this group will press the party for greater influence and representation (Hero, 1992). Since the 1970s, the Democratic party also gained a decisive advantage over the GOP in the recruitment of women voters

(Stanley and Niemi, 1994); they, too, are likely to press the party for increased numerical representation.

During his first year in office, President Clinton has installed a record number of Blacks in his administration—this despite having served as chair of the Democratic Leadership Council when it adopted a resolution denouncing the use of racial and gender quotas (Kelly, 1993). Of the 21 cabinet posts, five went to African Americans, while it is estimated that about 12 percent of the subcabinet posts went to Blacks. Nowhere is Clinton's diversity pledge more evident than in his selection of federal judges during his first year in office. One journalist found that "only 18 of Clinton's 48 nominees [were] white men. Carter during his first year nominated 30 white men out of 34; Ronald Reagan picked 41 out of 45, and Bush 17 of 23. Clinton's 11 African American nominees so far represent three more than Reagan nominated *during his eight years in office*" (Marcus, 1994; emphasis added).

## Conclusions

Clinton's popularity among Blacks remains exceptionally strong. Although he earned a rather low overall public approval rating for his first year in office relative to past presidents, Blacks' approval rating for Clinton, nevertheless, averaged around 74 percent compared to the national average of 49 percent (Bowman and Ladd, 1994). As a "new Democrat," Clinton's extraordinary popularity with African Americans is only possible given two recent developments in Black politics. First, as Blacks' policy agenda has continued its shift away from civil rights concerns to social welfare issues, they have advocated instead greater efforts by the national government toward improving the economy. In addition, although unemployment remains for many Blacks a more important issue than discrimination or crime, nevertheless crime has become more politically salient within the Black community today. Reflected in Black public opinion, this shift is also evident in the statements made by national Black leaders, including Jesse Jackson. In calling Black-on-Black crime the number one civil rights issue confronting Black America today, Jackson has redirected the focus away from his earlier agenda of racial justice.

President Clinton has seized on Jackson's new agenda. In a November 1993 speech given to a conference of Black ministers of the Church of God in Christ held in Memphis, the President called on Blacks to take greater responsibility for solving such pressing social problems as lawlessness, the dissolution of the Black family, and the welfare dependency that often accompanies it. While emphasizing that he would work with Congress to enact appropriate legislation, he warned that government alone could not conquer the multitude of social ills confronting Black America today. Thus far, this message of greater self-reliance has been positively received by most Blacks. Although the more liberal Blacks have greeted the President's new rhetoric skeptically, many others have responded more favorably. Blacks welcome the new level of attention given by the President to their community's victimization by America's crime problem. Moreover, this de-emphasis on government comes at a time when the ranks of those disappointed by more than a generation of Black elected leadership have increased. Growing numbers of African Americans no longer express confidence in the government's ability to improve economic and social conditions in their community. Nowhere has this pessimistic view of government taken greater hold than in America's urban centers. In Washington, D.C., a city with one of the nation's highest per capita murder rates but without the financial base to hire additional police officers, Mayor Sharon Pratt Kelly made an appeal to President Clinton to send in the national guard to help fight the city's crime. The 1992 riot in Los Angeles provoked by the failure of an all-White jury to convict four White police officers who had been videotaped savagely beating a Black suspect, Rodney King, has become the new symbol of the general powerlessness of Black mayors to effect change. Limited by the city's governing charter, the Black mayor of Los Angeles, Tom Bradley, had been unable to promptly fire L.A.'s police chief, which might have lessened some of the Black community's outrage over the verdict and possibly averted the riot that followed.

In fact, further erosion in Blacks' feelings of external political efficacy or optimism could become a new and grave crisis in Black politics. While the message of greater Black self-reliance is hardly new, it comes at a time when Blacks' level of political influence has expanded and when the national policymaking environment is more favorable to Black interests. Thus it is not at all clear whether this message will, in fact, motivate more Blacks to take greater responsibility for the community's problems and work collectively toward solving them, or, conversely, increase the ranks of those in the community most cynical about government. In the end, only the policy record and responsiveness of the Clinton administration to Blacks' interests will determine whether their faith in government and the political process will rebound or continue to spiral downward.

In formulating a domestic agenda that focuses on health insurance, welfare reform, and crime, President Clinton has the capacity to affirm Blacks' faith in government as well as strengthen the already remarkably high level of support shown to his party by Blacks. First, empirical evidence indicates that the Democrats' social welfare agenda is perhaps the party's most salient political feature among African Americans; this agenda, in addition to the party's record on race, explains their high rates of attachment to the party. The passage of new and significant social welfare legislation would likely reaffirm and solidify Blacks' Democratic loyalties. Second, Clinton can amplify the party's appeal to Blacks without undermining its standing among Whites. Health insurance, welfare reform, and crime are all issues on which there is a consensus in both communities. Blacks and Whites express near-identical views in their desire for government to take a more active role in providing health insurance, reforming the welfare system, and combating crime. Finally, even though Blacks as a group are disproportionately affected by such policies relative to Whites, these issues do not necessarily invoke the divisive issue of race. Thus, if President Clinton is successful in pushing his domestic agenda through Congress, he will have reaffirmed the primary basis that explains the high level of Black identification with the Democratic party without losing White support. If, however, the President is unsuccessful, then while most Blacks will continue to vote Democratic lacking other alternatives, increasing numbers of Blacks will exercise their last-resort strategy of "exit," voting for neither party. In such a scenario, the racial gap in voter participation that has been increasing since 1988, rather than decreasing, as had been the trend since 1968, is likely to rise further through the 1990s.

Appendixes · Notes
References · Index

# The National Black Election Study

The data utilized in this study are from a longitudinal telephone study of Black political attitudes and electoral behavior conducted during the 1984 and 1988 national elections. The study was
conducted by the Program for Research on Black Americans, the
Institute for Social Research, University of Michigan. The 1984 pre-
election interviews were conducted from late July through November 6, 1984, while reinterviews followed immediately after the election. The 1988 pre-election reinterviews were held in August
through November 8, 1988, while reinterviews began after the election. A total of 1,150 voting-age Black voters was obtained in the
first wave, 872 in the second wave, 473 in the third wave, and 418
in the fourth and final wave.

The 1984–1988 NBES is, in many respects, unique. First and
foremost, the sample size is sufficiently large to accommodate sys-
tematic and robust analysis techniques. Past political studies of
Black Americans have tended to rely on samples containing typically 200 to 250 Blacks. Oversamples, that is, attempts to interview
more than the 10 to 12 percent proportion of Blacks found in a
given survey, have been infrequent. The usefulness of these
oversamples has been limited by the fact that they do not very often
contain questions of special relevance to the Black community. The
Harris Polling Organization was the first research organization to
conduct a national sample of Blacks in the 1960s. Since then, there
have been only a handful of high-quality national samples of Black

Americans comparable to the National Black Election Study. (See Smith, 1987.)

Because the NBES is also a panel study, it permits unique glimpses into the nature of change and continuity within the Black electorate over a four-year period. Specifically, shifts in Blacks' support for the Democratic party, participation rates, and candidate evaluations during the 1984–1988 period can now be ascertained. Furthermore, because NBES is a survey of Black Americans, it contains items of special relevance to the Black community such as measures of race awareness and identification, attitudes toward Jesse Jackson, and a host of other Black-oriented questions.

Data from the 1984 and 1988 National Election Studies, a cross-sectional, face-to-face survey of voting-eligible Americans, are also utilized so that comparisons can be made between Blacks and Whites. The 1984–1988 National Black Election Study's questionnaire formats were modeled after the National Election Study, and NBES replicated many of the standard political items carried in the 1984 and 1988 National Election Studies. Major differences between the two studies include the survey mode (NES is a national face-to-face study, while NBES is a national telephone survey) and the sampling frame (NES is based on an equal probability multistage or cluster design, while NBES is based on a disproportionate probability Random Digit Dial design [see Kish, 1965]). Finally, NES contains interviews with a cross-section of voting-eligible Americans, while NBES has interviews with voting-eligible Black Americans.

## The Original 1984 Study: Waves 1 and 2

Because results from a pilot study in 1983 revealed that the number of working numbers for Black households would be too low and thus costly in an equal probability design (Inglis, Groves, and Heeringa, 1987), the sample for the first wave of the National Black Election Panel Study was derived using a disproportionate Random Digit Dial design. In this design, all telephone exchanges in the United States were assigned to one of three "Black Household Density" strata. These strata were as follows:

1. High Black Density: exchanges in all large Standard Metropolitan Statistical Areas (SMSAs) with Black density of 15 percent or more.

2. Medium Black Density: exchanges in small SMSAs and non-SMSAs in Alabama, Florida, Georgia, Louisiana, Mississippi, North Carolina, South Carolina, and Virginia.
3. Low Black Density: all remaining exchanges.

The selection rate for the high-density stratum was three times that for the low-density stratum. The rate for the medium-density stratum was twice that of the low-density stratum. Given the non-equal probability design, the 1984 samples require weighting. The appropriate weight is equal to the stratum number (that is, the weight for cases that originated in the first stratum is "1," and so on).

All working numbers of households with at least one Black occupant were eligible. Two hundred secondary numbers were generated from each eligible primary. The overall Waksberg cluster size was 7.5 and included the primary. The racial composition of the household was determined by a direct question about race in the screening instrument. The household informant was asked: "Would you mind telling me your race? Are you White, Black, American Indian, or Alaskan Native, Asian, or Pacific Islander?" The informant was then asked the race of each household member.

Members of eligible households found in the screening of the secondaries were eligible for the study if they were Black American (or a self-identified member of another Black ethnic group and a naturalized citizen), and would be at least eighteen by election day. Respondents were selected randomly from all eligible persons within the household (Kish, 1965). The overall response rate in the first wave (1984 pre-election study) was 57 percent. The rate is comparable to other surveys conducted by the Survey Research Center during the same period. The study most similar to the NBES was the 1984 National Election Study Continuous Monitoring telephone survey. That survey's final response rate was 62 percent. The response rate for the regular face-to-face National Election pre-election survey was 71 percent. The response rate for the second wave of the 1984 NBES post-election survey was 76 percent.

## The 1988 Reinterview: Waves 3 and 4

Because the original survey was not intended to be a longitudinal study, more than half of the original 1984 pre-election study respondents were lost in the 1988 reinterview. Most of the nonrespondents had no forwarding numbers, or had nonworking numbers; a few respondents were lost because of death or illness.

Interviewers attempted to contact respondents first by calling persons named as contact persons during the 1984 study. When that failed, a few respondents were contacted by calling the information operator. Because the 1988 interview was done using a computer-assisted telephone interviewing system (CATI), before the interview began the respondent's race, gender, and age were checked to verify that the person being interviewed was in fact the original 1984 respondent. The 1988 screening also included the following question: "Do you remember being interviewed around the time of the 1984 presidential election?" Interviews were immediately terminated if the respondent, most of whom interviewers were able to identify by name, was not Black. Cases with discrepant ages or gender were eliminated in the process of merging the 1984 and 1988 data sets.

The response rate for those contacted was generally high. The percentage of refusals in the third wave was 22 percent, and also 22 percent for the fourth wave.

## Methodological Issues

Because they exclude people without telephones, telephone surveys usually obtain respondents with a higher than average national socioeconomic profile. People without telephones tend to have lower incomes and are more likely to reside in the South (see Gurin, Hatchett, and Jackson, 1989 for further discussion of these issues). When NBES respondents were compared with data from the 1980 U.S. Census, the NBES respondent in general was found to be better educated and slightly more affluent. Approximately 41 percent of the sample had obtained one or more years of college education, while it is estimated by the Census Bureau that 22 percent of the Black population had received some college training. Thirty-three percent of the sample reported incomes of less than $10,000, while 40 percent of the Black population was estimated to be in a similar income bracket. The effects of noncoverage differ for various statistics. But, in general, bias can be minimized by controlling for variables that are most affected by the survey mode or sampling frame (for example, educational attainment, region, gender). The weight variable used in the 1984 data set was not designed to compensate for noncoverage but rather was established to correct for the non-equal probability design as discussed above.

The noncoverage and nonresponse bias, however, was compounded in the 1988 surveys. In the 1988 pre-election survey, approximately 49 percent had attended one or more years of college, and only 15 percent of the sample reported incomes of less than $10,000. It is clear that wave nonresponse, that is, the high proportion of missing respondents in waves 3 and 4, resulted in a socioeconomically skewed sample.

To compensate for the effects of this type of bias found in panel studies, a new weight variable was created for the 1988 surveys. Essentially, the effects of wave nonresponse were minimized by placing more weight on the responses of those Blacks less likely to be interviewed in 1988 than those more likely to turn up in the 1988 survey. Because the characteristics of the nonrespondents in 1988 could be exactly determined, it was possible to weight more accurately subgroups that were more likely to be underrepresented in the 1988 reinterviews. Weighting was the preferred choice over imputation (that is, estimating missing values using complex statistical models) primarily because of its simplicity. In general, studies have found little difference in the effects of weighting versus imputation on cross-sectional analyses (Lepkowski, 1989). Furthermore, Lepkowski (1989) notes that weighting is preferred over imputation for longitudinal analyses.

The 1988 weight variable is a cell-based adjustment. Separate analyses were run on both the weighted version of the 1984 pre-election and the unweighted 1988 pre-election data sets. The data were stratified by the following four variables: region, educational attainment, age, and gender. Neither this weight nor the 1984 weight, however, compensates for noncoverage present in telephone surveys.

# Methodological Notes

## Structural Equation Model of Black Policy Attitudes

The policy models were estimated using the full information maximum likelihood procedures available in LISREL VI. The equation for the policy item is shown below:

Policy item = $\beta_3$race identification + $\beta_4$social class identification + $\beta_5$ideological self-identification + $\beta_6$party identification + $\gamma_3$income + $\gamma_4$education + $\gamma_5$age + $\gamma_6$gender + $\gamma_7$region + $\gamma_8$urbanicity + $\varepsilon_1$.

For full details about the development and estimation of this structural equation model, see Tate (1989). The identification of this model is difficult to establish empirically given the set of correlated equation errors. The various rules of identification (null-B, rank and order identification tests) do not apply. This model, however, passed the $t$-rule, which is a necessary, though insufficient, test of identification for all parameters. A method that is not one hundred percent reliable but reasonable is to compare the effects of the addition of two unknowns on the estimated values. LISREL VI will provide estimates for models that are underidentified, although such estimates are often bad, either not reflecting the possible range of values, or having large standard errors or negative error variances and covariances, etc. When such a procedure was carried out, none of the models yielded wildly different estimates or negative variables which would suggest that one or more of the models was underidentified (see Tate, 1989: Appendix C).

The unstandardized ML coefficients and goodness of fit indices are reported in Tables 2.6 and 2.7. The fit of the general model to the data for all the policy models obtained was generally poor. The average chi-square statistic obtained for each policy structural equation model was 62.05 with 31 degrees of freedom. The probability value associated with this chi-square statistic is less than .001. Modifications of the general model were tried, but no significant improvement in fit could be obtained for identifiable versions of the policy models. The poor fit could be due to a variety of factors, including general problems such as model misspecification or correlated measurement error. Since the submodel specifying the reciprocal relationship between race and class identification obtained a reasonably good fit (see Tate, 1989: chap. 4), the poor fit of many of the policy models is more likely the result of the low squared multiple correlations (SMCs) obtained for each policy model. The SMCs, comparable to $R^2$'s in regression analysis, ranged from .03 to .15. These low SMCs, in turn, most likely reflect the general skewness of the policy measures. Blacks' policy preferences on average are located on the far left of a left-right policy continuum. This problem can be corrected with the development of better policy measures—ones that extend the range of possible responses for the majority of Black Americans who fall in the far left region of most policy items.

Consequently, the assumption of normality on which the chi-square test is based may have been violated (Bentler and Chou, 1988; Hanushek and Jackson, 1977: 321–322). Although statistical tests based on data with small deviations from normality are generally sound (Hanushek and Jackson, 1977: 68), nonnormal measures require estimation procedures that are not widely available in most statistical software programs. Bentler and Chou note that simulation evidence thus far indicates that normal theory ML estimators are "almost always acceptable even when data are nonnormally distributed" (1988: 171–172). Therefore, if the policy variables are nonnormal, the chi-square test and standard errors are less reliable, but this problem does not necessarily affect the consistency of the ML estimates themselves.

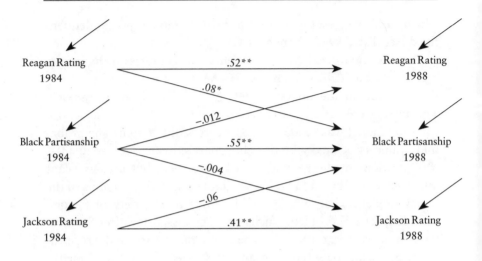

*p < .05; **p < .01

**Figure B.1**   Cross-Lagged Model of Jackson and Reagan Impact on Black
Partisanship, 1984–1988 (standardized WLS coefficients). *Note:* Not shown
are the exogenous variables (gender, region, age, and race identification) and
their pathways. (*Source:* 1984 NBES.)

## Structural Equation Model of Jackson Impact
## on Black Partisanship

To estimate the impact of Jesse Jackson's 1984 candidacy on Black
partisanship in 1988, a cross-lagged structural equation model was
developed using the 1984–1988 NBES panel data. Because negative
impressions toward Ronald Reagan also may have affected Black
partisanship in 1988, Reagan evaluations in both 1984 and 1988
were also included. A schematic depiction of this model, along with
the estimated beta coefficients, is shown in Figure B.1.

Estimation of the model was based on the number of complete
cases (380). Given the extent of Black identification with the Democratic party, Blacks' party identification is highly skewed. Output
from the PRELIS program in LISREL 7 revealed that Black partisanship is not only positively skewed, but also nonnormally distributed.
The skewness and kurtosis statistics reported in PRELIS are both
zero for a normal distribution. The skewness statistics for Blacks'

party identification in 1984 and 1988 were 1.8 and 2.0 respectively; the kurtosis statistics were 3.3 and 3.9, indicating severe kurtosis. Accordingly, the Weighted Least Squares (WLS) estimation procedure in LISREL 7 which allows for nonnormality was employed (see Bollen, 1989: 415–432). To control for spurious results, in both models the Jackson evaluation in 1984 is predicted by gender, racial identification, age, and region; party identification in 1984 is predicted by gender and age; and the Reagan evaluation in 1984 is predicted by gender.

Given the preliminary nature of the model, the fit obtained in its estimation, including the final model, was unacceptable. The chi-square statistic was 64.49 with 25 degrees of freedom. This statistically significant chi-square suggests that the implied covariance matrix is not an adequate representation of the data. The goodness of fit indices (.999), in contrast, imply that the model's fit is reasonably good. Moreover, impressions of Reagan and Jackson as well as partisanship among Blacks are relatively stable across the four-year period. The cross-lagged model confirms that Reagan, not Jackson, evaluations in 1984 are positively related to Black partisanship in 1988. In other words, those who rated Reagan more favorably in 1984 were more likely to identify with the Republican party in 1988. Given the slight movement away from the Republican party and political independence in this four-year period, it appears that negative affect toward Reagan in 1984 increased Black support for the Democratic party in 1988. Jackson, in contrast, had no lagged effect on Black partisanship in 1988. Nor did Black partisanship in 1984 have any impact on the two candidate ratings. However, given the lack of fit of the implied covariance structure to the data, these results should be viewed as merely suggestive.

## The Effect of Education on Black Political Participation

Political interest, partisanship, and, to a lesser extent, system responsiveness were shown to be important determinants of Black electoral participation in Chapter 4. Political trust, in contrast, was not related to Black voter participation and campaign activism in 1984. Table B.1 displays the results of the regression of these variables on gender, age, education, family income, region, home ownership, and urban-

**Table B.1** Demographic Determinants of Civic Attitudes, Political Interest, and Partisanship among Blacks (OLS coefficients)

| Independent Variables | System Responsiveness | | Political Trust | | Political Interest | | Partisanship | |
|---|---|---|---|---|---|---|---|---|
| | B | (SE) | B | (SE) | B | (SE) | B | (SE) |
| Constant | 1.85** | (.26) | 2.46** | (.22) | -4.53** | (.29) | .54** | (.17) |
| Gender (female) | -.05 | (.08) | -.10 | (.07) | -.23* | (.09) | .14* | (.06) |
| Age | -.002 | (.003) | .002 | (.002) | .02** | (.003) | .01** | (.002) |
| Education | .07** | (.02) | -.00 | (.01) | .09** | (.02) | .01 | (.01) |
| Family income | .04** | (.01) | -.02 | (.01) | .01 | (.02) | .00 | (.01) |
| Region (non-South) | -.11 | (.08) | -.21* | (.07) | -.07 | (.09) | -.07 | (.06) |
| Homeowner (yes) | -.01 | (.09) | -.11 | (.08) | .26* | (.10) | .11 | (.06) |
| Urbanicity (low-high) | .06* | (.03) | -.00 | (.03) | .04 | (.03) | .01 | (.02) |
| Total cases | 924 | | 923 | | 962 | | 959 | |
| $R^2$ | .07 | | .02 | | .09 | | .05 | |

*Source:* The 1984 National Black Election Study.

$*p < .05; **p < .01.$

icity. System responsiveness is a mean sum index of the following three Likert-scaled items: (1) "People like me have no say in government"; (2) "Public officials don't care"; and (3) "White officials always get their way." Political trust is a mean sum index of responses to two questions: (1) "How much of the time do you think you can trust government to do the right thing?" and (2) "Would you say government is pretty much run by a few big interests? . . . Or is it run for the benefit of all the people?" This indicator is scaled from low to high trust. The measure of political interest is standard; Blacks were asked, "Would you say that you have been very much interested, somewhat interested, or not much interested in the political campaigns so far this year?" Finally, partisanship is a categorical variable having three levels: (1) no party affiliation (independent) or other party affiliation; (2) weak partisan of either major party; and (3) strong partisan of either major party.

This analysis reveals that college-educated and affluent Blacks were more likely to feel that the government is responsive to their political demands and interests than less-educated and poor Blacks. Highly educated Blacks were also more likely than less-educated Blacks to express stronger interest in the 1984 political campaigns. Homeowners were also more likely to be more interested in the campaigns under way than renters. Black women had higher levels of political interest and were more likely to be stronger partisans than Black men. Finally, Blacks living outside the South were less trusting of government and government officials than those living in the South, but Blacks in rural areas were more likely to feel that the government is less responsive to their political needs than Blacks in urban areas.

Because many of the demographic variables related to Black electoral participation are also related to Black political and civic attitudes, another picture emerges if these attitudinal variables are dropped from the analysis of Black electoral participation and only the demographic variables are included, as shown in Table B.2. Many of the demographic variables which were not significantly related to Black political participation are now strongly related to these measures of participation. Education in particular, which was not significantly related to Black electoral participation when the attitudinal variables were present, is now an important determinant

**Table B.2** Demographic Determinants of Black Electoral Participation Only

| Independent Variables | Logit Coefficients | | | | OLS Coefficients | | | |
|---|---|---|---|---|---|---|---|---|
| | Registered to Vote | | Voted for President | | Voter Type Scale | | Campaign Activism | |
| | B | (SE) | B | (SE) | B | (SE) | B | (SE) |
| Constant | -2.24 | (.92) | -2.11** | (.62) | -2.69** | (.15) | -.68** | (.26) |
| Gender (female) | .67* | (.26) | .17 | (.19) | .04 | (.05) | -.18* | (.09) |
| Age | .05** | (.01) | .03** | (.01) | .01** | (.001) | .01* | (.003) |
| Education | .17** | (.06) | .15** | (.04) | .04** | (.01) | .09** | (.02) |
| Family income | .07 | (.05) | .03 | (.03) | .02** | (.01) | .04** | (.01) |
| Region (non-South) | .19 | (.27) | -.16 | (.19) | .03 | (.05) | .13 | (.09) |
| Homeowner (yes) | .45 | (.31) | .46* | (.21) | .17** | (.05) | .32 | (.09) |
| Urbanicity (low-high) | -.08 | (.10) | .00 | (.07) | .02 | (.02) | .00 | (.03) |
| Log likelihood | -214.12 | | -373.77 | | — | | — | |
| Predicted correctly | 90% | | 78% | | — | | — | |
| Total cases | 751 | | 751 | | 728 | | 745 | |
| $R^2$ | — | | — | | .12 | | .13 | |

*Source:* The 1984 National Black Election Study.

$*p < .05$; $**p < .01$.

of all four voting measures. Family income and home ownership are also significantly related to voter type and campaign activism in this analysis. Thus, because educated Blacks, most specifically, are more likely to express greater interest in politics and to feel that the political system is responsive (and for that matter, are more likely to be strong race-identifiers and members of Black organizations and politically active churches, as other analyses in this book show) than less educated Blacks, the total effect of education is underestimated in Chapter 4. Education, in fact, is a very important individual-level determinant of Black political participation.

# Notes

## 1. The New Black Politics

1. Current Population Report, Series P-20, No. 435, U.S. Bureau of the Census, February 1989. The Census Bureau estimates that 44 percent of Blacks were registered to vote in the South in 1964, but the 1964 estimate includes Blacks and other minority groups in the South. Lawson (1985) reports that only 31 percent of Blacks in the South were registered to vote in 1965.
2. The reapportioning and redistricting taking place now could create new Black-majority congressional districts, however, and it is unclear if Blacks will be elected in these new districts.
3. See Cavanagh and Foster (1984), Barker and Walters (1989), and Morris (1990) for more information on Jackson's 1984 campaign for president.

## 2. Race, Class, and Black Policy Views

1. The Pearson correlation between common-fate racial identification and Blacks' relative influence and power is .23; the correlation between race identification and the economic position of Blacks versus Whites is .14.
2. The results are not presented here, but can be found in Tate (1989). This finding contrasts with the results of Jackman and Jackman (1983), who found that socioeconomic status was not related to social class identification among Blacks. The differences in result obtained from the NBES data set and the Jackmans' data set may reflect the quality of the samples. The NBES data set has over five times as many Black respondents as the data set that the Jackmans employ. Although the Jackmans' study was conducted in the 1970s, while the NBES data

were collected in the mid-1980s, there is no reason to suppose that social class has become more meaningful to Blacks over the past ten years. Sociological studies have established that Blacks have historically distinguished among themselves by class (Frazier, 1957; Kilson, 1983).

3. Vanneman and Cannon (1987) dispute Jackman and Jackman's (1983) contention that higher-status Blacks are more likely to identify with the working class because of expressed preference for their racial group. They maintain that the working-class identities of professional Blacks are more likely due to their families' working-class origins and to the fact that a professional Black may be less secure about his or her position than a White in a comparable position. These factors undoubtedly explain some of the reasons why higher-status Blacks are more likely to identify themselves as working class. However, in Tate (1989), I found that race identification among Blacks had a strong and direct effect on their social class identifications, such that strong race identifiers were more likely to identify with the poor and working classes, as the Jackmans suggest.

4. This question was asked using a slightly different format from the one found in the National Election Study and used to generate Figure 2.4. The NBES item is a branching version and represents an improvement over the seven-point NES version. The differences between the two are the following. First, the seven-point version has an explicit filter ("haven't you thought much about it") to exclude those who are unfamiliar with the terms "liberal"/"conservative." Second, the end points of the seven-point version are labeled "extremely liberal" and "extremely conservative," while the ends of the branching version are "strong liberal" and "strong conservative." Finally, the midpoint of the seven-point version is "middle of the road," while the branching midpoint is "moderate." The wording differences generate different distributions of liberals and conservatives, with the seven-point version having a higher percentage of moderates and missing responses.

5. Alternatively, some responses that were considered unintelligible, and thus considered a nonresponse, in actuality may have been meaningful. The scheme used to code the content of this open-ended question was originally developed by researchers interested in detecting ideological reasoning in the American electorate. Analyzing the current data using this borrowed and dated coding scheme may have inflated the number of uncodable responses because of the absence of applicable codes.

### 3. Blacks and the Democratic Party

1. As suggested by Schneider and Lewis, a race identification by ideological identification interaction term was also tested, but had no independent effect on Black partisanship in 1984.

2. This is contrary to what I had reported earlier in Tate (1990). Perhaps because of the addition and deletion of cases in the latter stages of data cleaning, Jackson's lagged impact on Black partisanship in 1988 was no longer statistically significant.

3. The quotation is taken from Germond and Witcover. According to these authors, Brazile was later fired from the Dukakis campaign for her remarks on this matter (1989: 451).

## 4. Group Resources and Black Electoral Participation

1. The National Survey of Black Americans, 1979–1980, available through the Inter-university Consortium for Political and Social Research, Ann Arbor, Michigan.

2. Voter validation is a procedure that compares and corrects the reported behavior in voter surveys against voter registration lists. The Center for Political Studies' National Election Studies (NES) contain validated voting behavior measures. Analyzing NES data, Abramson and Claggett (1984) discovered that Black Americans were twice as likely to overreport their voting as White Americans. They write that Blacks may be more likely to misreport their voting than Whites because they "have struggled to gain the franchise, and it may be difficult for many to acknowledge that they failed to exercise it" (1984: 720). Abramson and Claggett, however, suggested in this article that the relationship between race and overreporting may be an artifact of the data. Blacks may be more likely to be misclassified as nonvoting voters. The total numbers of Blacks that fall in a given NES survey are small, and many of them reside in the South, where voter registration records are often poorly maintained. Nevertheless, in recent work (1992), Abramson and Claggett argue that Black overreporting is not the result of poor record keeping.

Although the problem inherent in self-reported measures of political behavior is well documented, most researchers still ignore the problem in their work because the validation process itself is extremely costly. (In 1988, in fact, an unsuccessful attempt to gather funds for such a project was made by this researcher.) Nevertheless, until a voter validation check using a large, national sample of Blacks is carried out, the actual extent of Black overreporting (relative to Whites) will remain unclear (see also Williams, 1987b, who takes a similar position on this issue).

3. The campaign activism scale is an additive index of the following four items: (1) Did you talk to people about the campaign, (2) go to candidate dinners/meetings/speeches, (3) register or take people to the polls, and (4) give or raise money for the candidate. Factor analysis using LISREL 7 revealed that a one-factor model best fit the data. The chi-

square statistic obtained was 1.54, with 2 degrees of freedom, and was nonsignificant. The lambda-$x$'s (standardized) ranged from .61 for talking to people about the campaign to .91 for attending dinners/meetings/speeches for the candidate.

4. Factor analysis using LISREL 7 revealed a two-factor solution for the five church-based activism items. The one-factor model yielded a statistically significant chi-square statistic of 50.55, with five degrees of freedom, while the two-factor model separating the church's informational function and campaign activism function yielded a much better fit. The chi-square statistic for the two-factor model was 3.27, with four degrees of freedom, having a probability level of .514.

5. "Baptists" were those who identified themselves as Baptists, while "Methodists" included those who belonged to Methodist and African Methodist Episcopal churches. "Pentecostal" denominations consisted of the following churches: Church of God or Holiness churches, Church of God in Christ, Pentecostal, Assembly of God, Church of Christ, Missionary Fundamentalist, Gospel Baptist, Sanctified, and all other fundamentalist churches. "Catholic and Episcopalian" churches included the Roman Catholic, Anglican, and Episcopalian churches. Finally, "Jehovah's Witness" were those who reported being Jehovah's Witnesses.

## 5. Black Turnout in the 1984 and 1988 Presidential Primaries and Elections

1. Because political trust and system responsiveness were not related to Black electoral participation, as shown in Chapter 4, they were not included in any of the models developed in this chapter.

2. Given that the NBES survey is a panel study, participation in 1984 was added as an additional control variable in the 1988 models; coefficients and standard errors for these variables, however, are not shown in the tables.

3. See Shirley Chisholm, *The Good Fight* (New York: Harper and Row, 1973).

4. In the reinterview four years later, however, 83 percent reported voting in the 1988 presidential election. The 1988 voter turnout estimate is substantially higher than the U.S. Census estimate in part because of survey attrition: respondents less likely to vote were lost. Furthermore, the high turnout may also be a reflection of the politicizing effect of the 1984 interview. These 1988 respondents may have registered and voted in higher numbers as a result of having participated in the 1984 interview.

5. This interview is from an article by Joel Dreyfuss that was published in the *New York Times Magazine*, January 20, 1991.

## 6. The Black Vote in 1984 and 1988

1. In the 1984–1988 NBES, slightly higher percentages (17 percent) of the nonvoters, however, expressed support for Reagan in 1984 and Bush in 1988. More than a quarter of the nonvoters in the study, however, reported favoring no one for president, and about half expressed support for Mondale in 1984 and Dukakis in 1988.
2. In the 1988 NBES reinterview of Blacks, Dukakis received a rating comparable to and no less positive than Mondale's in 1984. The 1988 NBES reinterview, however, is not a representative sample of Blacks and their opinions in 1988.
3. *The American Enterprise*, "American Opinion on the Gulf."
4. In the twentieth century, there have been four such successful challengers—Wilson in 1912, Roosevelt in 1932, and Carter in 1976, as well as Reagan in 1980.
5. Still, there was considerable friction between Jackson and Democratic party leaders who formed an organization outside the national party organization called the Democratic Leadership Council (DLC). This organization of 400 or so elected officials has been highly critical of the party's links to organized interests, such as labor, Blacks, and feminists, and critical, too, of the "traditional Democrats" who continue to maintain close ties to these groups, which they feel has undermined public support for Democrats in national races. In the spring of 1991, the DLC had sponsored a conference, inviting potential candidates in the 1992 race for president to speak. This list included Al Gore, Richard Gephardt, Bill Nunn, Paul Tsongas, and Doug Wilder. Jesse Jackson and George McGovern had not been invited. The DLC's president, Al From, explained the snub of Jackson as an attempt to change the party's image, which for the DLC was the root cause of its losses: "Jackson and McGovern represent the ideological approach to government we are trying to change" (*The New Republic*, May 20, 1991).
6. Ted Kennedy, however, did not nicely step aside in the 1980 Democratic presidential nominating contest that Jimmy Carter won; nor did Gary Hart voluntarily drop out in 1984.

## 7. Black Power and Electoral Politics

1. Other Black activists of this period offered a broader definition that focused on cultural as well as sociopolitical concepts. Amiri Baraka

(LeRoi Jones), for instance, maintained that an implicit part of a Black power strategy was a "program of Black consciousness"—a cultural movement at the grassroots level to promote understanding of Blacks' African origins and history.

2. Income might explain the different levels of support Keyes received; most Blacks in Prince George's county are affluent, while Blacks in Baltimore tend to be poor. Thus, Black Republicans might receive higher levels of support from the Black poor, who, as Table 7.2 reveals, are more inclined to vote for Black candidates regardless of political stripe.

3. Reynolds ultimately won against Savage in the 1992 Democratic primary election.

4. These programs have not been implemented, however, since the constitutionality of publicly funded schools for Black boys has been successfully challenged in federal court by the ACLU.

5. "Farrakhan Hits Moral Leadership," *Washington Post,* May 6, 1990, pp. D1, D11.


## 8. Black Electoral Politics and Beyond

1. For a critical assessment of the pluralist model in ethnic and racial group politics, see Dianne Pinderhughes (1987).

2. See Zald and Garner (1987), who contest the "inevitability" of this process.

3. Jackson may simply be unable to overcome past personal antagonisms between him and other notable members of the Black civil rights establishment, including Dr. King's widow, Coretta Scott King.

4. Black opinion shifted in favor of Thomas mainly because race concerns (brought up by Thomas's lynching remark) outweighed the gender issues of sexual harassment and sex discrimination (see Tate, 1992, and Mansbridge and Tate, 1992).

5. Linda Williams, a political scientist at the University of Maryland, introduced this idea in a talk given at the Department of Government, Harvard University, January 1991.

6. Calculated from the data collected by the Joint Center for Political Studies (1989), as presented in table 1.

7. At least one researcher in this area contends that the "deracialized approach to campaigning" by Black politicians today is not a new development (Perry, 1992: 223).

8. Leaders of the National Urban League have been calling for a domestic Marshall Plan for Blacks since at least 1962, when Whitney Young, Jr., then head of the National Urban League, first presented this idea (see Graham, 1990: 111).

9. The 1980 National Survey of Black Americans, University of Michigan, Ann Arbor, Michigan.

10. See Carole Pateman (1972) for a brilliant, now classic, analysis of the normative underpinnings of this debate.

## 9. A Show of Loyalty: Black Voters in the 1992 Elections

1. Before the 1992 nominating contest had begun in earnest, Clinton as governor of Arkansas had refused to commute the death sentence of Rickey Ray Rector, a mentally impaired Black convict, over the appeals and objections of a number of prominent Democrats opposed to the death penalty, including Jesse Jackson.

2. While few in the Black community would probably endorse the rapper's hateful statement, even with the implied context of the Los Angeles riot (and the Rodney King verdict that provoked it), many still felt that Clinton's castigation of Sister Souljah—and implied criticism of Jackson—was inappropriate and politically motivated.

3. I analyze Black voting behavior in the 1992 election using data from a number of sources. A data set comparable to the 1984 and 1988 National Black Election Studies, on which I based many of the conclusions contained in the book, did not exist in 1992.

4. In Tate (1994), I present the results of a confirmatory factor analysis of the six items using Lisrel 7. The results, while more suggestive than conclusive given the model's fit, indicate that the three social welfare items correspond to a general social welfare factor.

5. These figures were based on Times/CNN surveys conducted by Yankelovich Clancy Shulman, May 13–14, 1992. In light of the numbers reported in Table 2.3, this 20 percent figure indicates that many Whites have changed their opinion on welfare spending. During the early to mid-1980s, substantial numbers of White Americans supported President Reagan's effort to cut welfare payments. (See also Bobo and Smith, 1994.)

6. Only 2.5 percent of those Blacks interviewed in the 1992 National Election Study claimed to have voted for Perot.

7. I would like to thank Gregory Strizek for his prompt and thorough research assistance here. This data set is somewhat limited. Even though approximately 1,539 voters surveyed in the exit polling were African American, certain key political items, such as the respondent's political ideology and educational attainment, were asked of only 764 Black respondents. Moreover, only 82 in all of the Black respondents claimed to have voted for Perot. Finally, the data are also weighted to take into account the different probabilities of selection based on the sampling frame. Predominantly Black polling areas that were oversampled have a smaller weight.

8. Edward Brooke, a Black Republican, was elected to the Senate from Massachusetts in 1966. Until Braun's election, he was the only Black in this century to have served in the U.S. Senate.

9. For a complete analysis of Braun's historic victory, see Katherine Tate, "Twin Assets or Double Liabilities: Race, Gender, and the Senatorial Bid of Carol Moseley Braun," Center for American Politics, Harvard Occasional Paper, no. 93-7, Cambridge, Mass., 1993.

10. In addition, House representatives Dan Rostenkowski (Democrat) and Philip M. Crane (Republican) won with less than three-fifths of the vote in their bids for renomination.

11. Three of these nine GOP wins were due to political factors other than minority redistricting, according to Lublin (1994).

12. The reorganization that is currently taking place in the House could affect Black legislators' advancement there, jeopardizing their command over some of these posts.

13. There is, without a doubt, considerable irony in the new opposition to the Voting Rights Act, fueled as it is on the basis of its characterization as a special and unfair privilege for Blacks. Segregationists in the aftermath of the Civil War contested the use of federal force to ensure Black voting rights as a "special privilege" as well (see Condit and Lucaites, 1993: 199). Moreover, it was Ronald Reagan's designation of Blacks as just another "special interest" group that has given this new assault on the Voting Rights Act as another "affirmative action" policy extraordinary resonance.

14. At this time the President has nominated Deval Patrick, a Boston-based Black attorney, who had worked with Guinier on a number of voting rights cases. Patrick is the President's third nominee for this post.

15. See, for example, Clint Bolick, "Clinton's Quota Queens," *Wall Street Journal*, April 30, 1993, p. 12; also "Black-Majority Districts: A Bad Idea," by Carol Swain, *New York Times*, op-ed page, June 3, 1993.

16. These figures were taken from those reported in *USA Today*, June 8, 1993.

17. See the "Minority Report," by Dick Kirschten, *The National Journal*, January 30, 1993.

18. O'Connor's ruling remanded the plan back to the district court to determine if there might be any other compelling state justification to preserve the oddly-shaped district.

19. As Pildes and Niemi put it: "The North Carolina districting story would reveal the way in which politicians have come to use civil rights and the VRA as a screen; while going to Machiavellian lengths to protect their seats and pursue their partisan agendas, politicians claim, 'The Voting Rights Act made me do it'" (1993: 518).

*References to Chapter 9*

Bobo, Lawrence, and Ryan A. Smith. 1994. "Antipoverty Policy, Affirmative Action, and Racial Attitudes." In *Confronting Poverty: Prescriptions for Change,* ed. Sheldon H. Danziger, Gary D. Sandefur, and Daniel H. Weinberg. Cambridge, Mass.: Harvard University Press.

Bowman, Karlyn H., and Everett Carll Ladd. 1993a. "Reforming Welfare." *The Public Perspective,* vol. 4, no. 6 (September/October), p. 86. Roper Center for Public Opinion Research.

—— 1993b. "Health Care: The Public Reacts." *The Public Perspective,* vol. 5, no. 1 (November/December), p. 74. Roper Center for Public Opinion Research.

—— 1994. "President Clinton at Year One." *The Public Perspective,* vol. 5, no. 2 (January/February), p. 82. Roper Center for Public Opinion Research.

Brownstein, Ronald. 1994. "Clinton's 'New Democrat' Agenda Reopens Racial Divisions." *Los Angeles Times,* February 9, p. A5.

Condit, Celeste Michelle, and John Louis Lucaites. 1993. *Crafting Equality.* Chicago: University of Chicago Press.

Dionne, E. J., Jr. 1992. "In Poll, Blacks Defy Political Stereotyping." *Washington Post,* July 9, p. A10.

Edsall, Thomas, and Mary Edsall. 1991. *Chain Reaction.* New York: W. W. Norton.

Hero, Rodney E. 1992. *Latinos and the U.S. Political System.* Temple, Pa.: Temple University Press.

Hirschman, Albert O. 1970. *Exit, Voice, and Loyalty.* Cambridge, Mass.: Harvard University Press.

Kelly, Michael. 1993. "A Left Turn by Clinton? Centrists Feel Left Out." *New York Times,* May 23, 1993, p. 14.

Lublin, David Ian. 1994. "Gerrymander for Justice? The Impact of the Voting Rights Act on Black and Latino Representation." Dissertation in progress, Government Department, Harvard University.

Marable, Manning. 1992. "Clarence Thomas and the Crisis of Black Political Culture." In *Race-ing, Justice, En-gendering Power,* ed. Toni Morrison. New York: Pantheon Books.

Marcus, Ruth. 1994. "The Judiciary: Building Diversity in Lifetime Positions." *Washington Post,* January 16, p. A27.

Meacham, John. 1993. "Voting Wrongs: Racial Reapportionment." *Washington Monthly,* vol. 25, no. 3 (March), p. 28.

Pildes, Richard H., and Richard G. Niemi. 1993. "Expressive Harms, 'Bizarre Districts,' and Voting Rights: Evaluating Election-District Appearances after *Shaw v. Reno.*" *Michigan Law Review* 92 (3): 483–587.

Pinderhughes, Dianne. 1992. "Divisions in the Civil Rights Community." *PS* 25 (3): 485–487.

Pomper, Gerald. 1993. "The Presidential Election." In *The Election of 1992.* Chatham, N.J.: Chatham House.

Reed, Adolph, Jr. 1986. *The Jesse Jackson Phenomenon.* New Haven: Yale University Press.

Russakoff, Dale. 1993. "Lani Guinier, in Person." *The Washington Post's National Weekly Edition,* December 20–26, pp. 6–9.

Stanley, Harold W., and Richard G. Niemi. 1994. "Partisanship and Group Support, 1952–1992." Forthcoming in *Democracy's Feast: The 1992 Elections,* ed. Herbert F. Weisberg. Chatham, N.J.: Chatham House.

Tate, Katherine. 1993. "Twin Assets or Double Liabilities: Race, Gender, and the Senatorial Bid of Carol Moseley Braun." Center for American Politics, Occasional Paper no. 93-7, Harvard University.

——— 1994. "Structural Dependence or Group Loyalty? The Black Vote in 1992." Forthcoming in *Democracy's Feast: The 1992 Elections,* ed. Herbert F. Weisberg. Chatham, N.J.: Chatham House.

Thernstrom, Abigail. 1987. *Whose Votes Count?* Cambridge, Mass.: Harvard University Press.

# References

Abramson, Paul R. 1983. *Political Attitudes in America*. San Francisco: W. H. Freeman.

Abramson, Paul R., John H. Aldrich, and David W. Rohde. 1990. *Change and Continuity in the 1988 Elections*. Washington, D.C.: CQ Press.

Abramson, Paul R., and William Claggett. 1984. "Race-Related Differences in Self-Reported and Validated Turnout." *Journal of Politics* 46:719–738.

——— 1992. "The Quality of Record Keeping and Racial Differences in Validated Turnout." *Journal of Politics* 54 (August 1992).

Asher, Herbert C. 1988. *Presidential Elections and American Politics: Voters, Candidates, and Campaigns since 1952*. Homewood, Ill.: Dorsey Press.

Barker, Lucius J. 1989. *Our Time Has Come*. Urbana and Chicago: University of Illinois Press.

Barker, Lucius J., and Ronald W. Walters (eds.). 1989. *Jesse Jackson's 1984 Presidential Campaign*. Urbana and Chicago: University of Illinois Press.

Barnes, James A. 1990. "Into the Mainstream." *National Journal* 22 (5): 262–266.

Barnett, Marjorie Ross. 1982. "The Congressional Black Caucus: Illusions and Realities of Power." In *The New Black Politics*, ed. M. B. Preston, L. J. Henderson, Jr., and P. Puryear. New York: Longman.

Bartels, Larry M. 1988. *Presidential Primaries and the Dynamics of Public Choice*. Princeton: Princeton University Press.

Bass, Jack, and Walter DeVries. 1976. *The Transformation of Southern Politics*. New York: Basic Books.

Baxter, Sandra, and Majorie Lansing. 1983. *Women and Politics: The Visible Majority*. Ann Arbor: University of Michigan Press.

Bentler, P. M., and Chih-Ping Chou. 1988. "Structural Modeling." In *Common Problems/Proper Solutions: Avoiding Error in Quantitative Research,* ed. J. Scott Long. Beverly Hills: Sage Publications.

Bobo, Lawrence D., and Franklin D. Gilliam, Jr. 1990. "Race, Sociopolitical Participation and Black Empowerment." *American Political Science Review* 84 (2): 379–393.

Bollen, Kenneth A. 1989. *Structural Equations with Latent Variables.* New York: Wiley.

Brisbane, Robert. 1970. *The Black Vanguard.* Valley Forge, Pa.: Judson Press.

Brown, Ronald. 1984. "The Determinants of Black Political Participation." Ph.D. dissertation, University of Michigan.

Browning, Rufus P., Dale Rogers Marshall, and David H. Tabb. 1979. "Minorities and Urban Electoral Change: A Longitudinal Study." *Urban Affairs Quarterly* 15: 206–228.

——— 1984. *Protest Is Not Enough.* Los Angeles and Berkeley: University of California Press.

Bullock, Charles S., III. 1984. "Racial Crossover Voting and the Election of Black Officials." *Journal of Politics* 46: 238–251.

Bush, Rod. 1984. "Black Enfranchisement, Jesse Jackson, and Beyond." In *The New Black Vote,* ed. Rod Bush. San Francisco: Synthesis Publications, pp. 13–52.

Button, James W. 1978. *Black Violence.* Princeton: Princeton University Press.

——— 1989. *Blacks and Social Change.* Princeton: Princeton University Press.

Button, James W., and Richard Scher. 1984. "The Election and Impact of Black Officials in the South." In *Public Policy and Social Institutions,* ed. H. Rodgers. Greenwich, Conn.: JAI Press.

Campbell, Angus. 1960. "Surge and Decline: A Study of Electoral Change." *Public Opinion Quarterly* 24: 397–418.

Campbell, Angus, Phillip E. Converse, Warren E. Miller, and Donald E. Stokes. 1960. *The American Voter.* New York: John Wiley and Sons.

Carmichael, Stokely, and Charles V. Hamilton. 1967. *Black Power.* New York: Vintage Press.

Carmines, E. G., and James A. Stimson. 1989. *Issue Evolution.* Princeton: Princeton University Press.

Cavanagh, Thomas E. 1985. *Inside Black America: The Message in the 1984 Elections.* Washington, D.C.: Joint Center for Political Studies.

——— 1987. *Strategies for Mobilizing Black Voters: Four Case Studies.* Washington, D.C.: Joint Center for Political Studies.

Cavanagh, Thomas E., and Lorn S. Foster. 1984. *Jesse Jackson's Campaign: The Primaries and Caucuses.* Washington, D.C.: Joint Center for Political Studies.

Colasanto, Diane. 1989. "Public Wants Civil Rights for Some, Not for Others." *The Gallup Monthly*, No. 291.

Conover, Pamela, and Stanley Feldman. 1981. "The Origins and Meanings of Liberal/Conservative Self-Identifications." *American Journal of Political Science* 25: 617–645.

Converse, Philip E. 1964. "The Nature of Belief Systems in Mass Publics." In *Ideology and Discontent*, ed. D. E. Apter. New York: Free Press.

——— 1976. *The Dynamics of Party Support*. Beverly Hills: Sage Publications.

Cotton, Jeremiah. 1989. "Opening the Gap: The Decline in Black Economic Indicators in the 1980s." *Social Science Quarterly* 70 (4): 803–819.

Dahl, Robert. 1961. *Who Governs?* New Haven: Yale University Press.

Dillingham, Gerald. 1981. "The Emerging Black Middle Class: Class Consciousness or Race Consciousness?" *Ethnic and Racial Studies* 4: 432–447.

Downs, Anthony. 1957. *An Economic Theory of Democracy*. New York: Harper and Row.

Duke, Lynne. 1991. "Whites' Racial Stereotypes Persist." *Washington Post*, January 9: A1, A4.

Edsall, Thomas, and Mary Edsall. 1991. *Chain Reaction*. New York: W. W. Norton.

Eisinger, Peter K. 1982. "Black Employment and Municipal Jobs: The Impact of Black Political Power." *American Political Science Review* 76: 380–392.

Erikson, Robert S., Gerald C. Wright, Jr., and John P. McIver. 1989. "Political Parties, Public Opinion, and State Policy." *American Political Science Review* 83 (3): 729–750.

Farley, Reynolds, and Walter R. Allen. 1987. *The Color Line and Quality of Life in America*. New York: Russell Sage Foundation.

Fiorina, Morris P. 1981. *Retrospective Voting in American National Elections*. New Haven: Yale University Press.

——— 1991. "Elections and the Economy in the 1980s: Short- and Long-Term Effects." In *Politics and Economics in the 1980s*, ed. Alberto Alesina and Geoffrey Carliner. Chicago: University of Chicago Press.

Foster, Lorn. 1990. "Avenues for Black Political Mobilization: The Presidential Campaign of Reverend Jesse Jackson." In *The Social and Political Implications of the 1984 Jesse Jackson Presidential Campaign*, ed. Lorenzo Morris. New York: Praeger.

Frazier, E. Franklin. 1957. *Black Bourgeoisie*. Glencoe, Ill.: Free Press.

Freeman, Jo. 1983. *Social Movements of the Sixties and Seventies*. New York: Longman Press.

Fulenwider, Claire K. 1980. *Feminism in American Politics*. New York: Praeger.

Germond, Jack, and Jules Witcover. 1989. *Whose Broad Stripes and Bright*

*Stars? The Trivial Pursuit of the Presidency, 1988.* New York: Warner Books.

Giddings, Paula. 1984. *When and Where I Enter: The Impact of Black Women on Race and Sex in America.* New York: Morrow.

Gilliam, Franklin D., Jr. 1986. "Black America: Divided by Class?" *Public Opinion* 8: 53–57.

Gilliam, Franklin D., Jr., and Kenneth J. Whitby. 1989. "Race, Class, and Attitudes toward Social Welfare Spending: An Ethclass Interpretation." *Social Science Quarterly* 70 (1): 88–100.

Graham, Hugh Davis. 1990. *The Civil Rights Era.* New York: Oxford University Press.

Greenstone, David J., and Paul E. Peterson. 1973. *Race and Authority in Urban Politics.* New York: Russell Sage Foundation.

Grofman, Bernard, and Lisa Handley. 1991. "The Impact of the Voting Rights Act on Black Representation in Southern State Legislatures." *Legislative Studies Quarterly* 16 (1): 111–128.

Gurin, Patricia. 1985. "Women's Gender Consciousness." *Public Opinion Quarterly* 49 (2): 143–163.

Gurin, Patricia, Shirley J. Hatchett, and James S. Jackson. 1989. *Hope and Independence.* New York: Russell Sage Foundation.

Guterriez, Armando. 1989. "The Jackson Campaign in the Hispanic Community: Problems and Prospects for a Black-Brown Coalition." In *Jesse Jackson's 1984 Presidential Campaign,* ed. L. J. Barker and R. W. Walters. Urbana and Chicago: University of Illinois Press.

Hagen, Michael G. 1989. "Voter Turnout in Primary Elections." In *The Iowa Caucuses and the Presidential Nominating Process,* ed. Peverill Squire. Boulder, Colo.: Westview Press, pp. 51–87.

Hamilton, Charles V. 1982. "Foreword." In *The New Black Politics,* ed. M. B. Preston, L. J. Henderson, Jr., and P. Puryear. New York: Longman Press.

———— 1986. "Social Policy and the Welfare of Black Americans: From Rights to Resources." *Political Science Quarterly* 101 (2): 239–255.

Hanushek, Eric A., and John E. Jackson. 1977. *Statistical Methods for Social Scientists.* New York: Academic Press.

Harris, Fred R., and Roger W. Wilkins. 1988. *Quiet Riots: Race and Poverty in the United States.* New York: Pantheon Press.

Hibbs, Douglas A., Jr. 1987. *The American Political Economy: Macroeconomics and Electoral Politics.* Cambridge, Mass.: Harvard University Press.

Huckfeldt, Robert, and Carol Weitzel Kohfeld. 1989. *Race and the Decline of Class in American Politics.* Urbana and Chicago: University of Illinois Press.

Inglis, K. M., Robert M. Groves, and Steven G. Heeringa. 1987. "Telephone Sample Designs for the U.S. Black Household Population." *Survey Methodology* 13 (6).

Jackman, Mary R., and Robert W. Jackman. 1983. *Class Awareness in the United States*. Berkeley and Los Angeles: University of California Press.

Jaynes, Gerald, and Robin M. Williams. 1989. *A Common Destiny: Blacks and American Society*. Washington, D.C.: National Academy Press.

Joint Center for Political Studies. 1989. *Black Elected Officials: A National Roster*. Washington, D.C.: Joint Center for Political Studies.

Karnig, Albert K., and Susan Welch. 1980. *Black Representation and Urban Policy*. Chicago: University of Chicago Press.

Keech, William. 1968. *The Impact of Negro Voting*. Chicago: Rand McNally.

Kilson, Martin. 1983. "Black Bourgeoisie Revisited." *Dissent* 33: 85–95.

Kinder, Donald R. 1983. "Diversity and Complexity in American Public Opinion." In *Political Science: The State of the Discipline*, ed. Ada W. Finifter. Washington, D.C.: American Political Science Association.

Kinder, Donald R., Gordon S. Adams, and Paul W. Gronke. 1989. "Economics and Politics in the 1984 Presidential Election." *American Journal of Political Science* 75: 436–447.

Kinney, Patrick J., and Tom W. Rice. 1988. "Presidential Prenomination Preferences and Candidate Evaluations." *American Political Science Review* 82 (4): 1310–1319.

Kish, Leslie. 1965. *Survey Sampling*. New York: Wiley and Sons.

Klein, Ethel. 1985. *Gender Politics*. Cambridge, Mass.: Harvard University Press.

Kleppner, Paul. 1985. *Chicago Divided: The Making of a Black Mayor*. Dekalb: Northern Illinois University Press.

Kluegel, James R., and Eliot R. Smith. 1986. *Beliefs about Inequality*. New York: Aldine de Gruyter.

Landry, Bart. 1987. *The New Black Middle Class*. Berkeley and Los Angeles: University of California Press.

Lawson, Steven F. 1976. *Black Ballots*. New York: Columbia University Press.

——— 1985. *In Pursuit of Power*. New York: Columbia University Press.

——— 1991. *Running for Freedom: Civil Rights and Black Politics in America since 1941*. Philadelphia: Temple University Press.

Lepkowski, James M. 1989. "Treatment of Wave Nonresponse in Panel Surveys." In *Panel Surveys*, ed. D. Kasprzyk, G. Duncan, G. Kalton, and M. P. Singh. New York: John Wiley and Sons.

Levitin, Teresa, and Warren E. Miller. 1979. "Ideological Interpretation of Presidential Elections." *American Political Science Review* 73: 751–771.

Lewis, I. A., and William Schneider. 1983. "Black Voting, Bloc Voting and the Democrats." *Public Opinion* 6 (5): 12–15, 59.

Lincoln, C. Eric, and Lawrence Mamiya. 1990. *The Black Church in the African American Experience*. Durham and London: Duke University Press.

Mansbridge, Jane, and Katherine Tate. 1992. "Race Trumps Gender: Black Opinion on the Thomas Nomination." *PS* 25 (3): 488–492.

Marable, Manning. 1985. *Black American Politics: From the Washington Marches to Jesse Jackson.* London: Thetford Press.

—— 1990. *Race, Reform, and Rebellion,* 2nd ed. Jackson: University Press of Mississippi.

Marx, Gary T. 1967. *Protest and Prejudice.* New York: Harper and Row.

Matthews, Donald R., and James W. Prothro. 1966. *Negroes and the New Southern Politics.* New York: Harcourt, Brace and World.

McAdam, Doug. 1982. *Political Process and Development of Black Insurgency, 1930–1970.* Chicago: University of Chicago Press.

Miller, Arthur, Patricia Gurin, and Oksana Malunchuk. 1981. "Group Consciousness and Political Participation." *American Journal of Political Science* 25: 494–511.

Miller, Arthur, Warren E. Miller, Alden S. Raine, and Thad A. Brown. 1976. "A Majority Party in Disarray: Policy Polarization in the 1972 Election." *American Political Science Review* 70: 753–778.

Mladenka, Kenneth R. 1989. "Blacks and Hispanics in Urban Politics." *American Political Science Review* 83 (1): 165–192.

Morone, James A. 1990. *The Democratic Wish.* New York: Basic Books.

Morris, Aldon. 1984. *The Origins of the Civil Rights Movement.* New York: Free Press.

—— 1992. "The Future of Black Politics: Substance versus Process and Formality." *National Political Science Review* 3: 168–174.

Morris, Lorenzo (ed.). 1990. *The Social and Political Implications of the 1984 Jesse Jackson Presidential Campaign.* New York: Praeger.

Morris, Lorenzo, and Linda F. Williams. 1989. "The Coalition at the End of the Rainbow: The 1984 Jackson Campaign." In *Jesse Jackson's 1984 Presidential Campaign,* ed. L. J. Barker and R. W. Walters. Urbana and Chicago: University of Illinois Press.

Moses, Wilson Jeremiah. 1978. *The Golden Age of Black Nationalism, 1850–1925.* New York: Oxford University Press.

Nelsen, Hart, and Anne Nelsen. 1975. *The Black Church in the Sixties.* Lexington: University of Kentucky Press.

Nelson, William E., Jr. 1987. "Cleveland: The Evolution of Black Power." In *The New Black Politics,* 2nd ed., ed. Michael B. Preston, Lenneal J. Henderson, Jr., and Paul L. Puryear. New York: Longman Press.

Nie, Norman, Sidney Verba, and John Petrocik. 1979. *The Changing American Voter,* enlarged ed. Cambridge, Mass.: Harvard University Press.

Nieman, Donald G. 1991. *Promises to Keep.* New York: Oxford University Press.

Oberschall, Anthony. 1978. "The Decline of the 1960's Social Movements." In *Research in Social Movements, Conflict and Change,* ed. L. Kriesberg. Greenwich, Conn.: JAI Press.

Orfield, Gary, and Carole Ashkinaze. 1991. *The Closing Door, Conservative Policy and Black Opportunity*. Chicago: The University of Chicago Press.

Parker, Frank R. 1990. *Black Votes Count*. Chapel Hill: University of North Carolina Press.

Pateman, Carole. 1972. *Participation and Democratic Theory*. New York: Cambridge University Press.

Perry, Huey L. 1992. "The Political Reincorporation of Southern Blacks: The Case of Birmingham." *National Political Science Review* 3: 230–237.

Peterson, Paul E. 1981. *City Limits*. Chicago: University of Chicago Press.

Pinderhughes, Dianne. 1986. "Political Choices: A Realignment in Partisanship among Black Voters?" In *The State of Black America*. New York: National Urban League.

——— 1987. *Race and Ethnicity in Chicago Politics*. Urbana and Chicago: University of Illinois Press.

Piven, Frances Fox, and Richard A. Cloward. 1977. *Poor People's Movements: Why They Succeed, How They Fail*. New York: Pantheon Books.

——— 1988. *Why Americans Don't Vote*. New York: Pantheon Press.

Plissner, Martin, and Warren Mitofsky. 1988. "The Changing Jackson Voter." *Public Opinion* 11 (2): 56–57.

Popkin, Samuel, John W. Gorman, Charles Phillips, and Jeffrey A. Smith. 1976. "Comment: What Have You Done for Me Lately? Toward an Investment Theory of Voting." *American Political Science Review* 70: 779–805.

Preston, Michael B. 1987. "The Election of Harold Washington: An Examination of the SES Model in the 1983 Chicago Mayoral Election." In *The New Black Politics*, 2nd ed., ed. Michael B. Preston, Lenneal J. Henderson, Jr., and Paul L. Puryear. New York: Longman Press.

——— 1989. "The 1984 Presidential Primary: Who Voted for Jesse Jackson and Why?" In *Jesse Jackson's 1984 Presidential Campaign*, ed. L. J. Barker and R. W. Walters. Urbana and Chicago: University of Illinois Press.

Ranney, Austin. 1972. "Turnout and Representation in Presidential Primary Elections." *American Political Science Review* 12: 224–238.

Reed, Adolph, Jr. 1986. *The Jesse Jackson Phenomenon*. New Haven: Yale University Press.

——— 1988. "The Black Urban Regime: Structural Origins and Constraints." In *Power, Community, and the City*, vol. 1, ed. Michael Peter Smith. New Brunswick, N.J.: Transaction Press.

Robinson, Pearl T. 1982. "Whither the Future of Blacks in the Republican Party?" *Political Science Quarterly* 97 (2): 207–231.

Rosenstone, Steven, Roy L. Behr, and Edward H. Lazarus. 1984. *Third Parties in America*. Princeton: Princeton University Press.

Rustin, Bayard. 1965. "From Protest to Politics: The Future of the Civil Rights Movement." *Commentary* 39 (2): 25–31.

——— 1966. " 'Black Power' and Coalition Politics." *Commentary* 42 (2): 35–40.

Sandefur, Gary D. 1988. "Blacks, Hispanics, American Indians, and Poverty and What Worked." In *Quiet Riots*, ed. Fred R. Harris and Roger W. Wilkins. New York: Pantheon Books.

Schuman, Howard, and Stanley Presser. 1981. *Questions and Answers in Attitude Surveys*. New York: Academic Press.

Schuman, Howard, Charlotte Steeh, and Lawrence Bobo. 1985. *Racial Attitudes in America: Trends and Interpretations*. Cambridge, Mass.: Harvard University Press.

Shingles, Richard D. 1981. "Black Consciousness and Political Participation: The Missing Link." *American Political Science Review* 75: 76–90.

Sigelman, Lee. 1982. "The Nonvoting Voter in Voting Research." *American Journal of Political Science* 26 (1): 47–56.

Sigelman, Lee, and Susan Welch. 1991. *Black Americans' Views of Racial Inequality: The Dream Deferred*. New York: Cambridge University Press.

Smith, Eric R.A.N. 1989. *The Unchanging American Voter*. Los Angeles and Berkeley: University of California Press.

Smith, Robert C. 1981. "Black Power and the Transformation from Protest to Politics." *Political Science Quarterly* 96 (3): 431–443.

——— 1990. "From Insurgency toward Inclusion: The Jackson Campaigns of 1984 and 1988." In *The Social and Political Implications of the 1984 Jesse Jackson Presidential Campaign*, ed. Lorenzo Morris. New York: Praeger.

Smith, Wade A. 1987. "Problems and Progress in the Measurement of Black Public Opinion." *American Behavioral Scientist* 30: 441–455.

Smothers, Ronald. 1984. "Bid by Jackson is Cited in Blacks' Big Turnout." *New York Times*, March 15.

Stone, Clarence N. 1989. *Regime Politics*. Lawrence: University of Kansas Press.

Stone, Walter J. 1986. "The Carryover Effect in Presidential Elections." *American Political Science Review* 80 (1): 271–279.

Tarrow, Sidney. 1987. "Struggle, Politics, and Reform: Collective Action, Social Movements, and Cycles of Protest." Cornell Western Societies Paper No. 2, Cornell University.

Tate, Katherine. 1989. "Black Politics as a Collective Struggle: The Impact of Race and Class in 1984." Ph.D. dissertation, University of Michigan.

——— 1990. "Bloc Voters, Black Voters, and the Jackson Candidacies, 1984–1988." Paper presented at the annual meeting of the American Political Science Association, San Francisco, 30 August–2 September.

———— 1991. "Black Political Participation in the 1984 and 1988 Presidential Elections." *American Political Science Review* 85 (4): 1159–1176.

———— 1992. "Invisible Woman." *The American Prospect* (8): 74–81.

Taylor, D. Garth, Paul B. Sheatsley, and Andrew M. Greeley. 1978. "Attitudes toward Racial Integration." *Scientific American* 238: 42–49.

Thernstrom, Abigail M. 1987. *Whose Votes Count?* Cambridge, Mass.: Harvard University Press.

Thompson, J. Phillip. 1990. "The Impact of Jackson Presidential Campaigns on Black Political Mobilization in New York, Oakland, and Atlanta." Paper presented at the annual meeting of the American Political Science Association, San Francisco.

Thompson, Kenneth H. 1982. *The Voting Rights Act and Black Electoral Participation.* Washington, D.C.: Joint Center for Political Studies.

Tienda, Marta, and Gary D. Sandefur (eds.). 1988. *Divided Opportunities: Minorities, Poverty, and Social Policy.* New York: Plenum Press.

Travis, Toni-Michelle C. 1990. "Boston: The Unfinished Agenda." In *Racial Politics in American Cities,* ed. R. P. Browning, D. R. Marshall, and D. H. Tabb. New York: Longman Press.

Useem, Bert, and Mayer N. Zald. 1987. "From Pressure Group to Social Movement: Efforts to Promote Use of Nuclear Power." In *Social Movements in an Organizational Society,* ed. Mayer N. Zald and John D. McCarthy. New Brunswick, N.J.: Transaction Books.

Vanneman, Reeve, and Lynn Weber Cannon. 1987. *The American Perception of Class.* Philadelphia: Temple University Press.

Verba, Sidney, and Norman H. Nie. 1972. *Participation in America.* Chicago: University of Chicago Press.

Verba, Sidney, and Gary Orren. 1985. *Equality in America.* Cambridge, Mass.: Harvard University Press.

Walters, Ronald W. 1988. *Black Presidential Politics in America: A Strategic Approach.* Albany: State University of New York Press.

Walton, Hanes, Jr. 1972a. *Black Political Parties.* New York: Free Press.

———— 1972b. *Black Politics.* New York: J. B. Lippincott.

———— 1985. *Invisible Politics.* New York: SUNY Press.

———— 1990. "Black Presidential Participation and the Critical Election Theory." In *The Social and Political Implications of the 1984 Jesse Jackson Presidential Campaign,* ed. Lorenzo Morris. New York: Praeger.

Wattenberg, Martin P. 1984. *The Decline of American Political Parties, 1952–1984.* Cambridge, Mass.: Harvard University Press.

Weir, Margaret, Ann Shola Orloff, and Theda Skocpol. 1988. *The Politics of Social Policy in the United States.* Princeton: Princeton University Press.

Weiss, Nancy J. 1983. *Farewell to the Party of Lincoln.* Princeton: Princeton University Press.

Welch, Susan, and Lorn S. Foster. 1987. "Class and Conservatism in the Black Community." *American Political Quarterly* 4: 445–470.

——— 1992. "The Impact of Economic Conditions on the Voting Behavior of Blacks." *Western Political Quarterly,* forthcoming.

Whitby, Kenneth J., and Franklin D. Gilliam, Jr. 1991. "A Longitudinal Analysis of Competing Explanations for the Transformation of Southern Congressional Politics." *Journal of Politics* 53 (2): 504–518.

Williams, Linda F. 1987a. "The 1984 Elections in the South: Racial Polarization and Regional Congruence." In *Blacks in Southern Politics,* ed. L. W. Moreland, R. P. Steed, and T. A. Baker. New York: Praeger.

——— 1987b. "Black Political Progress in the 1980's: The Electoral Arena." In *The New Black Politics,* 2nd ed., ed. M. Preston, L. Henderson, and P. Puryear. New York: Longman Press, pp. 97–136.

——— 1989. "White/Black Perceptions of the Electability of Black Political Candidates." *National Political Science Review* 2: 45–64.

Willie, Charles V. 1979. *Caste and Race Controversy.* Bayside, N.Y.: General Hill.

Wilson, William J. 1981. *The Declining Significance of Race.* Chicago: University of Chicago Press.

——— 1987. *The Truly Disadvantaged.* Chicago: University of Chicago Press.

Wolfinger, Raymond E., and Steven J. Rosenstone. 1980. *Who Votes?* New Haven: Yale University Press.

Zald, Mayer N., and John D. McCarthy. 1987. "Social Movement Organizations: Growth, Decay, and Change." In *Social Movements in an Organizational Society,* ed. Mayer N. Zald and John D. McCarthy. New Brunswick, N.J.: Transaction Books.

# Index